CONFUCIANISM IN MODERN JAPAN

CONFUCIANISM
IN
MODERN JAPAN

A Study of Conservatism
in Japanese Intellectual History

WARREN W. SMITH, JR.

1959

THE HOKUSEIDO PRESS

TOKYO

PRINTED
IN
JAPAN

THE HOKUSEIDO PRESS

To Mamacita
in Appreciation of
her Constant Encouragement

FOREWORD

It is a matter for great joy that scholars in Europe and the United States have been keenly interested in the study of Japanese culture and published a number of excellent researches. As a Japanese scholar of the same field of learning I take pleasure in paying my respects to Mr. Warren Smith Jr., the author of this book, which well represents this kind of endeavors by foreign scholars. The bibliography itself will testify to the comprehensive efforts made by the author.

Although the problems of Confucianism in modern Japan are very important for us Japanese, scholars in this country are not considered to have made adequate inquiries into them. The fact that the author has grappled with these difficult problems will give an impetus to the scholarship in our country. In this sense, I offer my hearty congratulations on the publication of Mr. Smith's researches by the Hokuseido Press.

Upon the whole, I agree to what is presented there by Mr. Smith, who tries to view the rôle of Confucianism in modern Japan in its close relationship with her political backgrounds. Yet, from our point of view, it is desirable that the author should have emphasized more strongly the implicit influence that Confucianism exerted upon the principle of Emperor worship through our family system and family morality.

I take the liberty of asking for thus much, because the bibliography includes no reference to the books on Japanese family system published since the Meiji Era.

September 20, 1958

Saburo Ienaga
Professor of Japanese Intellectual History,
Tokyo University of Education.

PREFACE

In most studies of modern Japan, Confucianism is scarcely mentioned, and perhaps statistically where importance is often measured by frequency and quantity, such omission is justified. Indeed, it is true that in such important changes as the development of mass movements in modern Japan, the growth of Japanese nationalism, or the industrial transformation of Japan, Confucianism played a minor role. Despite this, interest in Confucianism existed in modern Japan, and after some years of neglect, Confucianism began a period of recrudescence which reached a climax in the Second World War. From the historical standpoint, an investigation of this process of waxing and waning can lend great insight into Japanese intellectual and social development and suggest something of what the course of Japanese thought may be in the future.

The background to the influence of Confucianism in Japan lies in the early phase of Japanese history when Chinese culture was imported into the country over fifteen hundred years ago. Confucian thought was a basic concomitant of Chinese culture, coloring the values of nearly all fields of human endeavor, particularly those concerned with political, intellectual, and social activities. It was during the Tokugawa period (1603-1868) immediately preceding the modern era that Confucianism flourished most widely in Japan. One might interpret this by saying that during the Tokugawa period, there was the greatest proximity between the type of ethical and social problems dealt with by Confucianism and the problems facing the Japanese in the maintenance of stability in a feudal state.

It had already become apparent before the Meiji period (1868-1912), which ushered in so-called modern Japanese history, that Confucianism no longer satisfactorily explained natural phenomena or was effective in dealing with the kind of problems which Western industrial and commercial techniques were bringing to Asia. Under such circumstances, Confucianism suffered a severe decline and was notably disregarded during the first decades of the Meiji period. Nevertheless, in contrast to China, Confucianism never died out in modern Japan, and the Japanese increasingly took pride in the fact that they alone possessed such elements of traditional Asiatic culture as Confucian thought.

The purpose of this study is to trace the varying fortunes of Confucianism in modern Japan and in this way shed light on the particular kind of situations in which the Japanese have been attracted to Confucian thought rather than alternative philosophies. This is by no means simply an academic question, for in certain respects, Japan is today in the same position she was in at the opening of the Meiji period, when it was necessary to choose from a flood of divergent and conflicting ideas. Elements of Confucian thought remain deeply implanted in the minds of many Japanese and will undoubtedly affect the kind of reintegration that is attempted in future years.[1]

In this book, the translation of the titles of foreign works, as well as the titles themselves, have been italicized. Also all foreign words, except for proper names, place names, and personal names, are italicized. In the case of the translations of some titles, such as *Analects* for *Lun-yü* 論語, where the English translation is well known, the foreign title and the Chinese characters are left out after the first few references. The Wade-Giles system has been used for the romanization of Chinese; the Hepburn system for the romanization of Japanese; and the McCune-Reischauer system for the romanization of Korean. The following abbreviations appear in the book:

---

1. A striking example of this may be found in the "Outline of Ethical Practice for the Japanese People," proposed in 1951 by the Japanese Minister of Education to replace the old Imperial Rescript on Education of the Emperor Meiji. R.P. Dore, "The Ethics of the New Japan," *Pacific Affairs*, XXV, 2 (June, 1952), 147-159, analyzes the great debt which the new "Outline" owes to Confucian ideas.

F.E.Q. for *Far Eastern Quarterly*
H.J.A.S. for *Harvard Journal of Asiatic Studies*

J.N.C.B.R.A.S. for *Journal of the North China Branch of the Royal Asiatic Society*
T.A.S.J. for *Transactions of the Asiatic Society of Japan*
T.A.K.B.R.A.S. for *Transactions of the Korea Branch of the Royal Asiatic Society*
I.M.T.F.E. for *International Military Tribunal for the Far East*
I.P.R. for *Institute of Pacific Relations*

In the names of Japanese, Chinese, and Koreans, the customary fashion of presenting the family name first, followed by the personal name, has been used, unless the individual is well known in the West according to the Western style of personal name followed by family name.

A final word of acknowledgement is due to those who have encouraged and helped guide the author in the writing of this book. To Professor Delmer Brown of the Department of History at the University of California, Berkeley, I owe my original interest in Japanese history. It was under Professor Brown's guidance that the thesis topic of Japanese Confucianism, on which this book is based, was begun.

For completion of the thesis, as well as for suggesting many fruitful lines of investigation, a deep debt of thanks is due to Professor Joseph Levenson of the Department of History at the University of California, Berkeley. I am also grateful to Professor Woodbridge Bingham of the History Department, and Professor Donald Shively of the Oriental Language Department at the University of California for their guidance and corrections to the thesis. And to the many others at the University of California and elsewhere who contributed to the thesis in different ways, I also wish to extend my thanks.

The publication of this book was made possible through the kind efforts and assistance of Mr. Shindō Buzaemon who felt that a foreigner's interpretation of Japanese history could have a special value to the Japanese by allowing them to see themselves as others have. Professor Harashima Yoshimori and Professor Suematsu Yasukazu of the Gakushūin University have assisted Mr. Shindō with the publication, attending in particular to the many details and corrections involved in proof reading before the manuscript could be turned over to the publishers, the Hokuseido Press. To these Japanese collaborators, I am most grateful.

Warren W. Smith, Jr.

September, 1958

CONTENTS

LIST OF ILLUSTRATION

I

THE BACKGROUND OF CONFUCIANISM
AND THE TOKUGAWA LEGACY

1. Chinese Confucian Background.

Throughout the Tokugawa period (1603-1868), Confucianism as interpreted and synthesized by Chu Hsi 朱熹 (1130-1200) and his predecessors such as Ch'eng Hao 程顥 (1032-85) and Chou Tun-i 周敦頤 (1017-73)[1] dominated Japanese intellectual life. But before the advent of these men in China, Confucianism[2] already had passed through various stages of development, and it will be valuable briefly to trace these in order to have clearly in mind which elements of Confucian thought were the most basic and recurrent.

Confucianism in China seems originally to have been a system for regulating the relations of men according to certain beliefs concerning the fundamental forces in nature and society. These beliefs had a long history and were by no means the product of a single man or group, but may be considered to have been

---

1. For a discussion of the more important figures who contributed to this new Confucian synthesis, see: J. Percy Bruce, *Chu Hsi and His Masters*. Probsthain Oriental Series (London: Probsthain and Co., 1938), 3-96; Fung, Yu-lan, "The Rise of Neo Confucianism and its Borrowings from Buddhism and Taoism," *H.J.A.S.*, translated from Chinese by Derke Bodde, VII (July, 1942); and Fung, Yu-lan, *A Short History of Chinese Philosophy*, edited by Derke Bodde (New York: Macmillan Co., 1948), ch. 23-25.

2. Ordinarily, the term Confucianist is used vaguely for any supporter of Confucian philosophy, but since the latter went through many phases, more precise terminology is needed to specify what particular stage of development is being referred to. In this chapter, after finishing the first section, Confucianism of Sung times will primarily be dealt with, since it was predominant in the Tokugawa period; and so in using the words "Confucianism," "Confucianist," and so on, Confucianism based on the Sung interpretations will be meant, unless otherwise stated.

an integration emerging from the gradual uniting and dominance in China of certain tribes, culture patterns, and originally divergent elements.[3] By the time of the Han dynasty, when state Confucianism was officially established in the reign of the Emperor Wu 武 (140-87 B.C.),[4] a fairly well developed system with special ceremonies, rituals, and a peculiar philosophical basis had become standardized, though this system was quite different from earlier Confucianism of the time of Confucius. The cosmological explanation of the *yin yang* 陰陽 and five elements (*wu hsing* 五行) schools had become part of the Confucian canon, and the interpretations and writings of philosophers after Confucius such as Tzu Ssu 子思 (b. 500 B.C.), Mencius 孟子 (371-289 B.C.), and Hsuntzu 荀子 (298-238 B.C.) had become accepted as orthodox. There also arose at this time a group of historians and commentators who looked on social activity and government essentially as a right ordering of things under heaven, and in writing history, such men stressed the "praise and blame" principle (*pao-pien* 褒貶) found so strikingly in the interpretations of the *Chien Han-shu* 前漢書 (*History of the Former Han*), compiled by the famous Pan Ku 班固.[5] In their works they insisted that the "descriptive principle fit the reality" (*cheng-ming* 正名), and in their attempts to foster orthodox attitudes of political morality, they liberally borrowed and interpreted from the "classics,"[6]

---

3. Wolfram Eberhard, *A History of China*, (Berkeley and Los Angeles: University of California Press,1950), 27-32, 37-40.

4. An interesting discussion of the establishment of state Confucianism can be found in: Pan Ku, *The History of the Former Han Dynasty*, translation by Homer Dubs, (Baltimore: Waverly Press, 1944), II, 341-355. Also Hu Shih, "The Establishment of Confucianism as a State Religion during the Han Dynasty," *J.N.C.B.R.A.S.*, XL, (1929), 20-41. Another standard work on this subject is: John Shryock, *The Origin and Development of the State Cult of Confucius*, (New York: The Century Company, 1932).

5. Clyde B. Sargent, "Subsidized History," *F.E.Q.*, III, (Feb., 1944), 133-138.

6. The term "classics" (*ching-shu* 經書) as used in Tokugawa times usually meant the *Five Classics* (*Wu-ching* 五經) and *Four Books* (*Ssu-shu* 四書), although from the Sung 宋 dynasty (960-1280) on, a broader classification of *Thirteen Classics* (*Shih-san-ching* 十三經) also existed. The *Five Classics* consisted of the: *Book of Changes* (*I-Ching* 易經); *Book of History* (*Shu-ching* 書經); *Book of Odes* (*Shih-ching* 詩經); *Spring and Autumn Annals* (*Ch'un-ch'iu* 春秋); and *Record of Rites* (*Li-chi* 禮記); The *Four Books* comprised the: *Analects* (*Lun-yü* 論語); *Great Learning* (*Ta-hsüeh* 大學); *Doctrine of the Mean* (*Chung-yung* 中庸): and *Mencius* (*Mengtzu* 孟子). Each of all these had extensive commentaries, but the choice of these particular works as the basic Confucian "classics" was accomplished by Neo-Confucians who, for example, raised the *Mencius, Great*

especially the *Spring and Autumn Annals* and its commentary the *Tso-chuan* 左傳 claimed by them as rendering faithfully Confucius' intention in composing the *Spring and Autumn Annals*, wherewith "rebellious ministers and villainous sons were struck with terror."[7]

The Confucian tradition had crystalized for these men into a system in which the earth and everything in it was conceived of as subject to the laws of Heaven. To the extent that activity was in harmony with the laws of Heaven, justice, goodness, happiness, and benevolent government were secured. This harmony had been achieved by the "Sage Kings" of China,[8] and though it had since been lost, it could be restored by a study of the works of Confucius and his disciples who had transmitted the patterns for proper relationships, daily life, ceremony, and ritual observation. Man's place in the world was considered most important, as he was thought to be the highest manifestation of Heaven's activity, and therefore it was incumbent on him to live as closely as possible in harmony with the laws of Heaven. There were five fundamental relationships between men in society that were essential for harmony to exist in other spheres of the world, and as the *Doctrine of the Mean*[9] enumerates them:

Learning, and *Doctrine of the Mean* from relative unimportance to a position of outstanding prominence. At the time of Christ, though, Liu Hsin 劉歆 in his *Ch'i-lueh* 七略 (*Seven Summaries*), appears to have segregated as "classics" all those texts which were supposed to have been connected with Confucius [see Charles S. Gardner, *Chinese Traditional Historiography*, (Cambridge: Harvard University Press, 1937), 33-36, 86], and they comprised the books mentioned above as the *Five Classics*. Originally there was also said to have been a *Classic of Music* (*Yüeh-ching* 樂經), but tradition claimed it was destroyed by the first Emperor of Ch'in, Ch'in Shih Huang-ti 秦始皇帝 (221-209 B.C.) in his famous "burning of the books."

7. *Mengtzu* 孟子 (*Mencius*), Duke T'ang-wen 滕文公, pt. II, 9. Although modern scholarship has tended to discount Confucius as the author of the *Spring and Autumn Annals*, or at any rate to question that he had any ethical motives in mind in that dry recording of events, there is no doubt that later commentators interpreted as ethical judgements what appeared to them as evidence of the "pruning pencil of the sage." That is to say, in one place a man might be mentioned as a duke, and in another, his title would be left out, indicating, according to the commentators, Confucius' disapproval of the actions of the man. A summary of one of the most authoritative studies on the problem of the authorship of the *Ch'un Ch'iu* is Ssu-ho Ch'i, "Professor Hung on the *Ch'un Ch'iu*," *The Yenching Journal of Social Studies*, I, 1 (June, 1938), 49-71.

8. The mythological rulers usually referred to as "sage kings" were Yao 堯, Shun 舜, and Yu 禹. Traditionally they were supposed to have ruled respectively from 2356-2255 B.C., and 2255-2205 B.C., and 2205-2197 B.C., but actually, they seem to have been local deities euhemerized by early, pre-Han Confucianists.

The duties of universal obligation are five and the virtues wherewith they are practiced are three. The duties are those between sovereign and minister, between father and son, between husband and wife, between eleder brother and younger, and those belonging to the intercourse of friends. Those five are the duties of universal obligation. Wisdom, compassion and courage, these are the three universally recognized moral qualities of men.[10]

This was, then, a primarily social philosophy in which the forces of nature were brought to support the forms and standards of society that were considered desirable. The problem of government was reduced to the observation, by all, of the proper obligations, with the ruler setting the example for the rest of the people to follow. These points are emphasized in the *Great Learning*[11] as follows:

In the Book of Poetry it is said, "They can discharge their duties to their younger brothers." Let the ruler discharge his duties to his elder and younger brothers, and then he may teach the people of the state. In the Book of Poetry it is said, "In his deportment there is nothing wrong. He rectifies all the people of the state." Yes, when the ruler, as a father, a son, and a brother, is a model, then the people must imitate him. This is what is meant by saying "The government of his kingdom depends on his regulation of the family."[12]

Finally, Confucianism of Han times had little interest in mystical or metaphysical problems, which is well illustrated by a passage from the *Analects*.

[The disciple] Tzu Lu asked how the spirits of the dead and others should be served. The Master said, "If you fail to serve men alive,

---

9. The *Doctrine of the Mean*, attributed to Confucius' grandson Tzu Ssu 子思, was originally a section of the *Record of Rites*, but it was raised to special prominence by the Neo-Confucians because much of it could be reinterpreted in a metaphysical way to suit the change in philosophical outlook.

10. *Chung-yung* 中庸 (*Doctrine of the Mean*), ch. XX, 8, as translated by James Legge, *The Confucian Classics*, second edition, revised, (Oxford: Clarendon Press, 1893), I, 406.

11. The *Great Learning*, like the *Doctrine of the Mean*, was originally a section of the *Record of Rites*, and later was raised by the Neo-Confucians to hold an independent position for much the same reason.

12. *Chung-yung*, ch. IX, 7, as translated by Legge, *op. cit.*, I, 372.

how can you serve their spirits?" Tzu Lu then asked about death and the Master replied, "If you do not understand life, how can you understand death?"[13]

Buddhism and Taoism largely overshadowed Confucianism in the centuries that succeeded the fall of the Han dynasty, and with them came an intense search for answers to just those types of mystical and metaphysical problems with which earlier Confucianism had never dealt. The result of this was that from the middle of the T'ang dynasty 唐 (618-907) on, Confucianism began gradually to incorporate into itself many Buddhist and Taoist ideas related to the universe, nature and spirit, mind and feeling, and life and death.[14] This did not mean that the emphasis on social relationships and attention to proper ceremonies for maintaining harmony between heaven and earth were forgotten, but it did lead to attempts to find a purpose for them outside the ken of man himself. For example, music was no longer simply a means of allowing expression to human emotions so they would be prevented from going to excess, but it became the path through which men could reach the state of "absolute sincerity" which had an essential religious and mystical meaning.[15] The sage now was not one who had simply reached the apogee of human relationships as in Mencius, but he who had become a "Confucian Buddha" by uniting with the nature and destiny of the universe.

The stage of reference for Chu Hsi and his precursors was definitely a cosmological one. Man, though still the highest being in the universe, was but one aspect of the action of the Supreme Ultimate (t'ai-ch'i 太極) which was present in all things. His nature was the reflection of perfect principles of nature, and what he had to do was through self-discipline and constant investigation, attempt to comprehend the form of the whole uni-

---

13. *Lun-yü* 論語 (*Analects*), XI, 11, as translated by Legge, *op. cit.*, I, 240-241.

14. This development is briefly dealt with in an article by Fung, "The Rise of Neo-Confucianism and Its Borrowings from Buddhism and Taoism," *H.J.A.S.*, VII (July, 1942), 89-125.

15. *Ibid.*, 107.

verse, after which he could achieve the perfection of his own nature.

Borrowing from religious Taoism, which believed in a universe acting according to law and sought in the physical realm to apply this by controlling nature with magical potions and primitive science, the Sung dynasty Confucianists conceived of a logical and internally harmonious cosmos where men must seek to live socially in conformity with an immutable higher law. Chou Tun-i, for example, is said to have received his direct inspiration for the Diagram of the Supreme Ultimate[16] from a chart embracing the *yin yang*, five element, and eight trigram cosmogony, prepared by a Taoist seeker of immortality.[17]

2. Early Japanese Confucianism and Trends of Orthodox Confucianism in the Tokugawa Period.

In Japan, Han Confucianism according to tradition had been introduced from Korea about 404 A.D.,[18] but it remained for about two hundred years after this little more than a name associated with Japanese efforts to learn to read and write Chinese.

The really first example we have of Confucian ethical and political principles being understood and utilized in Japan is when Prince Shōtoku (572-621) promulgated the famous so-called

---

16. For a reproduction of this diagram with an explanation of its cosmogonic action, see Bruce, *op. cit.*, 128-133.

17. Fung, "The Rise of Neo-Confucianism and Its Borrowings from Buddhism and Taoism," *op. cit.*, 122-123.

18. W. G. Aston, "Nihongi," *Translations and Preceedings of the Japan Society*, (London: Kegan, Paul, Trench, Trübner and Co., 1896), I, 261-262. Basil H. Chamberlain, *Translation of Kojiki*, annotated by W. G. Aston, 2nd. ed. (Kobe: J. L. Thomson and Co., 1932), 305-306. The traditional date is 284 according to orthodox Japanese chronologies, but on the basis of modern Japanese and foreign research, 404 is considered more accurate. See Emile Gaspardone, "La Chronologie Ancienne du Japon" *Journal Asiatique*, CCXXX (April-June, 1938) for details on this subject. A summary of the views of some Japanese scholars on dating early Japanese history, with a corrected chronological table including these revisions, may be found in: ōhara Toshitake 大原利武, *Chōsen shi taikei, nempyō* 朝鮮史大系年表 (*Outline of Korean History, Chronological Table*), (Keijō: Chōsen Shi Gakkai 朝鮮史學會, 1927), V, supplement. After 645 and the adoption of *nengō* 年號 or year names, presumably all dates in the early histories are accurate. In any dates prior to 645 based on the chronologies of early Japanese histories, the corrected figures and not the traditional Japanese ones shall be used.

"Seventeen Article Constitution" in 604.[19] Prince Shōtoku seems to have considered Confucianism as having an important role to play in buttressing the position of the central government, and the main emphasis of the "Seventeen Article Constitution" was on the duties of people towards their sovereign and the need for harmony among inferiors and superiors.

This tendency to use Confucianism for political purposes characterized the Japanese attitude towards it from earliest times. It led to Confucianism being studied most by those who planned for careers in government service, and in the curricula of the government schools which arose in the Nara period (710-784) to meet this need for trained administrators,[20] the Confucian classics were predominant.[21]

Together with the growing influence of Confucianism in Japanese intellectual and political circles was Japan's increasing direct contact with China, to which the first official embassy was sent in 607.[22] As China was in a period of unusual artistic and intellectual growth, especially during the first hundred years of the T'ang dynasty (618-907), Japan profited much from this contact, and Confucianism was greatly stimulated.[23]

Certain aspects of the development of Japanese Confucianism, however, set it apart from Confucianism in China, for from the first, the teaching of Confucianism in Japan was limited to the aristocratic classes,[24] while in China Confucian learning was

---

19. Aston, op. cit., II, 128-133 gives a translation of the "Seventeen Article Constitution." Joseph John Spae, Itō Jinsai, Monumenta Serica Monograph Series, XII (Peiping: Catholic University of Peking, 1948), 19, has a comparative table arranged showing where the text of the "Constitution" parallels texts from the Confucian classics.

20. For briefly tracing education developments in the Nara and Heian periods, see Kumagai Kōjirō 熊谷幸次郎, "Ōchō Jidai no Daigaku to shigaku" 王朝時代の大學と私學 ("The University and Private Schools in the Nara and Heian Periods"), Rekishi to chiri 歴史と地理 (History and Geography), as translated and summarized in the H.J.A.S., II (Mar., 1937), 68-73.

21. Kubomi Masayasu 窪美昌保, Taihōryō shinkai 大寶令新解 (New Explanation of the Taihōryō), (Tōkyō: Meguro Jinshichi 目黒甚七, 1924), 314-315.

22. Nihon Jugaku nempyō 日本儒學年表 (Chronological Table of Japanese Confucianism), (Tōkyō: Shibunkai 斯文會), 1923, 3.

23. Iwahashi Junsei 岩橋遵成, Nihon Jukyō gaisetsu 日本儒教概説 (Outline of Japanese Confucianism), (Tōkyō and Ōsaka: Hōbunkan 寶文館, 1926), 30-31, 37. Spae, op. cit., 25-26.

24. Kumagai, op. cit., as summarized and translated in the H.J.A.S., II (Mar., 1937), 69-70.

theoretically available to all.[25] Furthermore, Confucian instruction in Japan began to be the monopoly of a group of hereditary
scholars increasingly attached to the Imperial Court.[26] The effect
of this was not only to circumscribe severely the influence of
Confucianism to certain classes, but as the Imperial court grew
weaker from the tenth century onward, the hereditary scholars
had correspondingly less opportunity to put their ideas and beliefs
into practice.[27] Perhaps as a result, these scholars began to follow
the pattern of late Han and T'ang Confucianists in devoting most
of their energies to problems of textual analysis and criticism,[28]
contributing little to help solve the pressing problems of land
and administrative reform.

Finally, by the tenth and eleventh centuries, the appeal of
Confucianism, whether among scholars, military men, or the
common people, had been nearly entirely replaced by Buddhism.[29]
The latter creed, offering salvation to all men regardless of station in life, seems to have been particularly attractive in an age
of constant uncertainty and continual warfare. Besides this,
Buddhism grew up independently and was not forced to rely
on the Imperial Court or any other group for its existence of
advance.

Despite the apparent antagonism between the metaphysical
philosophy of Buddhism and the socially-centered, humanistic

---

25. *Lun-yü*, XV, 38; translated by Legge, *op. cit.*, I, 305. In practice, of course,
the Chinese educational system was not generally open to members of all classes.

26. Kumagai, *op. cit.*, as summarized and translated in *H.J.A.S.*, II (Mar., 1937),
70-71. Iwahashi, *op. cit.*, 36, 39, 54. *Nihon Jukyō* 日本儒教 (*Japanese Confucianism*),
Nnhon Bungaku Kenkyūkai 日本文學研究會 (Tōkyō: Tōyō Shoin 東洋書院, 1936), 75-77.
The most famous of the hereditary families were the Ōe 大江, the Kiyowara 清原, and
the Sugawara 菅原.

27. Iwahashi, *op. cit.*, 54-55. The rapid decline of the fortunes of Confucianism
in this period is climaxed by a fire at the Daigakuryō 大學寮 in Kyōto in 1177. This
had been the cradle of Confucianism in Japan, where the spring and autumn Confucian
sacrifices (*sekiten* 釋奠) were carried out, and it was a number of years before the
destroyed buildings were partially rebuilt. In the meantime, flagrant larcenies of the
Temple of Confucius occurred, further attesting to the unattended and weak position
of Confucianism in this period. See *Nihon Jugaku nempyō*, 119, 138-139, 144-155, 153, for
the details of this decline.

28. Spae, *op. cit.*, 28. Ashikaga Enjutsu 足利衍述, *Kamakura Muromachi jidai
no Jukyō* 鎌倉室町時代之儒教 (*Confucianism of the Kamakura and Muromachi Periods*),
(Tōkyō: Nihon Kotenzenshū Kankōkai 日本古典全集刊行會, 1932), 4-5.

29. Iwahashi, *op. cit.*, 43-48.

philosophy of Confucianism, it was largely through the efforts of Buddhist priests that Confucian learning survived in Japan during the Heian 平安 (782-1185) and Kamakura 鎌倉 (1185-1333) periods. Buddhist priests studied and taught the Confucian classics,[30] and after the reinterpreted Confucianism of the Sung dynasty was brought to Japan in the twelfth century,[31] they were the group most responsible for its spread and gradual popularization.

Zen Buddhist priests were those who most actively supported Neo-Confucianism, probably because of the similarity of many of the principles in both philosophies.[32] But even though the influence of Neo-Confucianism greatly increased in scholarly and political circles, it was not before 1600 that it began to gain an independent position, separate from that of the Buddhists or the hereditary scholars of Confucianism supported by the Imperial Court. By 1647, however, with the Emperor Go-Kōmyō 後光明 (reigned 1644-54) commanding that the hereditary Confucian scholars abandon the use of the Han and T'ang commentaries on Confucian classics and adopt the new ones of the Sung,[33] the doctrines of Chu Hsi became fully supreme in Japan. This supremacy had in fact developed earlier when Fujiwara Seika 藤原惺窩 (1561-1619) broke with the tradition of being either a Buddhist priest or hereditary scholar associated with the Imperial Court and established, as it were, a new tradition that permitted

---

30. Uda Hisashi 宇田尚, Nihon bunka ni oyoboseru Jukyō no eikyō 日本文化に及ぼせる儒教の影響 (The Influence of Confucianism on Japanese Culture), (Tōkyō: Tōyōshisō Kenkyūkai 東洋思想研究會, 1935), 879-909.

31. Spae, op. cit., 31-38, covers this matter in some detail and seems to feel that Kiyowara Yorinari 清原頼業 (1102-1189) deserves credit for beginning the study of Sung doctrines in Japan. It is to be noted, though, that he mistakenly claims Yorinari as the author of the Daiki 臺記 (which is misprinted as 太記 in Itō Jinsai), and makes this one of the foundations for the proof of his stand. Actually, Fujiwara Yorinaga (1119-1156) was the author of this work. Spae also errs in calling the latter the brother of Kiyowara Yorinari, for although the two men were friends, they could not have been brothers because they had different fathers and mothers. A more accurate description of the earliest transmission of the Neo-Confucianism to Japan and its relation to these two men may be found in: Nihonbunka Kenkyūkai 日本文化研究會, Nihon Jukyō 日本儒教 (Japanese Confucianism), (Tōkyō: Tōyō Shoin 東洋書院, 1936), 98-99.

32. For an understanding of the relationship between Zen and Confucianism in Japan, the chapter entitled "Zen and the Samurai" in Suzuki Daisetz, Zen Buddhism and its Influence on Japanese Culture, (Kyōto: Otani Buddhist College, 1938), is valuable.

33. Nihon Jugaku Nempyō, 282-283.

and encouraged the widespread study of Sung Confucianism as a field in itself. This stimulated a revival of learning and provided the basis for the intellectual dominance of Confucianists in the Tokugawa period, especially since the founder of the Tokugawa Shogunate supported this new movement. Tokugawa Ieyasu 徳川家康 (1542-1616) was in the close touch with Fujiwara Seika, and on the latter's recommendation, Ieyasu employed Hayashi Razan 林羅山 (1583-1657) who from 1610 until Ieyasu's death in 1616 was a constant advisor on matters of governmental reorganization, ceremonies, and learning.[34] By this time, Ieyasu was looking for methods of effective administration in order to keep the country at peace. His belief that these ends could be achieved through the spreading of Confucian doctrines is illustrated by a statement in which he held that:

> ...if the Way of human morality is not understood, society will be chaotic, the nation will not be at peace, and disorders will never cease. To bring forth an understanding of the principles of the Way, there is no better means than books. The printing and diffusion of books is the most important task of a benevolent government.[35]

Ieyasu gave Hayashi Razan permission in 1614 to set up a school for training talented men, but this plan was never carried out.[36] In 1630, however, the third Tokugawa Shōgun, Iemitsu 家光 (1603-51), gave Hayashi land for establishing a school, and in 1632, Tokugawa Yoshinao 徳川義直 (1600-50) helped Hayashi set up a temple to Confucius on this land.[37] The founding of

34. Shibunkai 斯文會, *Kinsei Nihon no Jugaku* 近世日本の儒學 (*Recent Japanese Confucianism*), (Tōkyō: Iwanami Shoten 岩波書店, 1939), 23-25.

35. *Buya shokudan* 武野燭談, as recorded in the *Tokugawa jikki* 德川實記 (*True Chronicle of the Tokugawa*), included in the series *Zokukokushi taikei* 續國史大系 (*Continuation of the Outline of National History*), (Tōkyō: Keizai Zasshisha 經濟雜誌社, 1902), IX, 330. The actual passage referred to in the *Tokugawa jikki* as from the *Buya shokudan* does not appear in a modern reprint of the *Buya shokudan*, Kokushi sōsho 國史叢書 series (Tōkyō: Kokushi Kenkyūkai 國史研究會, 1917), although on p. 6 of the latter there is a similar passage. This discrepancy may be due to the fact that there were several versions of the *Buya shokudan* which were current in Tokugawa times. For the sake of students of Tokugawa Confucianism, it is worth noting that Bamba Masatomo 萬羽正明, *Nihon Jukyōron* 日本儒教論 (*Theory of Japanese Confucianism*), (Tōkyō: Mikasa Shobō 三笠書房, 1939), 84, incorrectly gives the *Musashi shokudan* 武藏燭談 as the source for this passage instead of the *Buya Shokudan*, and Spae, *op. cit.*, 56, repeats this error. No work called *Musashi shokudan* seems to exist.

36. *Kinsei Nihon no Jugaku*, 23. *Nihon Jugaku nempyō*, 269.

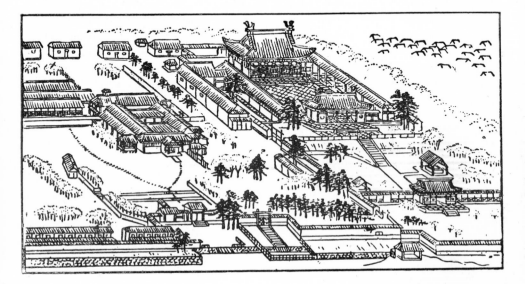

A birdseye view of the main building of Seidō and Shōheikō.

these two institutions[38] marks the genesis of a center for training Tokugawa officials along Confucian lines and for carrying out proper Confucian ceremonies by the Shōgunate's Confucian scholars. They were to be the mainstays of the government's control over educational and intellectual activities all over Japan, for they set the pace for most of the other clan schools and established a common Confucian basis for the consideration of all social problems. A glance at the more important books used in the curriculum of the Tokugawa and clan schools serves to indicate how this training assured the dominance of Confucian philosophy. These books included the *Lesser Learning* (*Hsiao-hsüeh* 小學), the *Five Classics*, the *Four Books*, and Chinese and Japanese histories stressing Confucian ethical relationships of cause and effect such as the *Ch'un-ch'iu*, *Tso-chuan*, *Han-shu*, *Shih-chi* 史記, an abbreviated version of the Chinese dynastic histories known in Japanese as the *Jūhachi shiryaku* 十八史略, and parts of the *Honchōtsugan* 本朝通鑑.[39]

Generally speaking, Confucianists during the Tokugawa period subscribed to similar views on cosmology, social organization, the nature of man, and epistemology. Because these men were the dominant intellectual force, it is necessary to try and assess what the results of such views were.

---

37. *Kinsei Nihon no Jugaku*, 950-951.

38. *Ibid.*, has two detailed articles on the growth and changes of both the temple to Confucius (pp. 947-1001) and the school (pp. 199-217). These can best be summarized by noting that the temple of Confucius and the school, under various names, remained from 1632 to 1690 at Shinobu-ga-oka 忍岡 in Edo 江戸. Throughout this period, though both institutions received aid and support from the Tokugawa, they were the private domain of the Hayashi family. In 1690, Tokugawa Tsunayoshi 徳川綱義 (1647-1709) had a temple of Confucius built at the Shōheizaka 昌平坂 in the Kanda area of Edo which replaced the old one at Shinobu-ga-oka, and the yearly Confucian sacrifices became official public ceremonies, with the Hayashi family presiding. Joined with the new temple was the school of the Hayashi, which though still private, was used for training many Tokugawa officials. This temple of Confucius, attached to the school, now came to be known as the Seidō 聖堂.

The next major metamorphosis was in 1797 when the Hayashi private school was made into an official Tokugawa school called the Gakumonjo 學問所, within which was the official temple of Confucius known still as the Seidō. The Gakumonjo is spoken of variously as the Shōheikō 昌平黌 (or 昌平校), and Shōheizaka Gakumonjo 昌平坂學問所. In 1868, its name was changed to Daigakkō 大學校, in 1869 to Daigaku 大學, but all Confucian sacrifices had ceased in 1868, and 1871, the Daigaku also was abolished.

39. Takahashi Shunjō 高橋俊乗, *Nihon Kyōikushi* 日本教育史 (*History of Japanese Education*), revised, 2nd ed. (Tōkyō: Kyōiku Kenkyūkai 教育研究會, 1934), 321-322

On the cosmological plane, there were commonly held to be metaphysical "above forms" (*keijijō* 形而上), and concrete or physical "below forms" (*keijika* 形而下). The Supreme Ultimate dominated the "above forms" and in effect consisted of the pattern or perfect principle of the universe. Within the Supreme Ultimate were an infinite number of principles (*li* 理) of metaphysical nature which when moved by the principles of motion and rest, *yin* and *yang,* produced through a primordial ether (*ch'i* 気) the five elements (*wu hsing* 五行). These in turn, through further combinations, produced all matter on the earth that became the "below forms," which were basically nothing more than reflections of the "above forms."[40] Without going into further detail, it will be sufficient to point out here that such concepts led logically to social and political views which claimed immutability and resisted change, for since man, society, and all the creatures of the world were formed according to perfect principles, it was simply a matter of determining what these were, and then striving to attain them. The Confucianists called this process the "extension of knowledge" and "investigation of things," and they claimed that it could be accomplished by studying the perfect examples that had existed in the past. This, in effect, established the position of the Confucian classics, for it was there that the "perfect examples" existed, and consequently any theory of knowledge not related to them was unthinkable.

The promised results of achieving an understanding of "fundamentals" were pictured in the Confucian classics in a way which would appeal to any ruler or administrator intent on maintaining the *status quo.* For example, proper loyalty on the part of samurai and retainers to their lord and superiors was a cardinal principle on which the stability of the feudal Tokugawa regime depended. The *Analects* described how filial piety led men to observe such loyalty as follows: "The philosopher Yu said, 'There are few who, being filial and fraternal, are fond of

---

40. The philosophy of Chu Hsi is clearly summarized and described by Fung, Yu-lan, "The Philosophy of Chu Hsi," *H.J.A.S.,* translated from Chinese by Derke Bodde, VII, (April, 1942), 1-51.

offending against their superiors. There have been none who, not liking to offend against their superiors, have been fond of stirring up confusion'."[41]

Another famous passage on how stable government could be attained through proper attention to Confucian principles is found in the *Great Learning*:

> The ancients who wished to illustrate illustrious virtue throughout the kingdom, first ordered well their own states. Wishing to order well their own states, they first regulated their families. Wishing to regulate their families, they first cultivated their persons. Wishing to cultivate their persons, they first rectified their hearts. Wishing to rectify their hearts, they first sought to be sincere in their thoughts. Wishing to be sincere in their thoughts, they first extended to the utmost their knowledge. Such an extension of knowledge lay in the investigation of things. Things being investigated, knowledge became complete. Their knowledge being complete, their thoughts were sincere. Their thoughts being sincere, their hearts were then rectified. Their hearts being rectified, their persons were cultivated. Their persons being cultivated, their families were regulated. Their families being regulated, their states were rightly governed. Their states being rightly governed, the whole kingdom was made tranquil and happy.[42]

It is little wonder that the Tokugawa Bakufu, in its attempts to perpetuate its rule in Japan, was drawn to such a philosophy that so logically and clearly related social stability, ethics and metaphysics. And although it is not fair to say that Confucianism and its precepts entirely captured the minds of the people, as happened in Korea, it seems in its fundamental forms to have been accepted by the people as the basic pattern for social relationships and the regulation of family life, while for the government and ruling classes, it extended to all fields of intellectual and social activity.

Perhaps the most outstanding example of the dominance of Confucian thought in intellectual circles would be the life of Arai Hakuseki 新井白石 (1650-1725), the brilliant advisor to the

---

41. *Lun-yü*, I, 4, as translated by Legge, op. cit., I, 138.
42. *Ta-hsüeh*, ch. I, 4-5, as translated by Legge, *op. cit.*, I, 357-359.

sixth and seventh Shōguns, Ienobu 家宣 (1662-1712) and Ietsugu 家繼 (1709-16). His famous interpretive history of Japan, *Doku-shi yoron* 讀史餘論, was almost entirely Confucian in its treatment, and as an illustration of how Confucianism was used by him in the highest levels of politics, his autobiography relates:

> The Korean ambassador objected to my use of a certain ideograph in our formal reply to their communication, because the ideograph occurred in the name of the seventh ancestor of their king. They insisted the word be mutilated, I refused. I told them the custom applied only in the relations of son and father, and vassal and lord, and not at all in international relations. Besides the rule applies only to the fifth generation, and when by mutual consent the rule is followed in international relations, it never applies beyond the fifth generation. Why should they forget too the precept that bids men never to do to others what they do not desire for themselves, since in their letter to the Shōgun, they had used an ideography which was part of the Shōgun's father's name.[43]

In addition to mentioning two of the five social relationships of the Confucian ethical code,[44] the precept of "men not doing to others what they do not desire for themselves" is taken directly from the *Analects*.[45] And the whole discussion above revolved around a point of great importance to Confucianists, that is the rectification of names.

Another example of Arai Hakuseki's use of Confucianism in dealing with problems of moment can be found in his advice to the government on economic matters when devaluation was proposed to deal with dwindling revenues.

---

43. George A. Knox, "Autobiography of Arai Hakuseki, Hyōchūoritaku Shiba no ki," *T.A.S.J.*, 1st series, XXX, pt. II, (1902), 155.

44. The social relations in Confucianism were five: those of ruler and minister, father and son, husband and wife, elder and younger brother, and friend and friend. Related to these were corresponding duties and obligations. The ruler was righteous, and the minister loyal; the father affectionate, and the son filial; the husband harmonious, and the wife submissive; the elder brother friendly and the younger respectful; and friends mutually sincere (君義臣忠父親子孝夫和婦順兄友弟恭朋信). There were also five fundamental virtues in Confucianism: humaneness, righteousness, wisdom, propriety, and sincerity (仁義知禮信).

45. *Lun-yü*, XV, 23, as translated by Legge, *op. cit.*, I, 301.

...I had another matter I wished to lay before the Shōgun, and so that night I wrote and on the morrow sent him two papers through Zembō. Their import is summed up in the words of Confucius in the *Analects,* when he undertook the government: "If producers are many and consumers few; if users use slowly and workers work fast, there will be enough." This I have taught so thoroughly in the past that I need not enlarge upon it now, but if we act on it, the treasury will be filled in a few years. To stop the debasing of the currency is to confer a blessing on the people.[46]

As evidence that Confucianism also was impressed on the people, the example of the decision to excute Sōgorō during the reign of the Shōgun Iemitsu is instructive, for Sōgorō, a mere peasant, had made a petition directly to the Shōgun, which breach of class could not be tolerated. Though ideally Confucianism did not rigidly differentiate classes, it did stress proper relationships between inferiors and superiors, and in the well-known story "Ghost of Sakura"[47] where Sōgorō's death is related, there are definite overtones of this attitude. As one of the councilors, beholding the execution, exclaimed:

Although you were but a peasant on this estate, you conceived a noble plan to succor the other farmers in their distress. You bruised your bones, and crushed your heart for their sake. Still, in that you appealed to the Shōgun in person, you committed a grievous crime and made light of your superiors; and for this it was impossible not to punish you.[48]

In the Confucian ethics found in the regulations of a guild (*kumi* 組) during Tokugawa times, however, it is possible to observe a more spontaneous expression by the people of their acceptance of Confucianism.

We shall require children to respect their parents, servants to obey their masters, husbands and wives, brothers and sisters, to

---

46. Knox, *op. cit.,* 139. The quotation from the *Analects* by Arai Hakuseki is apparently not from the *Analects* but from the *Great Learning* (*Ta-hsüeh* 大學), ch. X, 19.

47. A. B. Mitford, *Tales of Old Japan,* (London, Macmillan and Co., 1876), 193-233. I have been unable to determine what the title of this story was in Japanese, as Mitford gives no hint of it. He does mention that it was popular both as a story and a play in Tokugawa times, on page 197, in the preface to the translation. Sōgorō's whole name was Sakura Sōgorō 佐倉宗吾郎.

48. *Ibid.,* 218.

live in harmony, and the young to revere and cherish their elders, in short, we will endeavor to lead the people to walk righteously. Whoever fails to do so shall without fail incur your punishment...

On the other hand, if any person is distinguished by obedience to parents, diligence in their duties, or praiseworthy conduct in any other matters, he shall be reported by us and rewarded by you.[49]

Here are the five social relationships (*gojō* 五常) so emphasized by Confucianists as the basis of a harmonious social order, and an enumeration of some of the more important duties and obligations.[50] There is present also the idea that virtue should be rewarded, and a lack of virtue punished, a point of view stressed by Confucianists in their "praise and blame" principle.[51]

Despite the general agreement among Confucianists in their social and philosophical views, a number of schools arose in the Tokugawa period which differed quite radically from the orthodox Chu Hsi tradition on interpretations of the classics and philosophical points of emphasis. Such, for example, was the Kogakuha 古學派 which stressed going back to the original text to determine meanings, and the school of Ōyōmei 王陽明 (Wang Yang-ming) which emphasized intuition and the self as sufficient for attaining truth, as well as the Mito 水戸 school of Confucianism, the Ken'engakuha 蘐園學派, the Nangakuha, the Setchū Kōshō-gakuha 折衷考證學派 and others.[52] The reign of the early Tokugawa Sōguns, with the exception of the ban against Christianity, was a period of relatively few restrictions on the development of thought and ideas. And although the Bakufu supported Chu Hsi Confucianism, it did not actively suppress other schools as long as these did not directly oppose the government or malign the Tokugawa family.[53]

---

49. Simmons and Wigmore, "Land Tenure and Local Institutions," *T.A.S.J.*, 1st series, XIX, pt. 1, (1891), 188.

50. See note 44.

51. Sargent, *op. cit.*, 133-138, discusses how belief in this principle affected the writing of history in China. It was not conceived as being limited to this sphere alone, but was meant to be a principle active in every phase of life.

52. Spae, *op. cit.*, 51-80, briefly describes the history and doctrines of some of these schools. *Kinsei Nihon no Jugaku* also has chapters summarizing the development of schools not treated by Spae.

53. Spae, *op. cit.*, 52-53.

But by 1790, with political opposition to the Tokugawa becoming more open, and economic conditions shaking the foundations of the feudal system, it was natural that in dealing with the situation the Bakufu should make an attempt to bring the intellectual world in line in order to limit "subversive doctrines" to a minimum. The effort by the Bakufu to stabilize and control ideas and teachings is known as the *Kansei igaku no kin* 寬政 異學禁 (Prohibition of the Kansei era against heterodox teaching), and it was promulgated on the twenty-fourth day of the fifth month in 1790 by the president of the Daigaku, Hayashi Nobuyoshi 林信敬 (1767-93).[54] According to it, henceforth only Chu Hsi doctrine would be taught in government schools, and though not directly applied to the schools of clans other than the Tokugawa, it became the model for most clans to attempt some sort of intellectual control, ordinarily in favor of Chu Hsi Confucianism.[55]

Following soon after this was the reorganization of the Seidō in 1797, its name being changed to Gakumonjo and its curriculum being changed by the addition of stringent regulations and orders. These were no doubt meant to counter-act the atmosphere of demoralization and corruption that had prevailed in the years immediately preceeding,[56] when this so-called training center of officials had nearly ceased to attract men of talent to the government. Formerly, even men from clans outside the Tokugawa had been sent there, and now completion of the course was made a prerequisite to holding any high government office.

The effect of these measures was to produce a temporary revival of orthodox Chu Hsi Confucianism, especially when the

---

54. *Kinsei Nihon no Jugaku*, 160, for the text of the actual prohibition itself. The general effects of the prohibition are discussed in the pages following.

55. *Ibid.*, 158-159.

56. Some idea of the low state of Confucian studies previous to the *Kansei igaku no kin* can be gained from James Murdoch, *A History of Japan*, revised and edited by Joseph Longford (London: Kegan Paul, Trench, Trübner and Co., 1926), III, 421-425. Murdoch's picture of conditions must be modified, though, because he was anti-Tanuma. Tanuma Okitsugu 田沼意次 (1719-88) was one of the leading political figures of the latter half of the eighteenth century in Japan. He is referred to by Murdoch as Tanuma Mototsugu, apparently because Murdoch chose the reading *Moto* for 意, which can also be read *Oki*. Most Japanese biographical dictionaries prefer the latter reading.

strict and determined Hayashi Jussai 林述齋 (1768-1841) assumed the presidency of the Daigaku in 1793 and brought into the school as professors Shibano Ritsuzan 柴野栗山 (1734-1809), Bitō Nishū 尾藤二洲 (1745-1813), and Koga Seiri 古賀精里 (1750-1817).[57] These were all men of great ability and they became known as the "Three doctors of the Kansei Era" (1789-1803), each contributing a great deal to the renaissance of Chu Hsi doctrine.

In 1795 Hayashi Jussai enlarged the scope of the original *Kansei igaku no kin* to differentiate more drastically between orthodox and heterodox doctrines,[58] but in spite of such measures, the Chu Hsi philosophy of this period, as late as the Imperial Restoration in 1868, was not the same as that of Hayashi Razan in the seventeenth century. This was perhaps inevitable, due to the fact that the problems facing Japan in the nineteenth century were so different from those of earlier times, and the activity of the intellectual world reflected this change. Thus what was called Chu Hsi doctrine in the early nineteenth century in Japan in reality included the speculation and ideas of many of the schools outlawed in 1790. For example, Satō Issai 佐藤一齋 (1772-1859), one of the leading disciples of Hayashi Jussai, while outwardly professing to be a follower of Chu Hsi, was said actually to believe in the philosophy of Wang Yang-ming.[59] And the third son of Koga Seiri, Koga Dōan 古賀侗菴 (1788-1847), who like his father became a professor at the Seidō, wrote a volume on coast defense *Kaibō okusoku* 海防臆測, and in another work supported the theory of equality of the sexes, a point of view that would have been entirely impossible among earlier orthodox Confucianists.[60] Asaka Gonsai 安積艮齋 (1791-1860), who had studied

---

57. Iwahashi, *op. cit.*, 302-304, 306-310
58. *Ibid.*, 310.
59. *Kinsei Nihon no Jugaku*, 539-541.
60. *Ibid.*, 311-312. For a striking illustration of the low position of women in orthodox Confucianism, see the *Hsiao-hsüeh* 小學 (*Lesser Learning*), section of "Fu-fu chih pieh" 夫婦之別 ("The separation of men and women"), as quoted and translated by James S. Gale, "Selection and Divorce," *T.A.K.B.R.A.S.*, vol. IV, pt. III. (Yokohama, 1913), 21. One sentence of this section reads, "Confucius said, 'A woman's duty is to prostrate herself submissively before her husband, in such a way as to have no will of her own, but to demonstrate a perfect form of obedience,." Written as an ethics textbook for the young by a Chinese Confucian scholar about 1187, it became a regular part of every child's education in Tokugawa Japan and was a required text in all schools.

under Satō Issai and who also was a professor at the Seidō, clearly stated in his writings that while honoring Chu Hsi he would seek the good from all sides,[61] including Wang Yang-ming 王陽明 (1473-1529) and Lu Hsiang-shan 陸象山 (1139-93),[62] Chuang-tzu 莊子 and Laotzu 老子,[63] and Buddhism.

The sudden increase in the number of schools directly controlled by the Bakufu after 1790 may be taken as further evidence of the attempt by the Tokugawa to direct the intellectual activities of Japan. From 1615 to 1789, there were only three schools in the whole country administrered by the government, but immediately after 1789, five schools were organized by the government, and by 1847, three more had been added.[64] Though this list might not appear impressive today, one should remember that this was not a period of universal education, and the Tokugawa were interested primarily in the education of their own vassal samurai, hatamoto, and daimyō, for it was from these that most government officials were drawn. The effort to promote standardization and conformity along Confucian lines was seriously threatened after the opening up of Japan to the West in 1854, but even then the Bakufu attempted to meet the situation by the creation of more schools, and ten were set up between 1854 and 1867.[65] Not all of these were centers for training in Confucianism, which in itself shows how circumstances were forcing a modification of the rigid differentiation set up earlier between orthodox and heterodox, as well as causing a modification in the courses of study permitted in government schools.

---

61. Iwahashi, op. cit., 314.
62. Lu Hsiang-shan was a great opponent of Chu Hsi, being known as the developer of the "school of the mind" branch of Neo-Confucianism, in contradistinction to the "school of laws or principles" of Chu Hsi. Lu's ideas were further developed and completed by Wang Yang-ming 王陽明 (1473-1529). For details on this topic see Siu-chi Wang, Lu Hsiang-shan, a Twelfth Century Chinese Idealistic Philosopher, (New Haven: American Oriental Society, 1944).
63. Chuangtzu died about 280 B.C. and is considered as the greatest of the thinkers of philosophical Taoism. Traditionally he is said to have further developed and transmitted the ideas of Laotzu, the so-called founder of Taoism. In his writings Chuang-tzu showed great disdain for the Confucianists.
64. Uda Hisashi, op. cit., 625-626.
65. Loc. cit.

3.   Confucianism and Western Learning.

Confucianism in general, whether of the Chu Hsi, Wang Yang-ming, or any other school, was characterized by certain views that sought to explain in an internally harmonious fashion activity in the world in whatever form it appeared. This being so, it was inevitable that Confucianism in Japan would have to come to grips with the problems and data presented by Western learning.

Before 1790, the reaction had been mixed and varied, some Confucianists showing great interest in Western things, while others were hostile to an extreme. Arai Hakuseki, for example, had been intrigued by Western learning and discussed its meaning with Pere Giovanni Sidotti who secretly landed in Japan in 1708 and who was captured and incarcerated by the Bakufu.[66] Hakuseki's attitude seems to have been sympathetic, as he did not become hysterical in his recommendations to the Shōgun concerning what should be done with Sidotti, but simply suggested he be sent back to his own country.[67] And later Hakuseki published the *Seiyō kibun* 西洋記聞 in which he recounted his discussions with Sidotti including such information on the geography, history, and natural sciences of European countries as he had been able to glean from the prisoner. Another outstanding Confucian, Ogiū Sorai 荻生徂徠 (1666-1728), also showed an interest in Western science, writing a book on Western gunnery, *Seiyō kakō shinki setsu* 西洋 火攻神器説, based apparently on information taken from Chinese translations of such works.[68] During the reign of the Shōgun Yoshimune 吉宗 (1716-44), Western learning especially made progress when the ban against the reading and translating of Western books was removed.[69] This freer atmosphere made pos-

---

66. A partial translation by W. B. Wright of Arai Hakuseki's *Seiyō kibun* in which he relates his discussions and impressions of Sidotti can be found in "The Capture and Captivity of Pere Giovanni Batista Sidotti in Japan from 1709 to 1715," *T.A.S.J.*, 1st series, IX, (1881) 156-172.

67. Murdoch, *op. cit.*, III, 304.

68. Iwahashi, *op. cit.*, 351.

69. Murdoch, *op. cit.*, III, 356.

sible increased Japanese knowledge of Western science,[70] which though later to compete with Confucianism, was at this time still no threat to the dominance of Confucian thought.

With the promulgation of the *Kansei igaku no kin,* a serious blow was dealt to the modicum of free exchange of thought that had existed since the time of Yoshimune. Interest in Western learning and foreign countries began to be associated with plans to invade the country and overthrow Tokugawa rule. A Russian expedition in northern Japan in 1792-93, followed by continued Russian activity in northern Japanese coastal waters, increasingly disturbed many Japanese. After the refusal of the Bakufu to grant Russia trade privileges in 1806, Russian ships and gunboats appeared frequently off Japan, making particularly predatory attacks on Japanese settlements in 1806 and 1807. Constant British armed intervention and landings between 1808 and 1824 finally led the Bakufu to promulgate the famous "Expulsion Decree" of 1825 against foreigners.[71]

All this played into the hands of those Confucianists who were hostile to Western learning, for they now could associate the danger of the West to Japan with the increasing threat of Western ideas to Confucianism. It should be remembered that the Confucian philosophical world view was one based on certain premises such as the creation of all matter from a combination of five elements, the association of virtues, basic sounds and colors, and the seasons with these elements, and a dependence on Chinese classical literature as a basic source of knowledge. Western science would naturally undermine the whole cosmological explanation of Confucianism and prove Chinese literature inadequate for coping with modern technical problems. Confu-

70. *Ibid.*, 542-555. One of the most outstanding contributions to Japanese knowledge of Western science made in this period was Sugita Gempaku's 杉田玄白 (1738-1817) translation of Dutch books on anatomy and circulation of the blood.

71. *Ibid.*, 512-520, 528. For a more detailed account of the Russian attacks, see Emmett L. Murray, *Early Russian Contacts with the Japanese to 1855,* (M. A. thesis, University of California in Berkeley, 1950), 89-101. A complete translation of the "Expulsion Decree" is included in Yoshi S. Kuno, *Japanese Expansion on the Asiatic Continent, A Study in the History of Japan with Special Reference to Her International Relations with China, Korea, and Russia,* (Berkeley and Los Angeles: University of California Press, 1940), II, 320-322.

cianism was actually on the verge of receiving the same kind of
blow that scholasticism in Europe had received when science
began to destroy its basic premises.

The case of Watanabe Kazan 渡辺崋山 (1793-1841) is interesting from the point of view of this increasing conflict between
Confucianism and Western learning, for Watanabe himself was
a devout Confucian, daily reading the classics, and yet at the
same time he had become interested in Dutch studies and formed
a club for the investigation of Western science. Among the
members of this club were even Confucianists who had finished
the course at the Seidō, the Bakufu's leading Confucian school,
which serves to emphasize how interest in the West was increasing.[72] In any case, it seems that the "Morrison" incident of 1837,
when an American ship had tried to land but had been driven off,
provided the pretext for the anti-Western Confucianists to have
Western learning barred. With the subsequent repercussions to
the incident, they succeeded in having Watanabe sentenced to
confinement in his house, and Takano Chōei 高野長英 (1804-50),
the main source of Watanabe's information, was sent to jail.
Finally in 1843, the Bakufu was induced to promulgate the
Shibukawa 渋川 edict[73] by which only physicians in the future
would be allowed to study Dutch, and Western learning was
limited to medicine.[74]

Satō Issai, already mentioned as one of Hayashi Jussai's most
outstanding disciples and a leading Confucianist with many
students, also feared the encroachments of Western learning,
and in 1848 he published a treatise, Shiroku 誌録, in which he
wrote:

---

72. For a short biography of Kazan, see S. Ballard, "A Sketch of the Life of
Noboru Watanabe," T.A.S.J., 1st series, XXXII, (1905), 1-23.

73. Murdoch, op. cit., III, 564-565, refers to a decree issued by the Bakufu in 1843
on the basis of proposals put forward by Shibukawa Rokuzō 澁川六藏 (1811-1845) as
the "Shibukawa" edict. Hioki Shōichi 日置昌一, Kokushi dainempyō 國史大年表 (Great
Chronology of National History), (Tōkyō: Heibonsha 平凡社, 1936), III, 453, states that
Shibukawa Rokuzō (na: Yoshinao 敬直) actually submitted such a proposal to the
Bakufu, but when adopted, it was apparently not called the "Shibukawa" edict.

74. For the integrated details of this whole episode and its results see, Murdoch,
op. cit., III, 558-566.

The theories of the West have reached a flourishing state. Their so-called eternal truths are sufficient to alarm men. Confucianism, in the past, was harmed by the near-truths of the Buddhists, but today, the near-truths of Western theories are much more danger-ous.[75]

But despite everything, Western learning continued to gain more adherents in Japan, especially after Perry's arrival in 1854. The Bakufu in these later years began to revise somewhat its attitude towards the West, and in any case, realized that measures would have to be taken to modernize the country. This very position, though, seemed like a betrayal to many of the conser-vative Confucianists who had been responsible for the earlier attempts to have the government adopt a policy of restricting Western studies. Shionoya Tōin 塩谷宕陰 (1810-67) was a Con-fucianist of this type, and since he is fairly representative of this group, a brief resume of his activities will serve to gain an insight into their psychology.

When young, Tōin attended the Confucian lectures at the Seidō, but because of straightened circumstances was not able to finish the course. After a few years of eking out a precarious existence, he was introduced to Mizuno Tadakuni 水野忠邦 (1794-1851), lord of Hamamatsu 濱松, where he was appointed as a *jusha* 儒者 (Confucianist) with a fixed salary.

In 1841, Mizuno, who had been a members of the Shōgun's Grand Council (*Rōjū* 老中) since 1828, attained a position where he dominated the Council and became the actual leader of the Bakufu administration. In this capacity he attempted a large scale reform, issuing severe edicts in Confucian moralizing style. Tōin was one of Mizuno's advisors in drawing up these reform plans, so when they failed, he felt himself responsible. Never-theless, he was retained in Mizuno's service and presently became acquainted with foreign relations, when Mizuno was recalled to the Grand Council in 1844 to deal with a touchy

75. Iijima Tadao 飯島忠夫, *Nippon no Jukyō, Kokutai no hongi kaisetsu sōsho* 日本の儒教, 國體の本義解說叢書 (*Japanese Confucianism, Explanatory Series on the Meaning of National Polity*), fifth ed., (Tōkyō: Mombushō Kyōgakukyoku 文部省教學局, 1941), 88-89.

situation created by a letter from the King of the Netherlands
to the Bakufu. Mizuno was dismissed, however, in 1845 and
ended his official career, but Tōin continued his position with the
Bakufu.[76] In the meantime the Opium War had occurred in
China, and its results became known in Japan, arousing great
concern among Confucianists. Tōin was impelled to write an
essay, *Shin isei* 審夷情 (*Expose of the Nature of the Barbarians*),
in which he warned the Japanese against the British.[77] After
the opening up of Japan in 1854, he became increasingly critical
of the government's dealings with the foreigners, and finally in
1859 appeared his *Kakkaron* 隔華論. This was ostensibly a criticism of foreign aggression in China and of the weak policy
adopted by the Chinese authorities in dealing with the foreign
impact. In reality, however, it was directed against the Bakufu
officials and their treatment of the foreign problem, written in
allegorical form. One of the most informative section of this
work, which shows to what extent hatred of Western things could
move Confucianists like Tōin, is entitled "On the Barbarians
Invading Sinology." A passage in it reads:

> To like beauty and dislike ugliness, this is the nature of things.
> To hate coarseness and to rejoice in refinement, this is the nature of
> man. Now as regards the shape of foreign letters, they are confused
> and irregular, wriggling like snakes or larvae of mosquitos. The
> straights ones are like dog's teeth, the round ones like worms. The
> crooked ones are like the fore legs of a mantis, the stretched ones are
> like slime lines left by snails. They resemble dried bones or decaying
> skulls, rotten bellies of dead snakes or parched vipers.[78]

The ranting of Ōhashi Junzō 大橋順藏 (1816-62) against
Western science is indicative of the crumbling of the total world
philosophy of Confucianism at the end of the Tokugawa period.

---

76. This brief biography of Tōin has been taken from R. H. van Gulik, "Kakkaron, a Japanese Echo of the Opium War," *Monumenta Serica*, IV, (1939-40), 478-545.
A scholarly article, it deals exhaustively with Tōin's *Kakkaron*, and incidentally gives
much information on anti-Western Confucianists in the last year of the Tokugawa
period.

77. *Ibid.*, 539.

78. *Ibid.*

His vitriol was reserved especially for the study of Western science in Japan which was undermining the basis of Confucian metaphysics and cosmology. In his *Hekija shōgen* 闢邪小言 written in 1857, he warned:

> Followers of the Western learning steal this illustrious name [natural philosophy] and call themselves natural philosophers, shamelessly saying that the West knows the law of the universe. They are rebels who exhibit a forged seal of state and gather a vile rabble. True disciples of Confucius and Mencius should raise their banner, expose the counterfeit, and destroy these false scholars, that they may get their just regard from the spirits of the former Sages dwelling in Heaven... Fire and water are ki; and their burning and flowing too are ki. But that water being water flows and does not burn, and that fire being fire burns and does not flow, that such is the decreed nature of the two, this is of their ri.... The adherents of the Western philosophy indeed study carefully the outward appearances, but thus have no right to steal the honored name of natural philosophy. As when ki is destroyed ri too disappears, so with their analysis of ki, they destroy ri and thus their learning brings benevolence, righteousness, truth, and loyalty to naught.... Not reverent of heaven, and ignorant of the purpose of the Sages, they follow the custom of their land and study all the details, measure distances, observe the stars and make astronomy a toy.... Lights, comets, and shooting stars are ordinary things and not the reproofs of Heaven to the Westerners, who will not stand in awe of them.[79]

It was not along these lines of opposition to everything Western that Confucianism was to be redirected in Meiji times, but rather the path hinted at by Arai Hakuseki and attempted unsuccessfully by Watanabe Kazan. This latter current of Confucianism accepted the fact that Western science would preempt the explanation of the material world from the Neo-Confucian cosmologists, and it sought to create a new integration which, while giving Western learning a recognized position, would still keep Confucian ethics and certain features of its metaphysics dominant.

---

79. Knox, "Ki, ri, and ten," (a translation of part of the second volume of the *Hekija shōgen* by Ōhashi Junzō), *T.A.S.J.*, 1st series, XX, pt. I, (1892), 159, 161, 163, 166.

Already in the eighteenth century outstanding Confucianists such as Miura Baien 三浦梅園 (1723-89) had gone to the trouble of learning to read Dutch, and his writings on astronomy and economics show that he had borrowed from the West to develop his ideas along these lines.[80] Waki Gusan 脇愚山 (1764-1814), another Confucian scholar, was exposed to the Western ideas of Baien and reacted favorably to them, for he encouraged his disciples to study Western learning,[81] as a result of which one of them, Hoashi Banri 帆足万里 (1778-1852), spent seven years translating Western books. The remarkable part of this aspect of Hoashi's work, collected in a book called the *Kyuritsū* 窮理通, was that he began his translating endeavors at the age of forty without any adequate teacher. In his approach to Western learning, he did not show a great fear of it, despite the fact that he was a Confucianist, but instead applied a critical attitude in his selection of Western ideas.[82]

The famous Sakuma Shōzan 佐久間象山 (1811-64), ordinarily considered a Confucianist of the Ōyōmei school, in speaking of the opposition of Confucianists to Western things, shortly after the Opium War wrote in a poem:

China and Europe to us are both different territories. Our Imperial nation reveres the teachings of the gods, but [should] take their good points and make them into our support. Their things of beauty should firmly be incorporated, while their defects, why should they be hidden? The Way of the True King has no factional partiality. It is fair and arrives at the ultimate [of perfection]. Oh these ignorant Confucian philosophers. Aren't they cherishing great fallacies?[83]

Later on, after the arrival of Perry in Japan in 1854 and the signing of treaties with various foreign nations, Shōzan clearly expressed his attitude on the complementary position which Western learning and Confucianism should hold.

80. Iwahashi, *op. cit.*, 230, 353-354.
81. *Ibid.*, 249, 354-355.
82. *Ibid.*, 249, 355-356.
83. Iijima, *op. cit.*, 85.

People talk of the activity of the learning of the West and the inevitable decline of Confucianism. I say since the learning of the West is flourishing, the nourishment of the teachings of Confucius gains these resources. Now the learning of the West is science, [while] the teaching of Confucius is morality. Morality may be compared to food, and science may be compared to vegetables and meat which can help the savour of food. Who would say that with vegetables and meat you can destroy the essence of food?[84]

Even Satō Issai, who as late as 1846 had indicated his fear and opposition to Western learning, by 1851 had revised his views so that they coincided more or less with those of Shōzan and other more enlightened Confucianists who did not simply blindly attack the West. The type of integration he conceived of can be found in his *Shitetsuroku* 誌𧘯錄 in which he said:

The ultimate truths of the West are the mathematical principles of the material world, while the ultimate truths of the *Book of Changes* are the principles of the metaphysical world. Make these principles, for example, as the root and trunk [of a tree], and take the mathematical principles as the branches, and leaves will follow. Ultimate truths should be derived from the principles of the *Book of Changes*.[85]

The appointment of Koga Kin'ichirō 古賀謹一郎 (1816-84) in 1857 to head the Bakufu's newly founded school for the study of Western Learning,[86] the Bansho Torishirabejo 蕃書取調所,[87] serves to climax ironically the current of Confucianism that supported a synthetic policy toward Western learning. For it had been only sixty years before, in 1796, that Kin'ichirō's grandfather, Koga Seiri, had been appointed to the Seidō to help in carrying out the government's proscription against heterodox teachings.[88]

---

84. *Shōzan sensei bunko* 象山先生文稿 (*Writings of Shōzan*) as quoted by Iwahashi, *op. cit.*, 359.

85. *Shitetsuroku* 誌𧘯錄, as quoted by Iijima, *op. cit.*, 91.

86. Iwahashi, *op. cit.*, 312.

87. The Banshō Torishirabejo was a school founded in 1856 at Edo for the study of European sciences, the correction of translations, and similar work. It was moved in 1862 and its name changed to Yōsho Torishirabejo 洋書取調所, but in 1863 it was renamed Kaiseijo 開成所, which is often considered one of the precursors to Tōkyō Imperial University. *Ibid.*, 362-363.

88. *Ibid.*, 302.

4. The Fusion of Confucianism with the Imperial Restoration Movement.

The Imperial Restoration movement was fed mainly by two intellectual streams, the Kokugaku 國學 movement and the Mito 水戸 school of historical and philosophical writing. The first of these was basically anti-Confucian in its attempts to get back to nature and pristine Japanese ways, untainted by the influences of foreign cultures. By the nineteenth century, however, Kokugaku scholars and supporters were no longer adamant in their opposition to anything that smacked of Confucianism, and instead were associating particular Confucian concepts such as loyalty and filial piety with proper respect for Shintō deities and reverence to the Imperial line

The Mito school, unlike the Kokugaku movement, never opposed Confucianism as such, but rather made use of certain of the latter's historical and philosophical tenets to prove the legitimacy and ethical superiority of the Imperial line and its supporters.

In this way, Confucian ideas, while certainly not the core of the Restoration movement, had become in the nineteenth century a useful vehicle for directing the moral sense of men towards loyalty and devotion to the Imperial cause. Not only were Kokugaku and Mito supporters enlisted in this movement, but also Confucian scholars of other schools, and elements in society dissatisfied with the Tokugawa regime.

For all these men, however, the Restoration did not imply a social upheaval, but simply a change in the leadership and direction of the state. Under these circumstances, it is natural that Confucian ethical precepts would continue to have an appeal, since they could be used both to justify a change in loyalty from the Tokugawa to the Emperor and to maintain stability in society.

Examining the Kokugaku movement more closely, one finds its initiators were men such as Kada Azumamaro 荷田春満 (1669-1735) and his disciple Kamo Mabuchi 賀茂眞淵 (1697-1736). Though their primary interest was state of nature literature, as part of this they also desired a revival of pure Shintō and native

Japanese institutions, entirely apart from Confucian and Buddhist influences which they considered as having distorted the beauty and glory of Japan's divine succession. Mabuchi's anti-Chinese feelings are displayed clearly in his writings:

> In ancient time, when men's dispositions were straightforward, a complicated system of morals was unnecessary. It would naturally happen that bad acts might occasionally be committed, but the straightforwardness of men's dispositions would prevent the evil from being concealed and growing in extent. So that in those days it was unnecessary to have a doctrine of right and wrong. But the Chinese being bad at heart, in spite of the teaching which they got, were only good on the outside, and their bad acts became of such magnitude that society was thrown into disorder. The Japanese being straightforward, could do without teaching.[89]

What was necessary, according to these men, was a return to superior Japanese tradition. This point of view was emphasized even more by Mabuchi's successor, Motoori Norinaga 本居宣長 (1730-1801), whose ruling passion was a burning hatred of Chinese ideas, dominant in Japan in the form of Confucian philosophy. With Motoori, the attack on Chinese learning included statements that the relegation of the Emperor to a secondary role in previous periods had been a great wrong, rationalized on the basis of Confucian philosophy. And naturally it was only a short step further for his readers to take the same position in considering the role of the Tokugawa toward the Imperial House. A passage where this inference can easily be made is:

> The 'Holy Men' of China were merely successful rebels. The Mikado is the Sovereign appointed by the pair of deities, Izanagi and Izanami, who created the country. The Sun-Goddess never said "Disobey the Mikado if he be bad," and therefore, whether he be good or bad, no one attempts to deprive him of his authority. He is the immovable ruler who must endure to the end of time, as long as the sun and moon continue to shine. In ancient language the Mikado was called a god, and that is his real character. Duty therefore consists in obeying him implicitly without questioning his acts. During the Middle Ages such men as Hōjō Yasutoki, Ashikaga

---

89. Murdoch, *op. cit.*, III, 474.

Takauji and others violated this duty and took up arms against him. Their disobedience to the Mikado is attributable to the influence of Chinese learning.[90]

Motoori also stressed the inferiority of foreign nations to Japan and laid some of the groundwork for the "expel the barbarians" sentiment that ran so high just before the Restoration. But his extreme position on Chinese philosophy was impractical in view of the fact that the latter had such a strong hold on the nation. Besides, Shintō had little if any ethical system, and supporters of Shintō, realizing this weakness, began in the nineteenth century openly to equate Confucian rules of conduct with Shintō beliefs.[91] Hirata Atsutane 平田篤胤 (1776-1843), the most outstanding follower of Motoori, expressed this conciliatory attitude as follows:

> Devotion to the memory of ancestors is the mainspring of all virtue. No one who discharges his duty to them will ever be disrespectful to the gods, or to his living parents. Such a man will also be faithful to his prince, loyal to his friends, and kind and gentle with

---

90. Murdoch, op. cit., III, 486. Motoori was apparently criticizing the doctrines put forth by Mencius whereby an evil ruler was said to be no longer entitled to the throne. An example of such a saying by Mencius is, "A ruler who carries the oppression of his people to the highest pitch will himself be slain and his kingdom will perish.... If the sovereign be not benevolent, he cannot preserve the throne from passing from him." Mengtzu, bk. IV, pt. 1, ch. 3 and 4, as translated by Legge, op. cit., II, 293-294.

Motoori was correct in saying that Hōjō Yasutoki had justified his harsh treatment of the Imperial family on the basis of Chinese learning such as this. In the Myōe Shōnin (go) den 明惠上人後傳, as quoted by F. Brinkley, History of the Japanese People, (New York, London: Encyclopedia Britannica Co., 1915), 344-345, Yasutoki's actual words, recorded by the Buddhist priest Myōe Shōnin, testify to it.

91. The equating of Confucian ethics with Shintō beliefs and symbols actually already had a long history in Japan. Kitabatake Chikafusa 北畠親房 (1293-1354) in his Jinnōshōtōki 神皇正統記, for example, when speaking of the origin of the universe, intertwined the original Shintō deities with the Sung Confucian cosmogeny, relating them to the five elements and their corresponding virtues. Yamada Yoshio 山田孝雄, Jinnōshōtōki jutsugi 神皇正統記述義 (Explanation of the Jinnōshōtōki), (Tōkyō: Min-yūsha 民友社, 1932), 39-40.

Kumazawa Banzan 熊澤蕃山 (1619-91) is another good example of this synthetic tendency, for he insisted that just as ears and eyes existed before names were given them, so the power of virtue existed in Japan before these virtues were specifically named by Confucianists. Thus, the three divine implements, the jewel, the sword, and the mirror, represented the canon of the "age of the gods" in Japan, and stood for what Confucianists later called humaneness, wisdom, and courage, the virtues of the world. Kumazawa Banzan, Shūgi gaisho 集義外書 vol. 16, as quoted by Iwahashi, op. cit., 124-125.

his wife and children. For the essence of this devotion is in truth filial piety. These truths are confirmed by the books of the Chinese, who say that the 'loyal subject issues from the gate of the pious son,' and again, 'filial piety is the basis of all good actions.'[92]

Hirata was particularly skillful in redirecting the spirit of loyalty which was a basic Confucian moral teaching. Up through the eighteenth century loyalty ordinarily connoted the duty of a samurai to his immediate superior, or on a higher plane, of the *daimyō* to the Shōgun. The narrow confines of this relationship in early Tokugawa can be seen in the famous episode of the "Forty-seven Ronin" where samurai avenged the death of their direct superior, despite the fact that in doing this they were killing a lord who had been the direct superior of their own master.[93] What Hirata did, with the background of a revived Shintō that stressed the divinity and eternity of the Imperial line, was to question whether ultimate loyalty was not due to the chief and superior of all, the Emperor. His influence was widespread, both through his books and his lectures, especially in Kyōto where there was a tradition of Confucian heterodoxy and of fostering native studies as opposed to Chinese learning.[94] In addition, the Emperor and court nobility resided there, and they were becoming much more aware of their background and "rightful" position as the ideas in such historical works as the *Dainihon shi* 大日本史 (*History of Great Japan*) began to spread.

This brings up the second stream which nourished the Restoration movement, the development of the Mito school of historical and philosophical writing. The influence of the Mito school can be divided into two periods, the former being known as that of historical compilation begun by Tokugawa Mitsukuni

---

92. Murdoch, *op. cit.*, III, 494.

93. This story was known in many forms, but as a play it seems to have been most popular. Based on events occurring in the Tokugawa period, it ordinarily had to be presented in a somewhat diluted form, with names and dates changed because of the severe penalties imposed by the Bakufu on those publishing on recent or current events of a public character. An account based on a dramatic version of the story is V. Dickins, *Chiushingura* 忠臣藏: *The Loyal League*, (London: Allen and Co., 1880). Also see Mitford, *op. cit.*, 1-24, for a brief resume of the story in prose.

94. Murdoch, *op. cit.*, III, 494-496, aptly summarizes Hirata's contributions to the Restoration movement.

德川光圀 (1628-1700), and the latter as that of spiritual teaching extending from the sixth head of the Mito line, Harumori 治保 (1751-1805), through to the ninth head of the Mito line, Nariaki 齊昭 (1800-60).[95]

Mitsukuni's great task lay in the compilation and execution of the monumental history of Japan known as the *Dainihon shi* on which he began work in 1657. He spared no pains in searching for historical material throughout Japan, and his efforts in this regard no doubt stirred up a new interest in things Japanese. But it would be a mistake to imagine that Mitsukuni, because of his interest in the past of Japan, was in any way associated with the rabidly anti-Chinese movement represented by such members of the Kokugaku movement as Motoori. On the contrary, Mitsukuni was a devoted Confucianist, and he patterned the *Dainihon shi* after the *Shih-chi* 史記, following a system of "annals and biographies" (*chi-ch'uan t'i* 紀傳體) in writing the history, rather than simply a chronological style.[96] Furthermore, Mitsukuni employed the Chinese refugee scholar, Chu Shun-shui 朱舜水 (Japanese: Shu Shunsui) (1600-82),[97] and the latter is said to have emphasized the ethical view of history used by Chu Hsi in his *T'ung-chien kang-mu* 通鑑綱目, in which events were interpreted so that what was considered righteous was praised, and what was considered wrong was eventually

---

95. The two phases of the Mito school have been dealt with briefly in *Kinsei Nihon no Jugaku*, 95-120, 121-141.

96. *Ibid.*, 95-96. The *Shih-chi* was the first Chinese dynastic history, written by Ssu-ma Chien 司馬遷 (c. 145-85 B.C.), and highly valued by Confucianists. The reason the method of recording events in it is called the system of "annals and biographies" is that it arranged history under certain headings. According to the table of contents of the *Shih-chi*, these were: annals (*pen-chi* 本記), chronological tables (*nien-piao* 年表), histories of noble families (*shih-chia* 世家), essays on various topics (*shu* 書) ant biographies of famous people (*lieh-ch'uan* 列傳). This style was ordinarily contrasted with that of the *Ch'un-ch'iu*, or the *Tzu-chih t'ung-chien* 資治通鑑 of Ssu-ma Kuang 司馬光 (1019-86) which dealt with history in a direct chronological fashion.

97. Ernest Clement, "Chinese Refugees of the Seventeenth Century in Mito," *T.A.S.J.*, 1st series, XXIV, (1896), 12-20, describes Shu Shunsui, his background, and his activities in Japan. Also see, Arthur W. Hummel, *Eminent Chinese of the Ch'ing Period*, (Washington: United States Government Printing Office, 1943), I, 179-180. Hummel has a list of the writings of Shu Shunsui, as well as notes on modern studies made of him. In this work, however, he is to be found under his *na*, in Chinese, as Chu Chih-yu 朱之瑜.

punished.[98] It was natural for Shu Shunsui also to stress proper succession, since he himself had been forced to leave China when the usurping Manchus had overthrown the Ming dynasty, and in Japan this led him to glorify and honor the Imperial House. An example of how such fusion of historical and ethical judgments took place at this time is easily discernible in an inscription that was written by Shu Shunsui on a monument ordered set up by Mitsukuni in 1692 to honor Kusunoki Masashige 楠木正成 (1294-1336).　A part of the famous inscription reads:

> Loyalty and filial piety prevail in the universe; and the sun and the moon shine clearly in the sky. If there were no sun or moon in the universe, confusion would prevail in the world and stop everything. If the human mind should abandon loyalty and filial piety, heaven and earth would turn upside down. I hear that Masashige Nanko is a patriotic, brave and determined citizen, who has no equal; that his conduct is what no one could anticipate.... Since his mind is as constant as heaven and earth, and his resolution as hard as metal and stone, no injury could cause even a little fear, and not even his own advantage could shake his fidelity. By this he restored the Imperial government to the old city.... At last he sacrificed himself. Before his death he strictly enjoined his son to strive for the Emperor; but not a word [did he speak] for his own family. Unless his loyalty were so great as to reach heaven, he could not act so.[99]

Masashige had been one of the devoted retainers of the Emperor Go-Daigo 後醍醐 (1287-1338) who had fought against Ashikaga Takauji 足利尊氏 (1305-58) when the latter revolted in 1335. Masashige had perished in the unsuccessful attempt to stem Takauji, but as a result of his steadfast loyalty, even unto death, he had earned the reputation of being the ideal faithful minister. By making of Masashige a type to be admired, Mitsukuni was implying that loyalty and filial piety expressed in their highest form should be directed toward the Emperor.

Despite the importance of Mitsukuni's historical endeavors, it was really the second period of development of the Mito school

---

98. T. Haga, "Notes on Japanese Schools of Philosophy," *T.A.S.J.*, 1st series, XX, pt. I, (1893), 144-147.

99. Clement, *op. cit.*, 39-40.

that stimulated the Imperial Restoration movement. Regarding Confucianism, the leaders of the Mito school who wished to restore Imperial prestige openly attempted to redirect this social and intellectual force so that people would feel that their loyalty and moral duties were bound up with the Imperial nation and the Imperial family. In doing this, they showed great foresight and ability, as they apparently realized that it would be necessary to harness as many as possible of such influential forces to their cause. It is interesting to speculate on whether this had anything to do with the decline of anti-Confucian feeling among the Kokugaku scholars, for Hirata Atsutane, as has already been mentioned, greatly watered down the fiery anti-Confucian views of Motoori Norinaga, and accepted Confucian social and ethical precepts. In any case, by the early nineteenth century Mito scholars were claiming that loyalty and filial piety were most clearly exhibited in reverence to the gods, and the three men outstanding in Mito circles who took an active part in spreading these ideas were Aizawa Seishisai 會澤正志齋 (1782-1863), Fujita Tōko 藤田東湖 (1806-55), and the ninth head of the Mito clan itself, Tokugawa Nariaki 德川齊昭 (posthumous name: Rekkō 烈公, 1800-60).

Seishisai was the first of these to publicize such views in his *Shinron* 新論, written in 1825.[100] There he stated that the basic spirit upon which the Japanese state had been founded was loyalty and filial piety. These in turn were derived from the naturally virtuous conduct of the Japanese people, as a consequence of which the national polity (*kokutai* 國體)[101] of Japan

---

100. Iijima, *op. cit.*, 74, notes that the *Shinron*, while written in 1825, was not actually published until 1857. It apparently had been copied and printed from wooden blocks earlier, for it was known throughout the country.

101. National polity is a translation of the word *kokutai* 國體. This is inadequate, and perhaps the Japanese transliteration alone would be best, since it is difficult to find a word in English that includes the wide context of historical, emotional, and geographical connotations found in the Japanese *kokutai*. Ichimura Sanjirō 市村瓚次郎 "Kokutai to chūkō" 國體と忠孝 ("The National Polity and Loyalty and Filial Piety"), *Kokugakuin zasshi* 國學院雜誌, XXIII, (Jan., 1917), 17-20, discusses briefly the history of the meaning of this word, and he states that it is generally considered that *kokutai* was first used in its modern, more all-inclusive sense in the *Shinron*. But he himself feels that the first clear definition of the word had to wait until 1913, when Ishikawa Iwakichi石川岩吉, wrote his *Kokutai yōgi* 國體要義.

was peerless in the world. Since the Emperor was the head of this national polity, Seishisai deduced that the Emperor theory must be the ideal of the people, and he attempted to explain this theory and its relationship with loyalty and filial piety through Confucian ethics.[102] Seishisai also sought to awaken the people to the dangers to the national polity of heterodox doctrines and the impending threat from the West, and in this way helped sow the seeds for the *Sonnō jōi* 尊王攘夷 (Revere the Emperor; expel the barbarians) movement which characterized the Restoration movement during the last years of the Tokugawa period.[103] This opposition to the West coincided with one of the currents of Confucianism already described, and it is significant in that it shows how the Restoration movement was able to mobilize other trends in support of its cause.

Fujita Tōko was an advisor to Tokugawa Nariaki, and there is no doubt that he influenced the latter in his identification of the "Way of Confucius" with the "Way of the gods." This view of Nariaki's is found in his *Kōdōkanki* 弘道館記, written in 1838 with the help of Tōko, as well as Aizawa Seishisai and the Confucian scholar Satō Issai.[104] Since Nariaki was one of those who gave great impetus to the restoration of Imperial prestige, and was in a position to make his influence felt, his views toward Confucianism are worth noting. The *Kōdōkanki* mentioned above was engraved on a stone in 1838 at the establishment of his school, the Kōdōkan 弘道館, and it was meant to set forth the object of the school. In the last part of the inscription Nariaki wrote:

> To Takemikazuchi no kami[105] who wrought immortal deeds in primitive ages and still lives in the memory of inhabitants of this province, I have here dedicated a temple. I have done this for the sake of rewarding his benevolence and of making our people understand that

---

102. *Kinsei Nihon no Jugaku,* 135-136.

103. *Ibid.,* 136.

104. *Ibid.,* 123-124. For the text of *Kōdōkanki* 弘道館記, see the Gakkōhen 學校編 of the *Nihon kyōiku bunko* 日本教育文庫 (*Library of Japanese Education*), (Tōkyō: Dōbunkan 同文館, 1913), IXX, 197-198. According to the *Kinsei Nihon no Jugaku,* 123-126, for a real understanding of this inscription, one has to be acquainted with Fujita Tōko's *Kōdōkanki jutsugi* 弘道館記述義, and Aizawa Seishisai's *Taishokkanwa* 退食間話. Both of these men were very close to Nariaki.

this inviolable truth originated in such antiquity. I have also built a shrine to Confucius who propounded the moral doctrine of the Tō, Gu, and three other dynasties, doctrines that our countrymen adopted and amalgamated with, thus modifying the original truth. This I have done for the purpose of having our people know that the fact that this original truth became brighter and more beautiful is not without its cause.... Hold firmly to the truth of this holy nation; and at the same time adopt the principles of the Western land, China; respect both the gods and Confucianism.[106]

In this passage, the original truth which has been modified and become brighter is that of the Shintō gods. Without questioning exactly what Nariaki meant by "original truth," it is clear he was attempting to harmonize Shintō tradition with Confucianism. That this was not just a passing interest is proved by the fact that eight years before, Nariaki had commissioned his advisor Fujita Tōko, to make a study of Shintō, and in the *Shintō bikō sōron* 神道備考総論 written by Tōko to comply with this request, the unity of Confucianism and Shintō was proclaimed as being the characteristic Japanese way of virtue.[107]

The identification of Confucianism with Shintō was not limited alone to the Mito clan and its supporters, for the ideas of Tōko and Seishisai apparently had wide circulation. An important example of this is found in the regulations of the Gakushūin, a special school established in 1846 by the Emperor Ninkō 仁孝 (1800-47) for the education of the children of *kuge* 公家 (nobles).

...tread the 'Perfect Way' of the Sages and exalt the beautiful customs of our Imperial nation. If one does not read the Confucian classics, how can one cultivate the body? If one is not conversant

105. Takemikazuchi no kami 健御雷神 was the Shintō god sent to earth with Futsunushi no kami 經津主神 to obtain the submission of the ōkuninushi 大國主 prior to the descent of Ninigi no mikoto 瓊々杵尊 to Japan from heaven. Otsuka Tatsuo 大塚龍夫 and Uematsu Yasushi 植松安, *Kojiki zenshaku* 古事記全釋 (*Complete Explanation of the Kojiki*), 5th ed. (Tōkyō: Fukyūsha 不朽社, 1935), 150-162.

106. Clement, *op. cit.*, 25-26. As to the doctrines of "Tō" and "Gu," Nariaki was referring to Yao 堯 and Shun 舜. They were two of the legendary Chinese "sage kings" so revered by Confucianists, and the reason they were referred to as "Tō" and "Gu" is because these were the places where they held fiefs before becoming emperor. The "three other dynasties" apparently refers to the Hsia 夏 (2205-1766 B.C.), the Shang 商 (1766-1122 B.C.), and the Chou 周 (1122-221 B.C.) dynasties.

107. *Kinsei Nihon no Jugaku*, 137-138.

with the national records, how can one develop that which is just? One should clearly be aware of [both of] these and practice them with fervor.[108]

Associated with the Gakushūin was a scholar by the name of Saida Koresada 座田維貞 (1800-50). As an illustration of the sort of influences at work at the school, it is enlightening to note that he wrote a book called the *Kokki* 國基 in 1835 in which he said that the duty of revering the king, enunciated by Confucius in the *Spring and Autumn Annals,* in Japan was the same as revering the eternal Imperial line. In this book he also pointed out that environment and particular circumstances were important factors in determining the course of a nation. He claimed that with this in mind, Confucius had not criticized Kings T'ang 湯 (1766-53 B.C.)[109] and Wu 武 (1122-15 B.C.)[110] for their overthrowing evil dynasties, but that once these special Chinese characteristics were weeded out of Confucianism, its essentials were applicable everywhere.[111]

The famous loyalist Yoshida Shōin 吉田松陰 (1831-59), who did so much in a brief lifetime to stir up support for the Imperial Restoration, also appears to have approved of the fusion of Confucian morality into the national tradition, despite the fact that he was often critical of over-adulation of Confucianism. Thus, like Saida Koresada, he warned that the "way of the ruler" was different in China from that in Japan, and though it might be proper to praise abdication to another line and the overthrowing of rulers in China, this was unthinkable in Japan.[112] Concerning ethics, he had the following to say:

---

108. Iijima, *op. cit.,* 87. For details on the Gakushūin see footnote 118.

109. T'ang was the first ruler of the Shang dynasty (1866-1122 B.C.) and traditionally was meant to have driven out Chieh 桀 (1818-1766 B.C.), the last evil ruler of the Hsia dynasty 夏 (2205-1766 B.C.), who epitomized in Chinese thought cruel and despotic rule. In China, orthodox Confucianists ordinarily praised T'ang for this, claiming it was the inexorable action of Heaven moving when a limit of evil had been reached.

110. Wu was the first king of the Chou dynasty 周 (1122-255 B.C.) and traditionally is spoken of as having destroyed the last wicked ruler of the Shang dynasty, Chou 紂 (1154-1122 B.C.), who died in flames. Like many last rulers in Chinese history, Chou was considered as having reached the height of evil, due to which Heaven acted to destroy him, while Wu was said to be virtuous and was revered by orthodox Confucianists.

111. Iijima, *op. cit.,* 87.

112. Hagura Shinichirō 羽倉信一郎. "Yoshida Shōin no Jukyō shichō to sono kokkakan" 吉田松陰の儒教思潮と其國家觀 ("The Confucian Intellectual Trend of Yoshida Shōin and his National Views"), *Shibun,* XV, 1 (Jan., 1932), 42.

> If we are born as men, we must be able to distinguish between men and beasts or birds. For men there are five relations, among which that of lord and retainer, father and son are most important. Loyalty and filial piety are essential to perfection.... If we are born in Japan, we must know the excellence of Japan. The Imperial line is one. The lords and their retainers have loyally served the Mikado for centuries. If we are filial to our parents, then we shall be loyal to the Emperor. Filial piety and loyalty under such conditions as exist in Japan are one.[113]

In the first phrase above, "to distinguish between men and birds and beasts," Yoshida accepts a basic Confucian concept, namely that man must have moral training to set him apart from other beings in the world.[114] Furthermore he mentions the five social relations so stressed by Confucians as the basis of social life, and then proceeds to show how two of these have a special application in Japan. In doing this, he clearly associated himself with the current in the Imperial Restoration movement which since the early part of the nineteenth century found Confucian ethics a useful and valuable ally in strengthening its cause.

The problem of how Japan should deal with Western learning and foreign nations was a particularly acute one during the last years of the Tokugawa period. Its relation to the Imperial Restoration was very close, for the Imperial Court used the Bakufu's dealings with Western powers as the excuse for touching off the period of active opposition to the Tokugawa government begun in the late 1850's. The conflict over Western learning that had divided Confucianists also seems to have existed in the ranks of the loyalists. Among them, however, the conservative, anti-Western faction seems to have been even more dominant, although anti-foreign Confucian sentiment no doubt helped fan this flame, especially in view of the redirection and acceptance of many of its principles into the Imperial cause in the preceding

---

113. Robert C. Armstrong, *Light from the East*, University of Toronto Studies, (University of Toronto, 1914), 191.

114. The view that human nature must be differentiated from that of animals is most clearly expressed in *Mengtzu* 孟子, one of the books most used to educate the young in Tokugawa times. See *Mengtzu*, bk. III, pt. 1, ch. 4, 7-8; Legge, *op. cit.*, II, 250-251.

years. Ōhashi Junzō, who was already mentioned earlier when discussing the anti-Western current of Confucianism, is an example of this type, for besides being a staunch Confucian, he was devoted supporter of the Imperial Restoration movement.

But among the loyalists themselves there were men who realized that a policy of blind antagonism to the West was futile, and they were impressed by the technical superiority of the foreigners, particularly after the bombardment of Kagoshima by the British in 1863 and of Shimonoseki by an allied force in 1864. Yet they rarely were interested in going further than adopting these technical innovations, as they felt that after the country had been strengthened materially, the problem of preserving Japan's unique traditions and peerless Imperial line was paramount. Thus Yoshida Shōin wanted to adopt Western military methods in order to help protect the country, but did not have in mind any steps to modify thereby the Japanese national polity.

Hasegawa Akimichi 長谷川昭道 (1815-97), both a loyalist and a Confucianist, is representative of those supporters of the Restoration who foresaw the most practical way of dealing with Western learning, for he claimed that the strong points of any learning, after being critically analyzed, might be used to strengthen and supplement the Imperial way (Kōdō 皇道).[115] He had already done this with Confucianism in a book he wrote in 1852 called the Kōdō jutsugi 皇道述義. In it he said that the "way" was derived from the sun and not from heaven as in Confucianism, and developing this further, showed how the so-called Confucian six virtues, as well as the related six social relationships of Confucianism,[116] were formed from the action of the sun. This latter idea appears to have been borrowed by Akimichi from the Confucian cosmological theory which asserted that through the action of the yin and the yang in heaven, the five elements and corresponding virtues, social relationships,

---

115. Iijima, op. cit., 95.
116. Ordinarily in Confucianism there were five virtues, as well as only five fundamental social relationships. Sometimes, however, courage (yū 勇) was included in the category of essential virtues, and the five social relationships were increased by the addition of that between elder and younger (chō yō 長幼). An enumeration of the five virtues and five social relationships may be found under footnote 44.

and other phenomena were produced.[117] Akimichi was also active in popularizing such words as "Imperial way" (Kōdō 皇道), "Divine Imperial way" (Shinkō no michi 神皇の道), "Imperial law" (Kōhō 皇法), and "Imperial learning" (Kōgaku 皇学). Finally, in an article of the "Study Regulations" of the Kōgakusho 皇学所 [118] founded in 1868, with which Akimichi was prominently connected, the form of the full synthesis he conceived of can be observed. The particular article went as follows: "...clarify the 'national polity' and justly carry out obligations. Chinese and Western learning together [are] to become the wings of the Imperial way."[119]

And indeed, this is essentially the position that both Western and Chinese learning were to hold in modern Japan, the former giving the Imperial way a strong right arm, while the latter provided it with the moral basis for receiving absolute loyalty and obedience from its subjects.

---

117. Iijima, op. cit., 95.

118. In the opening year of the Meiji era, 1868, the Gakushūin 學習院, founded in Kyōto in 1846 for the education of nobles, had its name changed to Daigakuryōdai 大學寮代, but in the 9th month of the same year, its functions were transferred to the Kangakusho 漢學所 in Kyōto. The Kangakusho was amalgamated in 1869 with its brother institution, the Kōgakusho 皇學所, and here the tradition of a special school for teaching the nobility was preserved. Due to the change of capitals from Kyōto to Tōkyō, however, the Kōgakusho declined, and despite an effort to revive it in Tōkyō under the name of Daigakkōdai 大學校代, it was abolished in 1870. For the details of the books and courses proposed for the Kōgakusho and other institutions listed above, see Shibunkai 斯文會, Shibun rokujūnen shi 斯文六十年史 (A History of Sixty Years of Confucian Studies), (Tōkyō: Shibunkai 斯文會, 1929), 5-28. Although books on Japanese history and literature predominated, there were also a large number of Confucian works and Chinese histories included.

It is interesting to note that the tradition of a special school for nobles went back to 701 when the Taihōryō 大寶令 specified that a Daigakuryō 大學寮 would be set up where nobles of the fifth rank or above could attend. The Gakushūin of 1846 is said to have been an attempt to revive this, as the Daigakuryō ended its existence hundreds of years before. The present-day Gakushūin was founded in Tōkyō in 1877 when the Emperor Meiji personally gave land and money for it. Kokushi jiten 國史辞典, (Dictionary of National History), (Tōkyō: Fuzambō 富山房, 1940-42), II, 440; III, 740.

119. Iijima, op. cit., 96. Sansom, op. cit., 452, states that the idea of Western learning and Confucianism as the two wings of the Imperial way was not well received by Confucianists. While this may be true for the period immediately following the Restoration, the metaphor seems to have been widely accepted by 1910, and can be found, for example, generally used by Iwahashi in the last pages of his book Nihon Jukyō gaisetsu when describing the future of Confucianism in Japan. The term also occurs in many essays and speeches that were included in the magazine Shibun 斯文, the Confucian publication which first appeared in 1919.

II

CONFUCIANISM THROUGH THE MEIJI PERIOD AND FIRST PART OF THE TAISHŌ PERIOD TO 1913

1. The Decline of Organized Confucianism.

With the advent of the Restoration, the decline of Confucianism became rapid and severe, and as a strong organized movement it almost disappeared for a number of years. Probably the most important immediate cause for this was that organized Confucianism had been tainted as the "social philosophy" of the previous government of the Shogunate, and so would naturally be out of favor with the new ruling groups who tried to develop a vigorous National Shintō[1] which might in some measure attract the loyalty and emotions of all.

Most notable in this process was the abolition of the Shōheizaka Gakumonjo, its attached Seidō, and all similar institutions over Japan which had been directly controlled by the Tokugawa. These had served, it will be remembered, to train officials and Tokugawa retainers,[2] and the courses of study there had been primarily the Confucian classics, while the instructors ordinarily

---

1. Masaharu Anesaki, *History of Japanese Religion*, (London: Kegan Paul, Trench, Trübner and Co., 1930), 334-336, briefly describes this movement. For more details, see William M. Osuga, *The Establishment of State Shintō and the Buddhist Opposition in the Early Meiji Period*, (M.A. thesis, University of California in Berkeley, 1949), 1-7.

2. It is interesting to note that as late as 1867, the Tokugawa government decreed that all boys of over eight of *hatamoto* 旗本 or *gokenin* 御家人 families had to attend the Confucian Shōheizaka Gakumonjo, *Nihon Jugaku Nempyō* 日本儒學年表, (*Chronological Table of Japanese Confucianism*), (Tōkyō: Shibunkai 斯文會, 1923), 418. The *hatamoto* were the direct vassals of the Tokugawa who lived in Edo and guarded the Shōgun. In rank they were below the *daimyō* 大名, but above the *gokenin*, who constituted all samurai in the service of the Shōgun inferior in rank to the *hatamoto*.

had constituted the outstanding Confucianists in Japan. The Shōheizaka Gakumonjo was first transformed radically into a Daigakkō 大學校 in 1868, a Daigaku 大學 in 1869, and its life was finally terminated in 1871 when a Mombushō 文部省 (Ministry of Education) was established, and fu 府 (urban prefecture) and ken 県 (prefecture) set up to replace the old han 藩 (clan) organization.[3] This last action is significant, for previously, many of the han had had their own Confucian schools for training local administrators and samurai, but now a standardized educational pattern was imposed throughout the country in which, at first, Confucianism played no organized part whatsoever, while Western learning was stressed.

The Seidō and similar Confucian temples attached to all the major Tokugawa schools and to many of the han schools, where the important Confucian spring and autumn ceremonies called sekiten 釋奠 had been carried out, all disappeared with the abolition of organized Confucian educational institutions. No sekiten was carried out regularly again in Japan until 1907.[4]

Closely related to the decline of organized Confucianism was the craze for Western learning which swept Japan in the years immediately following the Restoration, when everything new was revered, and everything old was despised. This naturally placed Confucianism under attack, for to the popular mind it was associated with the rigid social order of Tokugawa times, opposition to the West and to Western learning, and a slavish and useless attachment to the literature and morality of Chinese antiquity.

The words of Fukuzawa Yukichi 福澤諭吉 (1835-1901), one of the most influential and prominent educators of the Meiji period, reflect this sentiment, for in his Gakumon no susume 學問のスゝメ (Encouragement of Learning), a book published in installments between 1872 and 1876, he said:

---

3. W. W. McLaren, "Japanese Government Documents, 1869-89," T.A.S.J., series 1, XLII, pt. 1, (1914), 20. Takahashi Shunjō 高橋俊乘, Nihon kyōiku shi 日本教育史, (History of Japanese Education), (2nd ed., revised and enlarged; Tōkyō: Kyōiku Kenkyūkai 教育研究會, 1934), 323, 386, 457.
    4. Nihon Jugaku nempyō, 431.

The only purpose of education is to show that man was created by Heaven to gain the knowledge required for the satisfaction of his needs for food, shelter, and clothing, and for living harmoniously with his fellows. To be able to read difficult old books or to compose poetry is all very nice and pleasant, but it is not really worth the praise given to great scholars of Chinese and Japanese of the past.

How many Chinese scholars have been good at managing their domestic affairs? How many clever men have been good at poetry? No wonder that a wise parent, a shopkeeper, or a farmer is alarmed when his son displays a taste for study.... What is really wanted is learning that is close to the needs of man's daily life.

A man who can recite the Chronicles but does not know the price of food, a man who has penetrated deeply into the classics and history, but cannot carry out a simple business transaction—such people as these are nothing but rice-consuming dictionaries, of no use to their country, but only a hindrance to the economy. Managing your household is learning, understanding the trend of the times is learning, but why should reading old books be called learning?[5]

Here indeed was the pragmatic spirit expressed forcefully, and it is clear that the long training necessary to produce competent Confucian scholars was considered utterly worthless by Yukichi. The influence of his book *Gakumon no susume* can be estimated from the fact that it sold over three million parts in installment.[6]

Itagaki Taisuke 板垣退助 (1837-1919), another prominent Japanese of the Restoration period who became one of the leaders of the abortive liberal movement of Meiji times, in a speech in 1882 on the obstacles to achieving liberty in Japan, described Confucianism as follows:

Again in Confucianism we have a mixture of politics and religion, the principles controlling either being held to emanate from the same source, government being regarded as a paternal institution whose main office is to instruct and protect the people. Thus government and religion trespassing on each other's domains have interferred, here with the private life of the people, there with the

---

5. Fukuzawa Yukichi 福澤諭吉, *Gakumon no susume* 學問のスヽメ, (*Encouragement of Learning*), as quoted by G. B. Sansom, *The Western World and Japan*, (New York: Alfred A. Knopf, 1950), 454.

6. *Loc. cit.*

administration of public affairs, inflicting injury on one side and another.[7]

And in 1884, Niishima Jō 新島襄 (1843-90), the most outstanding early Japanese Christian, in emphasizing the moral aspects of education severely criticized attempts to revive Confucianism, asserting that:

> There are many who are seeking to improve the public morality on the basis of Chinese philosophy. We cannot rejoice in their efforts, for the moral code of China had no profound hold on the minds of men.... It is the spirit of liberty, the development of science, the Christian morality which gave birth to European civilizations.... We cannot therefore believe that Japan can achieve this civilization until education rests on the same basis. With this foundation the state is built upon a rock.... Resting on the old moral code of China, it stands upon the sea-sands, and, when rough waves beat upon it, falls to ruin.[8]

The attempts to revive Confucianism mentioned by Niishima will be described in detail later, but it should be noted here that these efforts apparently had little appeal to the public, or even to the intellectuals and better educated classes. This can be deduced from the fact that the Tōkyō Shūshin Gakusha 東京修身學社, a Confucian organization founded in 1876,[9] and its successor society, the Nippon Kōdōkai 日本講道會 (the characters for this name were changed in 1886 to Nippon Kōdōkai 日本弘道會), had been unable to attract more than a few tens of members by 1884, despite eight years of constant endeavor.[10]

By 1881, many of the Confucianists who had carried on the tradition of the outstanding Tokugawa Confucian schools had died, and this also became a contributing factor to the rapid decline of Confucianism in the first half of the Meiji period.[11]

---

7. McLaren, op. cit., 608.
8. Anesaki, op. cit., 341-342.
9. Nihon Jugaku nempyō, 341-342.
  10. Kiyowara Sadao 清原貞雄, Kaishū Nippon dōtoku shi 改修日本道德史, (History of Japanese Morality, revised edition), (Tōkyō: Chūbunkan Shoten 中文館書店, 1937), 626.
  11. Between the years 1868 and 1891, the Nihon Jugaku Nempyō, 419-427, lists forty-nine Confucianists of note that died. Also, in the years immediately preceeding the

These men had been the principal proponents of carrying on instruction in Confucian philosophy, and in Confucian social and literary values, but with the number of those qualified to continue this tradition having shrunk greatly, there were fewer and fewer men in Japan who could understand the former total, all-encompassing sweep of Confucianism. This is not to say that men would know nothing of Confucianism, for they might still be acquainted with certain precepts from the classics, or quotations illustrating Confucian points of view, but the organization of the schools after 1868, their curricula, and the trends and exigencies of the times were all tending to lessen its influence.[12] This can be appreciated by noting that for a while after the Restoration there was no department of Chinese or Japanese literature at the government universities throughout Japan,[13] while in some schools English but not Japanese literature and history were taught, and morals text-books were even said to be translations of foreign readers.[14] Under such circumstances, the fading away of many of the old Confucian scholars at this time naturally meant that Confucianism would have few followers among the rising generation, unless the government or people of influence took an active interest in reviving and perpetuating it. It was not until 1877, following the establishment of Tōkyō Imperial University, that courses specifically on Chinese and Japanese literature were offered,[15] but it was 1882 before a special department for the Chinese classics was first set up at Tōkyō Imperial University.[16]

Restoration, a large number of outstanding Confucianists died without leaving well-established successors to carry on their teachings. Iwahashi Junsei 岩橋遵成, *Nihon Jukyō gaisetsu* 日本儒教概説 (*Outline of Japanese Confucianism*), (Tōkyō and Ōsaka: Hōbunkan, 寶文館, 1926), 364.

12. Shibunkai 斯文會, *Shibun rokujūnen shi* 斯文六十年史 (*A History of Sixty Years of Confucian Studies*), (Tōkyō: Shibunkai, 1929), 181-184.

13. *Shibun rokujūnen shi*, 184. Sansom, *op. cit.*, 461.

14. Sansom, *op. cit.*, 461.

15. *Shibun rokujūnen shi*, 185-187.

16. *Ibid.*, 232-236.

2. The Adjustment of Confucianism to the Times and its Re-
    currence in Various Fields.

Despite the eclipse of Confucianism in its organized "civil
service," educational, and ceremonial forms, as a pattern of
thought and frame of reference, particularly for social and ethical
problems, it continued to play an important part in Japanese
life in Meiji times. This fact is quite evident from only a cursory
observation of some of the regulations, statutes, and literary and
political trends of the day.

For example, in the *fu* and *ken* regulations of 1869 is the following: "Good customs and usages shall be maintained; frugality
shall be encouraged; good behavior shall be encouraged."[17] This
is reminiscent of the *kumi* regulations of the Tokugawa period,[18]
and is Confucian in its position of rewarding the good and ostensibly punishing the bad. Then in the very setting up of a Board
of Censors (*Danjōdai* 彈正台) in 1870, who were to exercise a
moral supervision over the acts of civil officials, a Confucian
principle of government was implied.[19] And among the principles
of Great Education (*Daikyō* 大教) announced in 1872 by the
Ecclesiastical Board (*Kyōbushō* 教部省) was one stating: "The
Way of Humanity shall be promulgated." It was meant to be
realized by seeing that: "The morality of the five relationships
shall be observed."[20] In the following year, Great Religious
Institutes (Daikyōin 大教院) were founded to carry out the aims
of the Ecclesiastical Board, and included in the two sets of topics
to be stressed were the relations between sovereign and subjects,
father and child, and husband and wife.[21] These are the first
three of the five Confucian social relationships. In addition, the
difference between man and birds and beasts was to be considered,[22] which already has been mentioned as reflecting a basic

---

17. McLaren, *op. cit.*, 27.
18. See ch. I, 16, of this study.
19. McLaren, *op. cit.*, 16.
20. Anesaki, *op. cit.*, 335.
21. Toyoda Takeshi 豊田武, *Nippon shūkyō seido shi no kenkyū* 日本宗教制度史の
研究 (*A Study of the History of Japanese Religious Systems*), (Tōkyō: Meguro Shoten
目黒書店, 1935), 217.
22. *Ibid.*, 217.

Confucian view as to the nature of man.[23]

A little later on in 1881, the Minister of Education, Fukuoka Takachika 福岡孝弟 (1835-1919), at a meeting of *fu* and *ken* educational officials held for the purpose of stressing the necessity of moral education, asserted: "In the teaching of discipline, we must make the unique moral teachings of this Imperial land the basis and require a following of the doctrines of Confucianism."[24] And in 1887, the Minister-President of State (*Dajōdaijin* 太政大臣) appealed to the public on the basis of Confucian-like virtues as follows: "It is therefore the earnest desire of the government that the people prove their loyalty and patriotism by faithfully discharging the two duties of paying taxes and performing military service."[25] The ideas of faithfully carrying out one's duties and of loyalty to the government, while certainly not existing only in Confucianism, had attained special ethical significance to Confucianists because of the emphasis by Chu Hsi on the theory of the "true relations between sovereign and subjects" (*taigi meibun* 大義名分). According to this, everyone was conceived of as having definite duties to carry out depending on his particular position in society. To the extent that these duties were respectively carried out, a nation flourished and declined. With the tendency of most Japanese government officials to think in terms of a corporate state, such Confucian ideas naturally recommended themselves.[26]

In the movement for constitutional government in Japan in the 1870's, Confucian reasoning appeared in several guises. For example, the appeal in 1874 by the samurai of Kōchi prefecture 高知縣 to the throne, on the occasion of the announcement of the creation of a deliberative assembly, is an extremely reactionary memorial in which Western learning is attacked and where the

---

23. See ch. I, 38, of this study. Also ch. I, foot note 114.
24. Iwahashi, *op. cit.*, 374.
25. McLaren, *op. cit.*, 328.
26. "Kōshi no taigi meibun setsu ni tsuite" 孔子の大義名分說に就いて ("Concerning Confucius's Theory of the True Relations between Sovereign and Subjects"), *Shibun* 斯文, XI, 6, (June, 1929), 423 ff. Also see Suzuki Daisetzu, *Zen Buddhism and its Influence on Japanese Culture*, (Kyōto: The Eastern Buddhist Society, Otani Buddhist College, 1938), 115-117.

natural and suitable doctrines for Japan are claimed to be those based on Confucianism.

> In this Empire there are Imperial institutions, Europe and America have institutions of their own, and the same is true in respect to other parts of the world. In this Empire the fundamental relations of lord and vassals, of parent and child, are established firm and unchangeable as a mountain.... But is it not enlightenment and civilization where lord and vassal, parent and child, husband and wife, each observe faithfully their relative duties; where governors and governed live amicably together?.... In education, however, the chief attention is directed to European studies, and the doctrines of the Chinese sages seem on the point of being discarded. It appears to us that the doctrines of the Chinese Sages accord well in many points with the Shintō religion, and 1600 years have now elapsed during which they have been held in high esteem by an unbroken succession of Emperors. Would it not be an error to do away with them entirely? Education should consist, first of all in the study of our native writings by which we learn the superiority of our national constitutions over those of all foreign countries, and next in acquiring a knowledge of the doctrines of the Chinese Sages, by which we learn the virtues of loyalty, filial piety, and justice.... What need have we to imitate the customs of foreign countries 10,000 ri away?[27]

The times were not propitious, though, for such precepts, and Western ideas were sweeping Japan. Yet even those who became fully attached to Western political and philosophical doctrines retained certain basic Confucian principles. Thus, Kōno Hironaka 河野廣中 (1849-1923), later one of the leaders of the democratic movement, in describing his first acquaintance in 1872 with John Stuart Mill's *On Liberty,* said:

> I bought a book called *Jiyū no ri* by John Stuart Mill and translated by Nakamura Masanao... I read this book on horseback while homeward bound, and there was a sudden great revolution in my thinking which had been nourished by Chinese studies and Kokugaku which tended to be anti-foreign. All my old ideas except those on loyalty and filial piety were completely destroyed. At the same time I learned that we should esteem man's liberty and rights.

27. McLaren, *op. cit.,* 449, 451, 457.

Furthermore I realized of my own accord that government must be on the basis of broad popular will.[28]

Although it would be unfair to characterize Japanese Confucianism of modern times as simply a propagation of and adherence to ideas of loyalty and filial piety, there is no doubt that these were the principles found most useful by the government authorities to maintain ideological uniformity. Before 1868, the emphasis put on loyalty and filial piety directed toward the Emperor had been of great importance in unifying public opinion, and the same was true in later periods of tension, crisis, or war. This is what makes Hironaka's statement illuminating, for he did not seem to realize that even loyalty and filial piety could make demands on the individual such that liberty and government based on popular will would be impossible.

But perhaps the most interesting example of an appeal to essentially Confucian ideals of harmony and mutual prosperity for justifying representative government is the following memorial, addressed in 1880 to the Minister-President of State on behalf of the local assembly of Miyagi prefecture 宮城縣:

His Imperial Majesty, the great and gracious Emperor who now rules over us with the assistance of your Excellency's wisdom and experience, leaves nothing to be desired in conducting the administration of the country, and yet dissatisfaction is prevalent at home, while abroad we suffer by reason of the exaction of foreigners. How is this to be explained? Is it not because no proper feeling of harmony has been established between the governors and the governed?

The prosperity of a country is inseparable from the prosperity of its inhabitants; the government and the people should therefore act in unison. Can it be right that the government should alone be charged with all the affairs that pertain to the welfare of the state?

It is indisputable that the most urgently pressing measure is the establishment of a constituent assembly, so that the people shall take part in legislative functions. Thus the three great bodies which go to build up prosperous communities would be working in har-

28. Nobutaka Ike, *The Beginnings of Political Democracy in Japan*, (Baltimore: The John Hopkins Press, 1950), 112.

mony, and the welfare of the Empire advanced as that of a single individual.[29]

The idea of the prosperity of the state depending upon the mutual harmony between governors and governed is one which is found constantly in all Confucian writings. Confucius had alluded to it in speaking of the advice that Yu Jo 有若 had given to Duke Ai 哀 on how to tax the people. There the latter had said: "If the people have plenty, their prince will not be left to want alone. If the people are in want, their prince cannot enjoy pleasure alone."[30] And Mencius had warned: "What the superior loves, his inferiors will be found to love exceedingly. The relations between superiors and inferiors is like that between the wind and the grass. The grass must bend when the wind blows upon it. The business depends on the prince."[31] The Japanese had learned to use such ideals of government in explaining the actions of praiseworthy rulers, soon after contact with China brought an appreciation of Confucian concepts of virtue. Thus in the *Nihongi*, written about 720 A.D., the Emperor Nintoku 仁徳 (ca. 395-427) is spoken of as having shown typical Confucian care and concern for his subjects, especially when he claimed that:

> The wise sovereigns of antiquity, if a single one of their subjects was cold and starving, cast the responsibility on themselves. Wherefore the people's poverty is none other than Our poverty; the people's prosperity none other than Our prosperity. There is no such thing as the people being prosperous and yet the Prince in poverty.[32]

Since Confucianism had been introduced into Japan only some fourteen years before this, about 384, it is highly unlikely that Nintoku ever said such a thing or had such ideas in mind. But Japanese historians and political figures constantly referred

---

29. McLaren, *op. cit.*, 481-482.
30. *Lun-yü* 論語 (*Analects*), Yen Yüan 顏淵 ch. 9. Legge, *The Confucian Classics*, 2nd ed., revised (Oxford: Clarendon Press, 1893), I, 255.
31. *Mengtzu* 孟子 (*Mencius*), Tangwen Kung 滕文公, pt. 1, ch. 2, sec. 4; Legge, *op. cit.*, II, 238.
32. W. G. Aston, "Nihongi," *Transactions and Proceedings of the Japan Society*, (London: Kegan Paul, Trench, Trübner and Co., 1896), I, 279.

to this as evidence that the Imperial line had through history
sought to rule harmoniously, with the welfare of the people as
its foremost aim.[33]

There is a hint of this in an Imperial message pronounced in
1874 at the setting up of a Prefectural Governors' Council, Chihō-
kan kaigi 地方官會議, in which one of the opening phrases went:
"I am convening an assembly of representatives of the whole
nation so as by the help of public discussion to ordain laws,
thus opening the way of harmony between governors and
governed..."[34] But the most significant allusion to this attitude
is found in a speech given by Itō Hirobumi 伊藤博文 (1841-1909)
in 1889 at the promulgation of the constitution. He was one of
its main drafters, and he said in reference to it:

> If we reflect upon the history of civilization in this country, it will
> be perceived, I think, that while several influences have been at
> work, still the introduction of such alien religious systems as Con-
> fucianism and Buddhism, which were largely instrumental in elevat-
> ing our people, and the development of such works as have conducted
> to their welfare, have been due to the benevolent guidance and
> encouragement of the sovereign. We may therefore say with truth that
> the civilization which we now possess is a gift from the throne....
> In a country under absolute rule the view of the sovereign is at
> once law; in a constitutional country, on the other hand, nothing
> being law without concurrence of views between the sovereign and
> the people, the latter elect representatives to meet at an appointed
> place and carry out the views of the sovereign. In other words,
> law in a constitutional state is a result of the concord of ideas be-
> tween sovereign and subject; but there can be no law when these
> two are in opposition to each other.... The case of Japan is totally
> different. The most cordial relations prevail between the Throne
> and the people while our constitution is granted. The position of
> our Court cannot be at all compared with that of England when the
> Magna Carta was granted, for we know that our Imperial House
> has a single aim, the welfare and happiness of the nation.... The

---

33. Reference to Nintoku's virtuous care for the people may be found in nearly
any Japanese school book on history or ethics. As a modern example of this, the
Shotō koku shi 初等國史 (*Elementary National History*), 2nd ed. revised (Keijō 京 城
Chōsen Sōtokufu 朝鮮總督府, 1937), I, 24-28, devotes a whole chapter to Nintoku's concern
for the welfare of his subjects.

34. McLaren, *op. cit.*, 506.

course which now lies before the Japanese Empire is plain. Both
Ruler and ruled should apply their efforts harmoniously to preserve
tranquility; to elevate the status of the people.... The great end
that we have in view must be attained by the cooperation of
Sovereign and people.[35]

The above, besides showing the rather narrow view of
constitutional government held by Itō, clearly indicates that
he conceived of the constitutional process in Japan as basically
one whereby a Confucian type of harmony and cooperation between sovereign and subjects could be attained. And his mentioning that this had been an ideal realized in the past by the
Imperial House shows that he was probably acquainted with
history of the Japanese use of this Confucian theory in praising
various emperors.

In the literary world too there were signs that Confucianism
still remained as a frame of reference and pattern of thought for
a number of writers, despite the fact that in general, Western
literary currents were ubiquitous and dominant in their influence.
Yano Ryūkei 矢野龍溪 (1850-1931), for example, in 1883 published
a political novel called *Keikoku bidan* 經國美談 which received
wide acclaim. Although the setting of the story was in ancient
Thebes, the author really was advocating a democracy based on
Confucian principles, in which the indivisibility of popular and
national rights were stressed.[36] In 1891 the story of *Keikoku
bidan* was dramatized, and apparently proved to be a great
success.[37] As to Ryūkei, though only a man of thirty-three when
his novel was published, he already was showing himself active
and able, having been the head of a school, an employee of the
Ministry of Finance, and secretary to the *Dajōkan* 太政官 (Office
of the Minister-President of State).[38] It may be possible to account
for his Confucian tendencies from the fact that he was a member
of the Shiseikai 思齊會, a Confucian society organized in 1868 for

---

35. *Ibid.*, 617-622.
36. Horace Z. Feldman, "The Meiji Political Novel," *Far Eastern Quarterly*, IX,
3, (May, 1950), 247-248.
37. Sansom, *op. cit.*, 409.
38. *Shinsen dai jimmei jiten* 新撰大人名辞典 (*Newly Edited Great Biographical
Dictionary*), (Tōkyō: Heibonsha 平凡社, 1941), VI, 308.

the purpose of considering wisdom, service, and the encouragement of public morals along Confucian lines. As this society
ended its existence in 1880, Ryūkei's contacts with it were before
his writing of the *Keikoku bidan*.[39]

A little earlier, in 1873, a literary organization called the
Meirokusha 明六社 had been formed by outstanding figures like
Katō Hiroyuki 加藤弘之, Mori Arinori 森有禮, and Fukuzawa Yukichi 福澤諭吉 for the purpose of fostering Western studies; yet
even among its members were men such as Nakamura Keiu
中村敬宇 (1832-91) and Nishimura Shigeki 西村茂樹 (1828-1902),[40]
both well-known Confucianists whose writings were widely read.

Nishimura, while well acquainted with Western learning,
seems to have become critical of its stress on material success
and sought to encourage Confucian ethics. In 1875, he is said
to have written on the subject of *Moral Training the Only Way
of Governing the Country*,[41] and in the same year he became
Chief of the Textbook Section of the Ministry of Education and
a Confucian lecturer to the Emperor.[42] From this time on Nishimura associated himself more and more with conservative Confucian organizations and became outspoken in his opposition to
Western style education.

Nakamura, on the other hand, did not lose his taste for
Western learning and became known as the outstanding synthesizer of Confucian ethics with European thought. In the late
1860's and early 1870's, he translated the American Constitution,
Washington's farewell address, John Stuart Mill's *On Liberty*,
and Smiles's *Self Help* and *Conduct*, nearly all of which appear
to have been quite popular.[43] He also organized a school in 1873,
the Dōjinsha 同人社, where the youth of the day were introduced

39. Yamamoto Kunihiko 山本邦彦 "Shibun Gakkai jidai no kaiko" 斯文學會時代
の回顧 (Recollections of the Period of the Shibun Gakkai), *Shibun*, IIX, 4 (July, 1926),
280.

40. *Nihon Jugaku nempyō* 421.

41. Sansom, *op. cit.*, 368. Sansom refers to this as a book entitled *Shūshin
chikoku hinoto ron*, but it does not appear among the titles of Nishimura's better known
writings. It is quite possible that it appeared in pamphlet form or as an article that
was incorporated into a larger work, under which it would have to be found.

42. *Nihon Jugaku nempyō*, 422.

43. Iwahashi, *op. cit.*, 371-372.

to Western learning, but not allowed to forget the Confucian basis of their ethics and customs.[44] In trying to assess the importance of Nakamura, it is not sufficient to say that he was simply a literary figure with an interest in Confucianism. He represents, rather, a continuation of that group of Confucianists of the Tokugawa days who advocated a complementary fusion of Western knowledge and Confucian ethics. And in general his position even in this regard was most moderate, for he did not differentiate on the basis of Western material civilization versus Eastern spiritual civilization, but recognized Western ethical theories as existing and having value.[45]

Another small but influential literary production, representative of a trend in intellectual circles, is Yasui Sokken's 安井息軒 *Bemmō* 辨妄 which was published in 1875.[46] Sokken had been one of the leading Confucianists in the last years of the Tokugawa period, and though he died in 1876, his trenchant attack on Christianity found in *Bemmō* was reprinted in 1881, and was still read by young men a generation after it was written. Sokken claimed in this work that the teachings of Christ were in conflict with those Confucian doctrines of loyalty and filial piety which were the foundations of the state. He also said that Christianity was not compatible with ancestor worship.[47]

Mishima Chūshū 三島中洲 (1830-1919) was still another literary figure in the Meiji era who maintained a strong predilection for Confucian learning and ideas. In 1877 he founded the Kangaku Semmon Nishō Gakusha 漢學專門二松學舍 where the study of the Chinese classics was encouraged, and in his numerous writings he constantly stressed moral and ethical themes related to Confucianism.[48] His style was considered excellent and was praised to the extent that he was dubbed one of the "Three

---

44. *Ibid.*, 372.
45. *Ibid.*, 373. Iwahashi refers readers who wish to become acquainted with these characteristics of Nakamura's ideas to the books *Keiu Nakamura sensei enzetsushū* 敬宇中村先生演説集 (*Collection of Speeches of Keiu Nakamura*), and *Keiu bunshū* 敬宇文集 (*Collected Writings of Keiu*).
46. Sansom, *op. cit.*, 369, 479. *Dai hyakka jiten* 大百科辭典 (*Great Encyclopedia*), (Tōkyō: Heibonsha 平凡社, 1931-35), XXIIV, 284.
47. *Ibid.*, 472.
48. *Shinsen dai jimmei jiten*, VI, 32.

Literary Masters of the Meiji Era" (*Meiji no Sandaibunsō* 明治の
三大文宗) along with Shigeno Yasutsugu 重野安繹 (1827-1910) and
Kawada Ōkō 川田甕江 (1830-96).[49] It is interesting to note that
these two other men were also outstanding Confucianists, Shigeno
being known particularly for his historical writings[50] and Kawada
for his acquaintance with Japanese studies.[51]

In considering this somewhat random sampling of men
engaged in literary activities who carried on Confucian traditions, it should be remembered that many others also contributed
consciously or unconsciously to it through their writings. The
important point to keep in mind, though, is that most of these
men had a background of study and scholarship going back to
Tokugawa times.[52] Once their generation died off, Confucian
traditions began to lapse seriously, as became evident in the first
two decades of the nineteen hundreds.

3. Attempts to Revive Confucianism on an Organized Scale
through 1890.

During the years preceding the Imperial Rescript on Education, despite the relative decline of Confucianism when compared
to Tokugawa times, there were a number of organized efforts made
to revive and stimulate Confucian points of view, especially those
related to ethics and man's moral duties in society. It is significant that none of these efforts were directed toward a restoration
of the old, detailed cosmological system of Confucianism, for it
was apparently recognized by all that Western science had dealt
this a fatal blow. Less well defined areas such as the nature of

---

49. *Ibid.*, VI, 32.

50. *Ibid.*, III, 232. Yasutsugu became in 1887 one of the founders of the Shigakkai
史學會 which still publishes the famous *Shigaku zasshi* 史學雜誌, and he was also
honored by the government and made a member of the House of Peers.

51. *Ibid.*, II, 209. Ōkō was lecturer at the Peers School for Women (Kazoku
Jogakkō 華族女學校), and also was made a member of the House of Peers. The year of
his death, he became advisor to the Imperial Household.

52. A number of men of this type are listed by Iwahashi, *op. cit.*, 376-377. Shimada
Jūrei 島田重禮 (1838-98, *gō*: Ōson 篁村); Kikuchi Sankei 菊池三溪 (1819-91): Namma
Kōki 南摩綱紀 (1823-1909); Okamatsu Ōkoku 岡松甕谷 (1820-95); Yoda Gakkai 依田學海
(1833-1909); Sakatani Rōro 阪谷朗廬 (1822-81); Nemoto Michiaki 根本通明 (1822-1906).

man, the problem of good and evil, and the aims of government occupied the speculation of Confucianists. Implicit in this choice of topics was an assumption that though Western science might have stolen the explanation of the material world from them, Confucianists still had special prerogatives and insight into the spiritual and ethical life of man. In other words, following the general pattern of the retreat of religion before science in the West, Confucianism too moved back into the area of ethics and human psychology where exact and scientifically verifiable data were insufficient to prove or disprove their basic assumptions.

Perhaps the first society that was formed after the Restoration in 1868 was the Shiseikai 思齊會.[53] Set up in 1868 for the purpose of considering wisdom, service, and the encouragement of public morality along Confucian lines, it initially had a fairly wide membership, but with the craze for Western things in the following years, interest in it declined.[54] Up to this time it counted among its members men like Yano Ryūkei, already mentioned as the author of the political novel *Keikoku bidan;* Ono Azusa 小野梓 (1852-87), a politician of the Meiji period who studied abroad and who held many government offices;[55] and Okamoto Kansuke 岡本監輔 (1839-1904), one of the founders of the society who led a varied life as explorer, Army General Staff employee, and writer and principal of a middle school in Tokushima prefecture 德島縣.[56]

With the gradual decline of the Shiseikai in the 1870's, its leaders attempted to gain the sympathy and support of men of importance in the government. This led to the founding of the

---

53. The name of this society is derived from a phrase in the *Lun-yün*, Le Jin 里仁, ch. 17. Legge, *op. cit.*, I, 170. "The master said, 'When we seek men of worth, we should think of equalling them'."

54. Yamamoto, *Shibun*, IIX, 4, (July, 1926), 280. Beginning with this number, Yamamoto wrote in the *Shibun* the most detailed history of the Shibun Gakkai 斯文學會 and its related organizations available, under the title, "Shibun Gakkai jidai no kaiko" 斯文學會時代の回顧 (Recollections of the Period of the Shibun Gakkai). The articles dealing with this subject continue through numbers 5, 6, 7, 8, and 9 of volume IIX, all the numbers of volume IX (1927) and volume X (1928), and the first number of volume XI (1929). Concerning the Shiseikai, Yamamoto wrote from memory because all of the records of this society had ben destroyed in the Tōkyō fire and earthquake of 1923.

55. *Shinsen dai jimmei jiten,* I, 628.

56. *Ibid.,* I, 623.

Motoda Eifu

Shibun Gakkai 斯文學會,[57] the most important Confucian organization in Japan in the years from 1880 to 1918.

Conditions were apparently propitious for this, as two years before, in the fall of 1878, the Emperor Meiji, on an inspection trip of the Hokuriku Tōkai 北陸東海 areas, had been shocked by the languishing condition of moral education observed there.[58] This resulted in the publication of a small tract in 1878 called "The Great Purpose of Teaching and Learning," *Kyōgaku taishi* 教學大旨, by Motoda Eifu 元田永孚 (1818-91), the Emperor's Confucian tutor and advisor. Motoda was very close to the Emperor, and apparently was ordered to write this to express the Emperor's feelings. Motoda, however, took the opportunity to include many of his own Confucian ideas in the essay.[59] For example, there is a phrase which reads: "From now on, based on the moral canons of our ancestors, we especially will clarify humaneness, righteousness, loyalty, and filial piety, and for moral teaching stress Confucius."[60] The point emphasized in the tract was that the infatuation of the people with Western things was leading the nation to a dangerous sort of ethical vacuum, for which Confucianism was the remedy.

Iwakura Tomomi 岩倉具視 (1825-83), who had returned in 1873 from his mission to Europe and America, was contacted

57. Yamamoto, *Shibun*, IIX, 4, (July, 1926), 280. The name of this society is derived from a phrase in the *Lun-yü*, Tzu Han 子罕, ch. 5. Legge, *op. cit.*, I, 217-218. "The Master was put in fear of K'wang. He said, 'After the death of King Wan, was not the cause of truth lodged here in me? If Heaven had wished to let the cause of truth perish then I, a future mortal should not have got such a relation to that cause. While Heaven does not let the cause of truth perish, what can the people of K'wang do to me?' "

Legge translates *shibun* 斯文 as the 'cause of truth' and in a footnote adds that, "It is the truth embodied in literature, ceremonies, etc., and its use instead of *tao* 道, 'truth in principles,' is attributed to Confucius's modesty." He also points out, though, that Confucius had identified himself with the great sages to whom Heaven had entrusted the instruction of men. With such connotations, isn't it significant that the founders of the Shibun Gakkai should choose such a name for their society, especially in view of the great need many of them felt for the proper guidance of the people along moral paths?

58. Watanabe Ikujirō 渡邊幾次郎, *Nippon Kempō seitei shikō* 日本憲法制定史講 (*Lectures on the History of the Formulation of the Japanese Constitution*), (Tōkyō: Chigura Shobō 千倉書房, 1937), 172.

59. Ienaga Saburō 家永三郎, "Kyōiku chokugo seiritsu no shisōshiteki kōsatsu" 教育勅語成立の思想史的考察 ("Historical Examination of the Ideological Formation of the Rescript on Education"), *Shigaku zasshi* 史學雜誌 LVI, 12, (Dec., 1946), 4.

60. *Ibid.*, 7.

by members of the Shiseikai to whose suggestions he was probably sympathetic in view of the disturbed times. In any case, in order to strengthen the foundation of the state by fostering reliable thinking based on Confucianism, he set about organizing the Shibun Gakkai in early 1880.[61]

Iwakura had been an influential man in engineering the Imperial Restoration, and since that time he had held various important positions in the government. In 1880 he was Minister of the Right (*Udaijin* 右大臣) the second or third most important political post in Japan, and taking advantage of this at a meeting of the prefectural governors in February, he gave Matano Taku 股野琢 (1839-1921) and Hirose Shin'ichi 廣瀬進一 (d. 1928) secret, private orders to ask the officials to become members of the society. These officials likewise were requested to collect members for the new organization from among their *gun* 郡 (sub-prefecture) chiefs after they returned to their respective prefectures. In this way over 1500 requests for membership were received by the Shibun Gakkai from all over Japan before the official opening ceremonies were held on June 6, 1880.[62]

Matano Taku was a staunch Confucianist who during his lifetime held important positions in the inner circles of government, such as chief recorder for the cabinet, Lord Keeper of the Privy Seal, Imperial Household secretary, and advisor to the Imperial House, through which he was able to assert influence in encouraging and spreading Confucianism.[63] There were others, however, of more prominence in the 1880's who associated themselves with the Shibun Gakkai and the movement to set it up. Thus Tani Kanjō 谷干城 (1837-1911), Shigeno Yasutsugu 重野安繹 (*gō*: Seisai 成齋), and Kawada Ōkō 川田甕江 (*na*: Takeshi 剛) met with Iwakura's representatives and published the aims of organizing the new society. Kanjō was a major general in the army who had played an important role in the campaign against

61. *Nihon Jugaku nempyō*, 423.
62. Yamamoto, *Shibun*, IIX, 4, (July, 1926), 280. The original announcement of the opening of the Shibun Gakkai and its aims can be found reproduced in this series by Yamamoto, *Shibun*, IIX, 6, (Sept., 1926), 429.
63. *Shinsen dai jimmei jiten*, V. 594.

the Satsuma rebellion in 1877. He later became a viscount, head of the Ministry of Agriculture and Commerce, and was an important figure in the House of Peers.[64] His deep interest in the Shibun Gakkai is evident from its earliest days, as he was its vice-head from 1883 to 1895, after which he was made the head of the society.[65] Yasutsugu and Ōkō have already been mentioned in connection with literary movements of the Meiji period, but to understand better the type of influence they exerted, a few more details are necessary.

Yasutsugu, after a brilliant record as student and teacher in the years before Meiji, became an employee of the Ministry of Education in 1871 and continued his connections with the government for nearly all of the rest of his life. Up to 1880, his main tasks were related to historical compilation, and by 1886 he had become head of the Temporary Historical Compilation Bureau (*Rinji Shūshi Kyoku* 臨時修史局). About this time he was appointed to be a member of the Genrōin 元老院, and in 1890 he became a member of the House of Peers. After 1893, he devoted himself exclusively to historical work, and while teaching at Tōkyō Imperial University, was known widely as one of those who contributed most to the progress of Japanese historical studies.[66] Ōkō worked in historical studies with Seisai in the 1870's, and his reputation as a teacher had become so well known that he lectured before the court. By 1881 he received court rank and was made reader to the Crown Prince, and maintained his connection with the Imperial family until his death in 1896.[67]

These men were among the most loyal supporters of the Shibun Gakkai from its inception onward, and from their general background it is evident that in high political and academic circles, Confucianism had a definite appeal.

This prominence of the Shibun Gakkai is indicated by the fact that its opening ceremonies were held at the Peers' School, Gakushūin 學習院, which was an honor granted to few organiza-

64. *Ibid.*, IV, 192.
65. *Nihon Jugaku nempyō*, 424-427.
66. *Shinsen dai jimmei jiten*, III, 239.
67. *Ibid.*, II, 209.

tions.[68] The roster of those present on this occasion and the list of those who supported the aims of the organization by donating money to it also emphasizes its importance. Over one thousand people of distinction, including Imperial Princes, took part, and Iwakura Tomomi, Imperial Prince Taruhito of the Arisugawa no Miya family 有栖川宮熾仁親王 (1835-95), the Minister-President of State, Sanjō Sanetomi 三條實美 (1837-91), and other men of importance gave considerable sums to the society. Direct Imperial favor was not wanting either, for Sugi Magoshichirō 杉孫七郎 (1835-1920), a palace official who had been among those who originally planned the organization, was sent with one thousand yen as a gift from the Emperor to the society, "for the purpose of arousing and strengthening public morals and encouraging literary arts."[69]

To carry out its tasks, the Shibun Gakkai planned to open up a school, conduct regular lectures, and publish articles and books related to Confucian topics. The moderate success of this program was largely due to the continuing close connections of the Shibun Gakkai with the Imperial family and the government. Thus it is significant that the first head of the society was the same Imperial Prince of the Arisugawa no Miya family who had contributed generously to it at its opening ceremonies.[70] In July, 1881, he addressed a meeting of the members of the Shibun Gakkai and exhorted them to steer a steady path, neither reactionary nor radical, to achieve the society's aims of preserving public morals, encouraging literary arts, and clarifying the meaning of the Confucian classics.[71]

The problem of land in Tōkyō for the school and for the headquarters of the organization was a pressing one in these early days. Temporarily, the Imperial Household Ministry loaned

---

63. Shibunkai 斯文會, "History of the Shibun Gakkai," *Shibun*, I, 1, (Jan., 1919), 105.

69. *Ibid.*

70. *Shinsen dai jimmei jiten*, IV, 226. Arisugawa was an important political figure in the first half of the Meiji period, having played a conspicuous part in the Imperial Restoration, and in government later on as chairman of the Genrōin in 1876, Minister of the Left (*Sadaijin* 左大臣) in 1880. and other similar positions. For outstanding military achievements, he was made Field Marshal in 1878.

71. Shibunkai, *Shibun*, I, (Jan., 1919), 105-06.

a building, and the Ministry of War also loaned the society land free of charge. Finally in April 1883, the Imperial Household Ministry granted a more permanent site, tax free, to the Shibun Gakkai for the purpose of building its school, and with this came a yearly stipend of 2,400 yen to support the operations of the school for ten years.[72]

Meanwhile there occurred an event of importance in tracing the development of Confucianism in Meiji times, which was mirrored in the activities of the Shibun Gakkai. This was the Imperial presentation in December 1882, of a book called *Yōgaku kōyō* 幼學綱要 (*Fundamentals of Education for the Young*), written by the Emperor's Confucian advisor, Motoda Eifu.[73] The book had had its inception in 1879 when the Emperor requested Motoda to write such a book on morals,[74] probably because of the conditions he had found in the schools on his inspection trip of the Hokuriku Tōkai area in the fall of 1878. In any case, after the book was formally published in December, 1882, it was distributed in 1883 under the copyright of the Imperial Household Ministry to every school in Japan.[75]

The Shibun Gakkai, having close relations with the Imperial House, naturally was sent official word of the publication of this work and of the reasons why such a book was necessary at the time. In February, 1883 the following Imperial message (*chokuyu* 勅諭) was delivered to the society by the Imperial Household Department with a copy of the book:

Proper social relationships and virtue are the principal basis of education. Our nation, despite the fact that China has its particularly lofty doctrines and that each European nation and America also have a moral science, has adopted these without attaining their essence. And today, under the pressure of various studies, many have also mistaken root and branch. In early years when at school,

72. *Ibid.*, 106.
73. *Nihon Jugaku nempyō*, 424.
74. *Ibid.*, 423.
75. Iijima Tadao 飯島忠夫, *Nihon no Jukyō; kokutai no hongi kaisetsu sōsho* 日本の儒教, 國體の本義解說叢書 (*Japanese Confucianism; Explanatory Series on the Meaning of National Polity*), (5th ed., Tōkyō: Mombushō Kyōgakukyoku 文部省教學局, 1941), 99.

it is most necessary to make loyalty and filial piety as fundamentals, and to put humaneness and duty in the forefront. Consequently, I have ordered my Confucian minister to edit this book, and bestowed it on the common people. The essentials of the clarification of human morality and the practice of virtue are found here and made known.... Readers of the great instructions of the Imperial exhortation, you must reverently obey them and lay them to heart.[76]

The contents of this book were largely Confucian, and it is little wonder that it should have recommended itself to the members of the Shibun Gakkai, many of whom were men in government. To them, such doctrines as utilitarianism, individualism, or theories claiming that sovereignty rested in the people and not in the ruler or in Heaven, as well as attitudes critical of loyalty and filial piety as the foremost virtues, were indeed dangerous, for they would tend to bring political disturbance and social unrest.

With this as a background, the Shibun Gakkai's long cherished plans for a school finally bore fruit when construction on the land leased by the Imperial Household Ministry was begun in May, 1883. At a banquet held in June in honor of this event, Imperial Prince Arisugawa no Miya made an address in which he said:

Now, relying on great Imperial favor, we have attained setting up [the school's] foundation. And the task of construction of the school already having begun, our feelings of joy indeed cannot be excelled. Therefore, considering this, our society is in the final analysis in such a situation due to being under Imperial protection. Imperial wishes lie in encouraging the cause of truth in literature and preserving the morality of the people, and this society has been given the responsibility [of carrying these out]. Already having this responsibility, the society will repay the Imperial favor by suitably gathering the strength of the people and reporting the collected result to the Throne.[77]

---

76. Shibunkai, *Shibun*, I, 1, (Jan., 1919), 106-107. Motoda Eifu and Sugi Mago-shichirō 元田永孚, 杉孫七郎 *Yōgaku kōyō* (and) *Fujokan* 幼學綱要, 婦女鑑 (*Essentials of Learning for the Young, Mirror of Womanhood*), (5th ed., Tōkyō: Kunaishō 宮内省, 1915), I, front page.
77. Shibunkai, *Shibun*, I, 1, (Jan., 1919), 106-107.

This statement unequivocably establishes the relationship between the Shibun Gakkai and the Imperial House, and more than suggests that the society had as one of its main purposes the fulfillment of the desires of the Emperor and his advisors. Since one of the Emperor Meiji's closest and most trusted advisors was his Confucian tutor, Motoda Eifu, the reason for this becomes clearer. Looking forward a little, the activities of the society greatly declined after Motoda's death in 1891, and examples of special Imperial favor to it also became rare.

The school itself opened in the fall of 1883, having twenty students enrolled as residents and fifty-six student commuters. Besides the Imperial House, support came from members of the Council of State and business figures like Iwasaki Yatarō 岩崎彌太郎 (1834-85). No tuition was required of the students, and in 1884 the school was expanded. It was known as the Shibunkō 斯文黌.[78] The curriculum of the Shibunkō is interesting, for there seems to have been an effort made in setting it up to imitate the curriculum of the Daigakuryō 大學寮, the government's Confucian school established in the Nara period (710-784). It consisted of six departments: Morals (Shūshin 修身); Literature (Bunshō 文章); Law (Hōritsu 法律); History (Shigaku 史學); Calligraphy (Sho 書); and Mathematics (Su 數).[79] The Daigakuryō had also been organized into six departments, but the names for some of these had been different, though the subjects taught were nearly identical.[80]

In 1887, after four years of operation, the Shibunkō had to be suspended due to lack of space brought about by the necessity of returning the land leased in 1883. During this period, the school graduated 113 students,[81] and among the best known of those who attended it was Konoe Atsumaro 近衛篤麿 (1863-1904),[82]

---

78. Ibid., 107.

79. Nihon Jugaku nempyō, 424. The teachers for each department, as well as the actual organization of classes at the school, can be found in A Brief Survey of Recent Sinological Studies in Japan, compiled and edited by Ku-lu Wang, (Shanghai: Life Publishing Co., 1935), 143.

80. Iwahashi, op. cit., 36.

81. Shibunkai, Shibun, I, 1, (Jan., 1919), 107.

82 Yamamoto, Shibun, XI, 1, (Jan., 1929), 82.

father of the late Prince Konoe Fumimaro 近衛文麿 (1891-1945).

Following the closing of its school, the Shibun Gakkai devoted its energies to daily public lectures which were well attended until fires in 1891 and 1893 destroyed the lecture halls. After this, people began to come to the lectures in smaller and smaller numbers until 1910, when the lectures were stopped entirely.[83]

The publications of the Shibun Gakkai also showed the same decline. They had been envisaged as an integral part of the original plans of the society, and were numerous in the first ten years or so, but appear to have nearly disappeared after 1900.[84]

Besides the Shibun Gakkai, a number of other organizations were set up in the first half of the Meiji period which also made Confucian principles a basic part of their program. The most important of these was the Tōkyō Shūshin Gakusha 東京修身學社' founded in 1876 by Sakatani Rōro 阪谷朗廬 (1822-81) and Nishimura Shigeki for the purpose of clarifying the path of "loyalty and filial piety, and humaneness and righteousness."[85] By 1884, despite nearly ten years of effort, it had been unable to attract more than a few tens of members, so it was reorganized as the Nippon Kōdōkai 日本講道會 under the auspices of two Imperial princes.[86] In 1886 the organization again changed its name to Nippon Kōdōkai 日本弘道會, and Nishimura Shigeki, who had been the head of the two previous societies, was also made the head of the new one.[87] Nishimura's early contact with Western learning already has been mentioned in speaking of literature, but his more mature and developed views can be seen in a three-day lecture series he gave in December, 1886, at Tōkyō Imperial University.[88]

---

83. Shibunkai, *Shibun*, I, 1, (Jan., 1919), 107.

84. *Ibid.*, 107. A partial list of these publications follows: *Shibun Gakkai hōkoku-sho* 斯文學會報告書, 20 numbers of this had been published by October 1883 when it was suspended; *Kōgi hikki* 講義筆記, beginning in June, 1881, 69 monthly issues were published through 1886; *Shibun ippan* 斯文一斑, beginning in 1881, with 30 odd issues printed by 1891; *Shibun Gakkai kōgiroku* 斯文學會講義錄 was published monthly from 1893, reaching some 50 issues.

85. *Nihon Jugaku nempyō*, 422.

86. Sansom, *op. cit.*, 369.

87. Iwahashi, *op. cit.*, 375-376.

88. *Nihon Jugaku nempyō*, 425.

The subject of the lecture series was "A Theory of Japanese Morals." Nishimura began by stating that Japan had become a nation without a firm moral base which was being threatened by Western ambitions. Consequently the nation was in danger, and it was imperative that a solid, new moral structure be constructed immediately. Western philosophy Nishimura concluded was unsuited to Japan, and moreover, it was tied up with Western ambitions, so it could not be used in making a new synthesis. Confucianism alone, though, had proved too narrow and tied to the past to be able to serve as a moral foundation in a rapidly changing world. But if its essential truths regarding human relationships and virtues were combined with a measure of the pragmatic, empirical characteristics of the learning of the West, it would provide the basis for Japanese morality. Nishimura listed five main tenets as necessary for achieving this type of moral standard. They were: develop yourself to a high degree; harmonize and help the family; promote peace and cooperation among villages and towns; seek the safety and well being of the nation; try to help the whole world and bring peace to all men.[89]

The outline of Nishimura's views above is significant because it shows how even a man who had reacted against Western learning, as he had earlier, still recognized that Japanese or Confucian teachings of the past were inadequate to deal with modern conditions. Under the circumstances, a synthesis with certain aspects of Western learning was a natural development which had been presaged by the more farsighted Confucianists of late Tokugawa times. It should be noted, though, that even in the construction of a synthesis, a process of selection is involved which may throw light on the beliefs and fundamental premises of the synthesizer. Thus while Nakamura Keiu was willing to include Western ethical precepts in his ideas concerning the evolution of a new ethical system for Japan, Nishimura apparently rejected these as valueless. He implied that Confucian

---

89. Kiyokawa, *op. cit.*, 628-638. According to the *Nihon Jugaku nempyō*, 425, these lectures were published as a book in 1887 called *Nippon dōtoku ron* 日本道徳論 (*A Theory of Japanese Morals*).

and Japanese spiritual and moral foundations were a unique, superior legacy which needed the support of Western learning only for reorientation. And the tenets for this moral standard would seem to attest to the high purpose and idealism which motivated it. Unfortunately, just such appeals to harmony, peace, and cooperation were to characterize the aims of Japan after she embarked on her program of expansion from 1931 onward. Therefore, even much earlier, such pronouncements by Nishimura may be questioned as merely an attempt to inculcate those attitudes which would keep political opposition to a minimum and discourage social unrest.

Although the Nippon Kōdōkai does not appear to have been very successful in arousing support among the people,[90] it continued its activities, publishing a magazine called the Kōdōkai zasshi 弘道會雜誌 in 1889, and giving public lectures at various intervals on national ethics.[91] In 1890, it announced its ten basic aims, the most important of which were: to strengthen filial piety and honor the gods; to revere the Imperial House and stress the importance of the nation; to protect national laws and plan for the nation's well being; to promote harmony in the household and mutual assistance among villages; to guard sincerity and carry out the good and the merciful.[92] The similarity of these with the tenets that Nishimura stressed is self-evident. One may likewise wonder if these did not have as aims creating a docile, obedient populace in view of the attitudes of many conservatives at the unrest of the times.

Later in 1890, a Woman's Department of the Nippon Kōdōkai was set up, and Nishimura made and address on the occasion in which he opposed Western style education and emphasized the importance of strengthening unique, Japanese womanly virtues.[93] Since these included obedience and proper attention to caring for the home, in contrast to developing more critical or analytical attitudes of mind as found in Western education, they

90. Sansom, op. cit., 369.
91. Kiyokawa, op. cit., 639.
92. Ibid.
93. Ibid.

stress the conservative position of the Nippon Kōdōkai and its tendency to equate virtue with stability and the *status quo*.

In 1888 another organization was set up called the Nippon Kokkyō Daidōsha 日本國教大同社.[94] Among its leaders was General Torio Koyata 鳥尾小彌太 (1847-1905), who as a member of the House of Peers and the Privy Council was known to be very conservative;[95] and Kawai Kiyomaru 川合清丸 (1847-1917), an educator and sociologist who took particular interest in Shintō and Japanese national traditions.[96] This organization probably grew up as one phase of the reaction against Western things which became widespread in 1887. Its avowed purpose attests to this, for it was meant to foster and support "National Teachings," including tenets of Buddhism, Confucianism and Shintō. The society published a periodical called the *Daidō soshi* 大同叢誌, where it was claimed that the "Great Way" in Japan was attained by amalgamating the three creeds above. Once the "Great Way" of the "National Teachings" was clarified, loyalty to the sovereign, love for the nation, and an avoidance of suffering would follow nearly automatically.[97] Here again, then, is an example of a society that associated virtue with loyal support for the state, a stand which could be justified on the basis of Confucian ethics. The Nippon Kokkyō Daidōsha claimed at one point a membership throughout Japan of over thirty thousand, but this was in its early years, and by the first decade of the twentieth century, it seems to have almost disappeared. Finally at the death of Kawai in 1917, the organization was disbanded.[98]

Although the Shibun Gakkai, the Nippon Kōdōkai, and the Nippon Kokkyō Daidōsha were the most active and influential organizations in the first half of the Meiji period which supported Confucianism, others sporadically arose impelled by some particular aims or special conditions, but would fade away soon afterwards. For example, the Daidōkan 大同館 was founded in

---

94. *Ibid.*
95. *Shinsen dai jimmei jiten*, **IV**, 485-486.
96. *Ibid.*, **II**, 188.
97. Kiyowara, *op. cit.*, 639-640.
98. *Dai hyakka jiten*, V, 627.

1880 by Katō Ōrō 加藤櫻老 (1811-84) and others in Tōkyō. They set up a temple to Confucius and carried out a *sekiten* or Confucian ceremony there.[99] Little is known of what happened to this society from then on, as it appears to have ceased all activity within five years. It did leave several issues of a publication called the *Daidō shimpō* 大同新報.[100] Even more obscure were the Rongokai 論語會 (Confucian Analects Society) and the Kōshikyō Kai 孔子教會 (Society for Confucian Teachings) which existed in the 1880's and perhaps later. The former carried on its meetings and discussions in the Gakushūin or Peers School and seems to have been mainly a literary society.[101] The impelling force behind the Kōshikyō Kai appears to have been the writer and political figure Yano Ryūkei, whose interest in Cofucianism already has been mentioned. A certain Matsui Kiyoshi 松井廉, who wished to spread the teaching of Confucius and Mencius among merchants and businessmen, also was active in this organization, but further information on it is unavailable.[102]

4. Motoda Eifu and the Imperial Rescript on Education.

Japanese and Western scholars alike have agreed that the Emperor Meiji was not just a passive figurehead in events occurring in Japan after 1868. It is therefore important to assess the types of influences that were strongest on him in order to understand what aims motivated his decisions and actions. The position of the Emperor was a peculiar one, for he was not directly involved in affairs as a strong executive would be, but his approval and support were always looked for. This was because measures or activities blessed with Imperial favor attained reverence and sanctity that would arouse the loyalty of the people. Japanese politicians and men of affairs were aware of this, and

99. *Nihon Jugaku nempyō*, 423.
100. Ibid., 423-424. Nakayama Yasumasa 中山泰昌, *Shimbun shūsei Meiji hennen shi* 新聞集成明治編年史 (*Meiji Chronological Collection of Newspapers*), (Tōkyō: Zaisei Keizai Gakkai 財政經濟學會, 1934-36), IV, 230.
101. Shibunkai, *Shibun*, I, 1, (Jan., 1919), 109.
102. Yamamoto, *Shibun*, XI, 1, (Jan., 1929), 81.

consequently they realized that a policy could be most effectively carried out if it were expressed as an Imperial edict or Imperial promulgation.

One of the men who was closest to the Emperor Meiji was Motoda Eifu 元田永孚 (1818-91). Trained as a Confucianist in Tokugawa times, Motoda had studied under the famous Yokoi Shōnan 横井小楠 (1809-69) who was outstanding because of his progressive stand on the necessity for a synthesis of Confucian and Western learning.[103] Motoda, however, living a generation later than his teacher, saw a dismaying flood of Western emulation seize Japan, and so he tended to view Western learning mainly as a threat to what had ethically and philosophically been the foundations of Japanese life. He was already a mature man with fixed ideas when he was appointed to the Imperial Household Ministry to be Confucian lecturer in 1871, and his increasing influence over the Emperor dates from these early years in the Meiji period. The Emperor was only eighteen or nineteen at the time, and Motoda seems to have had the determination and drive of one who sincerely felt he had a divine mission to perform in guiding his sovereign.[104]

This attitude of his is most clearly expressed in a remarkable letter he wrote to Iwakura in September, 1873, on "Essentials for the Virtuous Guidance of Emperors." The letters, written in cleassical Chinese style, is filled with Confucian metaphors and parallels which not only testify to Motoda's thorough acquaintance with Confucian literature, but also to his complete faith in

---

103. Ienaga Saburō 家永三郎 "Kyōiku chokugo seiritsu no shisōshiteki kōsatsu" 教育勅語成立の思想史的考察 ("Historical Examination of the Ideological Formation of the Rescript on Education"), Shigaku zasshi 史學雜誌, LVI, 12, (Dec., 1946), 3. G. B. Sansom, The Western World and Japan, (New York: Alfred A. Knopf, 1950), 366-369.

104. Tokutomi Iichirō 徳富猪一郎, Motoda sensei shinkōroku 元田先生進講録 (Record of Lectures before the Emperor of Mr. Motoda), 2nd popular ed., with supplement (Tōkyō: Min'yūsha 民友社, 1934), shogen 緒言 (Introductory remarks) 3, 8-9, 11-12. This book contains a short biography of Motoda and his own comments on how he became the official tutor of the Emperor. N. Asaji and J. C. Pringle, in their partial translation of Motoda sensei shinkōroku, "Lectures Delivered in the Presence of His Imperial Majesty the Emperor of Japan," T.A.S.J., series 1, XI, (1912), 47-48, also give a brief summary of Motoda's life, but say that he was first attached to the Imperial Household in 1868. On the basis of Tokutomi's information, this is incorrect, as well as some of the other general background about Motoda recorded by Asaji and Pringle.

them as a guide for directing the Emperor. He apparently felt that if the mind of the Emperor, as yet undeveloped, could be formed properly, benevolent government of the kind pictured in the *Shu-ching* 書經 (*Book of History*) during the reigns of such virtuous rulers as Yao 堯, or Shun 舜, or known in Japanese history during the reign of such a sovereign as Ōjin 應仁, would inevitably be achieved.[105] As to the means of accomplishing this, he almost directly recommended himself, saying:

> Again, all Emperors are born with similar characters. They cannot always be exactly like the holy Emperors of old. The selection of the reigning Emperor's tutor therefore becomes the supreme question.... The most supremely qualified person in the empire must be chosen; he must be as intimate with his master as a fish is with its native element water, as the vital organs of the body are with one another. Then and only then will the Emperor really benefit by the training and education he will give Him.[106]

Following in the best Confucian tradition, Motoda claimed that once the Emperor had attained virtue, it would permeate all society.

> Let however the mind of the Emperor be once formed, then, even though you neither see perfect administration everywhere, nor a complete set of codes in operation, you will find the heart of every subject throbbing with appreciation: the solid worth of the Emperor's work will appeal to them; His undertakings will prosper; and without waiting for specific commands, the people will fall into line behind Him like water finding its own level.[107]

The final picture he had in mind was one of minister and prince, and subject and ruler "advancing in the inevitable might of harmonious energy."[108] But it was an autocratic ideal monarch

---

105. Tokutomi, *op. cit.*, shogen 15. Asaji and Pringle, *op. cit.*, 57. Yao and Shun were Chinese legendary rulers, originally probably local nature deities that later were euhemerized by Confucianists. Their traditional dates are: Yao, 2356-2255 B. C.: Shun, 2255-2205 B.C. The Emperor Ōjin was the fifteenth Emperor of Japan during whose reign the Confucian classics are first said to have been brought to Japan. History records him as a ruler of virtue and benevolence. His traditional dates are 201-310 A.D., but modern research estimates he reigned from about 380 to 395 A.D.

106. Tokutomi, *op. cit.*, shogen 13. Asaji and Pringle, *op. cit.*, 53-54.

107. Tokutomi, *op. cit.*, shogen 13. Asaji and Pringle, *op. cit.*, 53.

108. Tokutomi, *op. cit.*, shogen 15. Asaji and Pringle, *op. cit.*, 58-59.

that he conceived of, for Motoda saw the Son of Heaven as acting for Heaven in supporting the helpless millions, and not as an instrument for expressing the sovereignty of the popular will. The latter would have been a theory entirely foreign to Confucian thinking where ultimate sovereignty lay in Heaven alone.

It seems that Motoda's hope of becoming the intimate tutor and unofficial advisor of the Emperor was realized to a large extent, judging from the statements that Motoda made, masquerading under the guise of Imperial wishes. The first important example of this was the *Kyōgaku taishi* 教學大旨, an essay published in 1878, on which the characters "Imperial Wishes" (*Seishi* 聖旨) were inscribed. The school inspection trip leading to the Emperor's willingness to give Imperial sanction to such a tract has already been mentioned on page 57. The moral degeneration found in the schools so shocked the Emperor that he resolved on the need for remedial measures.[109] Motoda's guidance of the Emperor was apparently beginning to bear fruit, as Imperial sanction for a criticism, based on Confucian standards, of the existing educational institutions had been nearly spontaneous. In one part of the *Kyōgaku taishi* Motoda was able to express his dislike for Western learning as follows:

> A leading aim of the Restoration was the destruction of harmful habits. With the excellent view of making the expanse of knowledge world-wide, we temporarily took the strong points of the West, and this daily brought results. But an evil from this current [of Westernization] is the placing of humaneness, rigteousness, loyalty, and filial piety in a secondary position. Striving uselessly over Western manners, one of the fears for the future is that of being unable to guess whether finally this will lead to ignorance of the great duties between sovereign and subject, and father and son. Such [ignorance] is not the basis of our nation's teaching.[110]

In 1879 the Emperor personally instructed Motoda to write a morals textbook, saying:

---

109. Watanabe Ikujirō 渡邊幾治郎, *Nippon kempō seitei shikō* 日本憲法制定史講 (*Lectures on the History of the Formulation of the Japanese Constitution*), (Tōkyō: Chigura Shobō 千倉書房, 1937), 172.

110. Ienaga, *op. cit.*, 6.

The essentials of learning and teaching lie in making clear the
root [from] the branch; once the root and the branch are clear,
then the will of the people is settled; and with the will of the people
settled, the Empire is at peace.   There is no learning for the young
which should take procedence over this [process of clarification].
You, together with the Minister of Education, should publish such
a book and therewith contribute to the learning of the young.[111]

The motivation for this order was probably the same as that
which had moved the Emperor to authorize Motoda to publish
the *Kyōgaku taishi*, except that now he was having his Confucian
lecturer take more drastic steps to deal with the situation. This
no doubt pleased Motoda, for it gave him another opportunity
to harp on his favorite themes of the necessity for a Confucian
moral renaissance and of the superiority of Confucian spiritual
values over essentially material Western ones. He emphasized
this in the preface to the *Yōgaku kōyō* 幼學綱要 (*Essentials of
Learning for the Young*), the book he wrote to comply with the
Emperor's order.

By making a foundation of morality, one attains wisdom, has
the beginning of social relationships, and extending to one's work,
it is the essential of teaching and learning. Therefore to follow this
principle, one uses loyalty and filial piety; and in this one fixes
the will of the people. Then when this wisdom progresses, and
when this talent is realized, it will come out in people's discourse
and in their actual carrying out of their work. In their behaviour
at their jobs, there will be none which is not derived from humaneness, righteousness, loyalty, and filial piety. But if the will of the
people is unsettled, and they seek only knowledge and try to develop
technical skill, then their moral culture will suffer, and the [result-
ing] ills will be legion....

The fact that even a small child of three feet understands dying
for loyalty and filial piety is a unique characteristic of our customs.
It cannot be doubted that our sacred ancestors, adhering to this, made
it into a long accepted custom. [But] ways and customs are changing, and the people only strive for knowledge and technical skill,
disregarding fundamentals, and seeking only results. Finally they
will become completely ignorant of the meaning of humaneness,

111. Motoda Eifu and Sugi Magoshichirō, *op. cit.*, I, preface, 1.

righteousness, loyalty, and filial piety, and in the end, where will this harm stop?[112]

Because Motoda's ideas constantly repeat themselves, it will be valuable to analyze them here in order to determine what were their most fundamental characteristics. He first of all indicated that he believed the basis of morality to be in the Confucian virtues of humaneness, righteousness, loyalty, and filial piety, which were also spoken of as the foundation of social relationships. Progress was simply living a daily life according to these precepts. Motoda next clearly presented the thesis that these so-called Confucian virtues, especially those of loyalty and filial piety, were uniquely Japanese. In doing this, he was carrying on the tradition developed and emphasized by the loyalists in the first half of the nineteenth century when they had associated Confucian ethical principles with pristine Japanese ways. This had been done to give the Imperial cause the added strength found in the Confucian moral code, and after the Restoration, the relationship was maintained and fostered because of its wide appeal and unifying tendency. Finally Motoda stressed the importance of putting moral and spiritual values before material Western ones, warning of the dangers of life without an ethical sense. This position was essentially a recurrence of the synthetic attitude in relation to Confucian morality and Western learning held by the more progressive Confucians of late Tokugawa times. These men had claimed that Western learning could supplement and help support Confucian ideals, but that it should never replace them.

There were other men about the Emperor Meiji who did not see matters in the same light as Motoda and who resented his unofficial position as advisor. The most important of these was Itō Hirobumi, who held a prominent place in Japanese politics during the whole Meiji period and is best known as the principal drafter of the constitution of 1889. Itō from the first seems to have felt that the system of Imperial Household officials taking

---

112. *Ibid.*, I, preface, 1-2.

part in major political decisions, as Motoda was wont to do, without bearing any of the responsibility for such actions, had to be abolished. This he partially accomplished in October 1879,[113] but despite it, the position of Motoda with the Emperor remained an intimate and confidential one, while the clash of ideas with Itō was constantly growing.

The genuine differences between these two men arose essentially because of the widely differing views of government that they held. Itō felt that Japan had to be modernized and that her governmental structure should be patterned along parliamentary lines. Strength and influence as a world power would be forthcoming to a Japan that absorbed the knowledge of Western science and modified her legal and governmental forms to fit in better with those of modern nation-states.[114] Motoda, however, conceived of government along Confucian lines, a system in which an absolute ruler, advised by virtuous ministers, would lead multitudes to live moral lives in accord with the laws of Heaven. To him the idea of division of powers and responsibility over narrow areas of governmental activity by the Emperor's ministers was anathema because it partitioned the unified and integrated moral life of man into subdivisions where over-all ethical values could no longer be the determining force.[115] Motoda saw constitutional government and representation in terms of Shōtoku Taishi's so-called "Seventeen Article Constitution" of 604, and Shun's consulting with the "four mountains" (ssu yo 四岳) before governing.[116] Shōtoku Taishi's "Seventeen Article Constitution" was not a constitution in any real sense, but had been promulgated apparently with the idea of strengthening the position of the Imperial House by the use of Confucian philosophy.[117] The

113. Watanabe, op. cit., 178.

114. Ibid., 126-130, 173-175.

115. Although this is a point of view implicit in nearly all Motoda's writings, a feeling for the earnestness with which he felt it can best be obtained by reading through his "Essentials for the Virtuous Guidance of Emperors." Tokutomi, op. cit., shogen 12-15. Asaji and Pringle, op. cit., 52-59.

116. Watanabe, op. cit., 169-71.

117. For a detailed analysis of the contents of this "Seventeen Article Constitution," see Joseph John Spae, Itō Jinsai, Monumenta Serica Monograph Series, XII, (Peiping: The Catholic University of Peking, 1948), 18-20.

story of Shun's consulting with the "four mountains" came from the Confucian *Shu-ching* 書經 (*Book of History*), but it hardly could be considered an example of representation in the modern sense, and in any case was an unreliable event, based on folklore and legend.[118] Nevertheless, these were the ideas that Motoda believed in, and in speaking of the functions of ministers and Imperial attendants in 1878, he compared them to the stomach, the heart, the ears, and the eyes of the sovereign which worked with a single end in view, the proper direction of their master.[119] This parallel is taken again from the *Book of History*, and it is nearly a paraphrase of Shun's message to his ministers which ordered them to act as his thighs and forearms, and eyes and ears.[120] That Motoda should use it, though, shows the extent to which he was imbued with ideals from the Confucian classics and felt they were applicable to conditions in his day.

In education, too, Motoda and Itō clashed, for while both agreed that Japan faced a crisis in this field, their analyses of it were poles apart. Thus the Emperor, disturbed by the educational conditions he had seen in Japan on his 1878 tour of inspection, in September of the next year ordered Itō, an advisor (*sangi* 参議) at the time, to present his views on the abuses and evils of the educational system. Itō was also given a copy of Motoda's *Kyōgaku taishi* which had been the latter's answer to the same question put to him earlier by the Emperor. After some days of consideration, Itō drafted his answer known as the *Kyōikugi* 教育議 (Views on Education) in which he stated that the evils in the educational system were more apparent than real. Educational methods stressing scientific and technical education were not invalid, he said, and vaunted educational abuses were simply a reflection of the rapid changes of the times and nothing more. He warned that if radical methods were used to try and extirpate these fleeting ills, the country might easily fall into the errors

---

118. *Shang-shu* 尚書 (*Book of History*), Yü *shu* 虞書, *Shun tien* 舜典. Legge, *Confucian Classics*, III, 41. *Shang-shu* is simply another name for the *Shu-ching*.

119. Watanabe, *op. cit.*, 171.

120. *Shang-shu* 尚書 (*Book of History*), Yü shu 虞書, Yi and Tsieh 益稷. Legge, *op. cit.*, III, 79-80.

that had plagued Tokugawa Japan. Accordingly, political moralizing and speeches were certainly not the need of the day.[121]

In considering these points above, it will easily be seen that this was a rebuff to Motoda's view that insufficient attention had been paid to moral education in contrast to technical training. And it was not long before Motoda countered Itō's *Kyōikugi* with a memorial entitled *Kyōikugi fugi* 教育議附議 (Opinion of Views on Education) in which he took special pains to criticize Western ethics as follows:

> As for good textbooks on ethics and customs, although there are such in Western moral science, they cannot excel the *Classic of Filial Piety*, the *Analects*, the book of *Mencius*, the *Great Learning*, the *Doctrine of the Mean*, the *Classic of Poetry*, and the *Book of History*. Furthermore, so-called Western moral science, by such things as making light of the loyalty between prince and minister, and placing the clandestine relations of husband and wife above the relation of father and son, contravenes the very foundation of the way [of virtue] in our nation. And for textbooks on morals, most of the [Western] ones are based on Christian doctrine. Therefore, making the [Confucian] *Four Books* and *Five Classics* the foundation, we may also use national literature related to ethics, but should choose [only] those Western books which are entirely satisfactory on morals.[122]

Meanwhile, there apparently had been germinating in Motoda's mind the idea that the most efficacious way of dealing with the decline of morality and the increasing dangers of Western materialism would be by having some sort of basic "national doctrine" (*kokkyō* 國教) promulgated which would become the final ethical standard of the nation. One of the first inklings of this came in 1880 when Motoda presented a memorial to the Emperor entitled "General Outline for a National Pattern (*Kokken daikō* 國憲大綱), in which he suggested that, "A national doctrine taking humaneness, righteousness, propriety, humility, loyalty, filial piety, and honesty as principles, could never be contravened by prince or minister, high or low, or government

---

121. Watanabe, *op. cit.*, 172-173
122. Ienaga, *op. cit.*, 7.

regulations and laws."[123] Motoda even contacted Itō in 1884 over the need he felt for the establishment of a "national doctrine."[124] Like his earlier proposal to the Emperor, he stressed making Confucianism its basic element, but Itō was critical of the idea, for he suspected that such a doctrine might become the vehicle for suppressing religious freedom, hindering the progress of education, and unnecessarily narrowing the activity of the intellectual world. Itō also feared an intermingling of religion and philosophy in government because it was not in keeping with the practice of modern states and reflected the weak and ineffectual policies of the nineteenth century Tokugawa regime.[125]

On almost every count, then, Motoda and Itō conflicted sharply, and the struggle between them continued up to Motoda's death in 1891. As early as 1879, Itō had tried to curb Motoda's influence in politics gained by his position as tutor to the Emperor, but he had been unsuccessful for the most part. This was because the Emperor continued to see Motoda and discuss matters of state with him, though according to the regulations, responsibility for such decisions was completely out of the hands of tutors attached to the Imperial Household. Moreover, Motoda's intimate relations and influence with the Emperor were made even stronger by the fact that he went freely to and from the palace and was scheduled to lecture regularly before the Emperor, the Empress, and the court.[126] These lectures were not simply exercises in literary exposition, but skillful attempts to analyze present-day problems in terms of the traditions and philosophy found in the Confucian classics. For example, in a lecture dealing with the results which would come from instructing the whole nation in Confucianism, Motoda said:

> The world is not being enlightened by a sound moral philosophy. Heterodox views of life and scraps of physical science are the prevailing substitutes. The individual is guided by his own opinions

123. *Ibid.*, 8.
124. *Ibid.*, 7-8.
125. Watanabe, *op. cit.*, 174-175.
126. Tokutomi, *op. cit.*, shogen 3, 6, 24, 31-32.

which he takes for eternal truths, thus effectively debarring himself from all possibility of developing a candid and serious spirit.

Unaware of the vital importance of bringing his passions and activities under systematic rules, he takes his own cleverness for a sufficient guarantee of the excellence of his own private opinions and actually proceeds to their propagation! If he is not successful in securing absolute agreement with them, he will probably have the presumption to rail at his superiors and abuse his fellows! Such men may pose as scholars and geniuses, "Choice and master spirits of the age," but they end by being drowned in the fountains of their precious wisdom. Ignorant of the road which leads back to the philosophic calm, in their fury they raise rebellious heads against those in authority, and take counsel how to work havoc in the state.... There is no remedy for their ailment, since they are without any course of study which can form character.... They are as far removed from the philosophic gentleman of Confucius, as the heavens are from the earth....

When the study of Confucianism holds its proper and supreme place in the national esteem, strength of character is cultivated at the expense of passion. The manners of the whole community are those which humility, its practices those which rectitude inculcates. The arts and sciences make due progress. Sin is entirely absent, and rebellion out of the question.[127]

In this way the mind of the Emperor became saturated with Motoda's Confucian ideas to which he often proved very sympathetic. Thus in November, 1886, the Emperor made a tour of inspection of the Imperial University in Tōkyō and returned scandalized at the lack of interest in Japanese studies, in Confucianism, and moral subjects in general. He ordered Motoda to visit the Imperial University and make a report to him on the causes of the bad conditions.[128] Motoda once again took advantage of this situation, as he had previously in 1878 in the *Kyōgaku taishi,* and levelled his attack against the current of Westerniza-

---

127. Tokutomi, *op. cit.,* 20-21. Asaji and Pringle, *op. cit.,* 83-84. Dating Motoda's lectures selected and included in Tokutomi's collection is difficult. In the shogen, 31-32, is a letter which helps somewhat, but even with it only chapters X, XII, and XIV can accurately be dated as taken from lectures delivered in 1876, 1879, and 1890. On this basis, however, it appears that the earlier chapters were taken from parts of earlier lectures.

128. Tokutomi, *op. cit.,* shinjo 新序 (New preface), 3-4.

tion prevalent at the time. Like the *Kyōgaku taishi,* this latest essay also masqueraded as an expression of Imperial wishes, which is shown by its title "Record of Imperial Instructions" (*Seiyuki* 聖喩記). After an exposition of the Emperor's fears over the trend in education which seemed to ignored moral training completely, Motoda gave his answer to the causes for this situation saying:

> ...from the time Your Majesty decided on the *Yōgaku kōyō* which was so important for education and to which you had given deep consideration, the evils of American education gradually were corrected, the world was once again returning to the principles of loyalty to the sovereign and love for the country; and there were also those who began advocating humaneness, righteousness, and morality. But from the year before last, there has been a tendency toward Western habits once more, and last year there was a trend to change exclusively to Western learning and entirely abolish Japanese and Chinese learning in the future, at which [suggestion] all patriots felt great anxiety.[129]

Besides condemning Western education here, Motoda was indirectly criticising Itō and the latter's choice for Minister of Education, Mori Arinori 森有禮 (1847-89), who was noted for his support of Western learning and technical education. Mori had entered the Ministry of Education 1884 and became Minister of Education in 1885, the years that Motoda specified as the ones when moral deterioration set in due to the overadulation of Western things.[130]

The conflict between Motoda and Itō had been reaching a climax during these years, especially because Motoda was continuing his position as special advisor to the Emperor, despite all that Itō could do. Motoda in his capacity as Imperial Household official would see the Emperor every day, ostensibly on palace affairs. But he would often spend so much time with the Emperor that Itō was hard pressed to find time to discuss

---

129. *Ibid.,* shinjo 3-6.
130. Watanabe, *op. cit.,* 181-182, and Sansom, *op. cit.,* 458-459, both note the significance of Mori becoming Minister of Education.

affairs of state with the Emperor to obtain his approval. Matters reached such an impasse that in July, 1884, Itō had written:

> Motoda's and Tokudaiji's audiences daily consume most of the time, with the result that time for our audience on matters of state is very short. From now on, how would it be to limit Motoda's and Tokudaiji's audiences to the morning, and those of ministers and advisors to the afternoon? If it goes on like it is now, there is nothing left for us but to resign.[131]

Motoda on hearing this was not in the least concerned, and on the contrary, expressed the opinion that as advisors outside the regular administrative structure, he and Tokudaiji had a special responsibility to be on hand to help and direct the Emperor at any time.[132] The final solution to this did not come until Itō became Prime Minister in 1886, when he had special rules of procedure drawn up for audiences with the Emperor. According to these, important matters of state brought by the Prime Minister or other ministers for Imperial consideration would receive immediate attention and the minister involved allowed an audience.[133] It was just this type of modification that Itō desired as part of his plans to give Japan and Japanese institutions the aura of Western constitutional government. And at the same time, Itō also may have had in mind some method of permanently restricting the influence that Motoda wielded over governmental affairs.

In 1887 with the failure of Japan to persuade Western nations to give up their special treaty rights, a wave of anti-foreign feeling began to sweep the country, and everywhere there was a revival of interest in things Japanese as opposed to Western importations. This is reflected in the rise of a number of organizations between 1887 and 1890 which were dedicated to the propagation of the "national essence" (*kokusui* 國粹). Among the more important of these were the Nippon Kokkyō Daidōsha

---

131. Watanabe, *op. cit.*, 179.

132. *Ibid.*, 179-180. Tokudaiji Sanenori 德大寺實則 (1839-1919) was an important Imperial Household official who often joined Motoda in his audiences with the Emperor.

133. *Ibid.*, 180-181.

日本國教大同社 already mentioned in the previous section, the Ishin Gakkai 惟神學會, the Tōyō Gakkai 東洋學會, the Kokugakuin Daigaku 國學院大學, and the Seikyōsha 政教社. This last organization was known for publishing the magazine *Nipponjin* 日本人 which strongly criticized the trend of indiscriminately imitating the West.[134] As an indication of its position, one of its leading editors, Miyake Yūjirō 三宅雄次郎 (1860-1945, better known by his *gō*: Setsurei 雪嶺), claimed that while it was proper for Japan to assimilate Western scientific thought, in philosophy, Buddhism and Confucianism were superior to anything the West had to offer.[135] This point of view is similar to that of the progressive Confucianists of late Tokugawa times, and was that subscribed to by Motoda and most other supporters of Confucianism in the Meiji period.

It is easy to imagine how men like Motoda and Nishimura Shigeki must have been elated at this reaction against what they had for over fifteen years spoken of as the dangers of Western material civilization. The immediate problem, though, was to find a suitable method of restoring a common moral standard which would call forth the loyalty and devotion of people. It was particularly pressing at this time because of the confusion in standards resulting from the competition of such varying ideologies as Christianity, Shintoism, Buddhism, Confucianism, Western utilitarianism and individualism. Reference has already been made to Motoda's early interest in having a "national doctrine" set up as the ultimate standard for proper conduct, and now in 1887, Nishimura once again brought this idea to the attention of important officials. He secured the approval and support of Soejima Taneomi 副島種臣 (1838-1905) and Sasaki Takayuki 佐々木高行 (1830-1910), both advisors to the Imperial Household, and that of the Minister of Home Affairs, Sanjō Sanetomi 三條實美 (1837-91). The latter felt that an Imperial edict could be issued and a textbook on ethics drawn up on Imperial direction that would be circulated all over the country. Together these could become the basis of the nation's moral education, much as Imperial injunctions by the

---

134. Kiyowara, *op. cit.*, 439-441. Iwahashi, *op. cit.*, 376.
135. Sansom, *op. cit.*, 371-372.

Chinese Emperors K'ang-hsi 康熙 (reigned 1662-1723) and Yung-cheng 雍正 (reigned 1723-36) had served as guiding ethical principles in every school in China. But as the Minister of Education, Mori Arinori, did not approve of the project, it did not get any further at this time.[136] Nishimura, however, had not changed his basic conviction that the center of moral and spiritual direction for the nation lay in an edict or rescript stemming from the Emperor. He presented these views in a statement to Hijikata Hisamoto 土方久元 (1833-1918), the Imperial Household Minister, in February, 1889, but apparently they had no direct effect.[137]

It was only a year later in February, 1890, at a meeting of prefectural governors that the Imperial Rescript on Education (*Kyōiku chokugo* 教育勅語) seems officially to have had its genesis. With educational aims still unsettled, the opinion was voiced that the emphasis on developing knowledge alone in the schools was having bad effects. Teachers were not following any fixed course as a basis for ethical teaching, and loyalty and filial piety were often put aside in favor of individual theories. Direction was needed from the educational authorities.[138]

According to Yoshikawa Akimasa 芳川顕正 (1841-1920), Minister of Education at this time, the Emperor was disturbed at these reports and ordered him to draw up the first draft of the Imperial Rescript on Education.[139] In view of the advice and suggestions that the Emperor had been receiving for over ten years from Motoda on the need for a "national doctrine," these actions are not surprising. In addition, other advisors influential with the Emperor like Soejima and Sasaki had supported the idea when it was presented by Nishimura; and although it had not succeeded at that time, it focused attention on the possibility of an Imperial edict restoring fixed aims in the turbulent ideological world.

Imperial edicts were not innovations to Japanese life, for they are reported as early as the mythical "Age of the Gods"

---

136. Watanabe, *op. cit.*, 384-385.
137. *Ibid.*, 385-386.
138. Ienaga, *op. cit.*, 8. Tokutomi, *op. cit.*, appended article on the "Kyōiku chokugo yonjūnen" 教育勅語四十年 ("Fourtieth year of the Imperial Rescript on Education"), 5.
139. Tokutomi, *op. cit.*, "Kyōiku chokugo yonjūnen," 5.

in the *Kojiki* 古事記. After the Meiji Restoration, they took on a new significance because they served to give special sanction to government policies and to lessen divergence or opposition. At the height of popular agitation for an assembly in 1875, there was an Imperial Rescript which stabilized the situation;[140] and in 1882, an Imperial Rescript to soldiers and sailors was promulgated that appealed to the loyalty and service of every man in the armed forces by making him directly responsible to the Emperor.[141]

With this background, it is easy to see how an Imperial Rescript on Education would be used, particularly in view of the general agreement that confused social conditions and a welter of conflicting foreign ideas were endangering the traditional "moral fiber" of the nation. Motoda expressed this succinctly in June, 1890, in an essay called the *Kyōiku taishi* 教育大旨 where he stated:

> Not following the teachings of our ancestors but rather accepting and using the culture and science of foreign nations, this is the same as adorning a man who has no soul. It is [like] taking the whole country and destroying its soul. There is no greater harm to the country than this. Isn't it like trying to have Germans imitate Frenchmen, or Russians imitate Englishmen? Seeing the other country's faults, it goes without saying that they never wish to imitate them. Ah, can the Japanese [then] voluntarily acquiesce and wish to become foreigners?[142]

The problem, though, was in actually drawing up the rescript and deciding what its contents would include. Tokutomi Iichirō 徳富猪一郎, writing in 1928 on the "Fourtieth Year of the Imperial Rescript on Education" ("Kyōiku chokugo yonjūnen" 教育勅語四十年), claims that Motoda's revisions and corrections of the original drafts of the rescript were those most highly valued by both the

---

140. W. W. McLaren, "Japanese Government Documents, 1869-1889," *T.A.S.J.*, series 1, XLII, pt. 1, (1914), 41-42.

141. Joseph H. Longford, *Japan*, The Nations of Today Series (Boston and New York: Houghton Mifflin, 1923), 313-315.

142. Ienaga, *op. cit.*, 7.

Emperor and the cabinet.[143] These assertions are questionable, though, because of Tokutomi's admiration for Motoda and his overadulation of the rescript itself. Furthermore, he does not present sufficient evidence to support his stand, but simply shows that Motoda did play a part in formulating the rescript. More enlightening on the way the contents took form is the information given by Tokutomi showing that Inoue Kowashi 井上毅 (1843-95) revised the original draft by Yoshikawa and played an important part in phrasing and perfecting the final document.[144]

Inoue intellectually and politically was a follower of Itō. He had worked with Itō in drawing up the constitution which was promulgated in 1889, and was a man of wide knowledge of the world. Aware of the aims that Motoda would be likely to have, he remarked in a letter to Yamagata Aritomo 山縣有朋 (1838-1922), Prime Minister at the time, that "according to principles of constitutional government, the sovereign does not interefere with the freedom of conscience of his subjects."[145] Motoda, in contrast, believed that the sovereign had the duty to lead his subjects in the way of virtue and must therefore direct their moral lives. Freedom of conscience undoubtedly sounded like license to him, and on numerous occasions he stressed that "the main point is we must take Confucianism and make it the object of moral teaching."[146] But besides Motoda's preference for a paternalistic political philosophy, it was to be expected from his previous statements that he openly would be opposed to Western learning, and Inoue seems to have realized this too. Though not directly mentioning Motoda, he spoke of the rescript in the letter to Yamagata already quoted, saying:

In this rescript, philosophical reasoning must be avoided, for philosophical reasoning always somehow arouses opposite ideas. The basic theory of the "Way" should be intrusted to the investigation

---

143. Tokutomi, *op. cit.*, "Kyōiku chokugo yonjūnen," 8.
144. *Ibid.*, 6-7.
145. Ienaga, *op. cit.*, 9.
146. *Ibid.*, 7.

of philosophers. It is something that should never be fixed by the ruler's decree.... No intimation of Chinese learning or Western ways should be expressed.... If one of the principles of the various groups in society should be felicited, there should be no wording such as to anger the others.[147]

From this one can see that the conflict between Itō and Motoda was continuing, only it was now being carried on by Inoue. Up to the present, there has been little information available showing exactly what Motoda proposed for inclusion in the Imperial Rescript on Education. On the basis of his earlier, adamant views, however, it is reasonable to assume that he would openly have criticized the West and mentioned Confucianism if his influence had been paramount. But while his full hopes for a Confucian "national doctrine" were not realized, the men responsible for drawing up the final rescript did not overlook the great value of Confucian ethics. What they wished to do, though, was to emphasize the national and Japanese character of these ethics and relate them to the new institutions of the state, without falling into a narrow dogmatism or taking a purely negative stand.

The opening sentences of the rescript itself show this first point, as loyalty and filial piety were spoken of as virtues implanted by Japan's founders and illustrated by succeeding generations. Loyalty having been placed at the head of the list of virtues, the people were next exhorted to practice the other virtues associated with the Confucian social relationships, although Confucianism was never mentioned by name.[148] Yoshikawa, Minister of Education at the time of the writing of the rescript, in 1912 described the process by which these Confucian virtues had been made an integral part of it. He said:

As people know, the Imperial Rescript on Education was based on four virtues: benevolence, righteousness, loyalty, and filial piety.

---

147. *Ibid.*, 12. Ienaga points out in footnote 8, p. 17, that Yamagata, Yoshikawa, and Aoki Shūzō 青木周藏 (1854-1914) did not fully support the idea of a rescript because they feared the possible effects of its philosophical and religious overtones.

148. The Confucian social relationships are described in detail in ch. I, footnote 44, of this study.

The making of these four virtues the foundation of the national education was, however, strongly criticized at the time, and some scholars even declared that these virtues were imported from China and ought never to be established as the standard of the nation's morality. Others again said that should such old-fashioned virtues be encouraged among the people it would mean the revival of the old form of virtue typified by private revenge, etc. But I strongly upheld the teaching of these four principle virtues, saying that the essence of man's morality is one and the same irrespective of place or time, although it might take different forms according to different circumstances, and that therefore, the aforesaid four virtues could be well made the moral standard of the Japanese people.[149]

Even a casual reading of the Imperial Rescript confirms Yoshikawa's statement regarding the integration of Confucian moral precepts into Japanese ethics; and besides this, many phrases in the rescript are direct Japanese translations of well-known Confucian terms occurring in the classics.[150] But probably most significant of all in explaining the state of mind and aims of the drafters of the rescript were the sentences relating virtue with proper conduct toward new institutions and the state. Such phrases indicate that the drafters were well aware that they must create a document which would bring with it a sense of national unity and purpose, and not simply be a set of ethical rules. Though Motoda himself did not lack national consciousness, with his primarily Confucian background he tended to think that moral tenets were sufficient to unite the aims of all Japanese. Once again, however, his views were not found acceptable to the other men drawing up the rescript, and this disagreement is strikingly put in the memoirs of Egi Kazuyuki 江木千之 (1853-1932).

149. *Kokumin shimbun* 國民新聞 *(The People's Newspaper)*, Aug. 5, 1912; translated by the Japanese Advertiser, Aug. 6, 1912, as quoted by D. C. Holtom, *Modern Japan and Shintō Nationalism*, (Revised ed.; Chicago: The University of Chicago Press, 1947), 79.

150. Ienaga, *op. cit.*, 9. Watanabe, *op. cit.*, 400-401. A Japanese copy of the Imperial Rescript on Education is readily available: Teikoku Chihō Gyōsei Gakkai 帝國地方行政學會, *Genkō hōrei shūran* 現行法令輯覽 *(Compilation of Present-day Laws and Ordinances)*, 12 vols.; Tōkyō: Naikaku Kambō Kirokuka 内閣官房記錄課, 1930), VII. Gakuji 學事 (Educational Matters), 1. For the authorized English translation of the Imperial Rescript on Education, see appendix of this study.

Concerning the phrase—always respect the Constitution and observe the laws—in the Imperial Rescript on Education, the Minister of Education Yoshikawa and the Imperial reader Motoda differed on it; and there were also various opinions on this among the cabinet ministers, so that it was difficult to come to any agreement. The Imperial reader Motoda claimed, with respect to this phrase, that it was unnecessary to include it in the Imperial Rescript on Education, for if the intention of loyalty and filial piety [already included in the rescript] were realized fully, these other aims would naturally follow. The Minister of Education Yoshikawa emphasized, though, that in these times and circumstances, such a phrase must be especially inserted, and its meaning made clear, but the discussion was unable to reach any final conclusion. The Emperor Meiji, after having this proposal in his hands for some time, spent much thought over these points and finally decided that in view of the times, the phrase was necessary.

Concerning the matter of Motoda's and Yoshikawa's disagreement, and the final Imperial decision, this is exactly the way I personally heard it from the former President of the Privy Council, Field Marshall Yamagata, who was Prime Minister at the time of the proclamation of the Imperial Rescript on Education.[151]

Motoda died on the twenty-first of January, 1891, not quite three months after the promulgation of the Imperial Rescript on Education (November 30, 1890). In retrospect, despite the fact that a number of important changes and additions were made to it with which he disagreed, the document is symbolic of the final victory of his idea that Japan needed a "national doctrine" in which Confucian ethical beliefs played a dominant role. Furthermore, his influence over the Emperor Meiji was tremendous, a fact which Itō recognized and spoke of to the Emperor after Motoda's death.[152] And in spite of the fact that the Emperor rejected Motoda's views on occasion as above, he and the leaders of Japan of that time essentially accepted Motoda's exalted

---

151. *Egi Kazuyuki-ō keireki dan* 江木千之翁經歷談 (*Narrative of Personal Experiences of the Aged Egi Kazuyuki*) as quoted by Ienaga, *op. cit.*, 13. Ienaga states in footnote 9, p. 17, that the same particular events quoted from Egi's memoirs above are described in *Yamagata Aritomo no kyōiku chokugo kampatsu ni kansuru danwa hikki* 山縣有朋の教育勅語渙發に關する談話筆記 (*Record of Conversations of Yamagata Aritomo related to the Promulgation of the Imperial Rescript on Education*).

152. Watanabe, *op. cit.*, 184.

Confucian concept of the Imperial institution.[153] According to it, an Emperor set the example of benevolence for his subjects, and thereby led them to attain virtue with him. This idea was expressed in the last sentence of the Imperial Rescript on Education as "It it Our wish to lay it [the Way of loyalty, humaneness, etc.] to heart in all reverence, in common with you, Our subjects, that we may all attain the same virtue." It had been one of the most constantly repeated ideals for rulers in the Confucian classics,[154] and its inclusion in the Imperial Rescript on Education emphasizes the appeal of Chinese ethical-political philosophy to the Japanese in a time of change and crisis.

5. Confucian Development after 1891.

After the death of Motoda and the acceptance of many of his Confucian ideas in the Imperial Rescript on Education, the general activity of Confucianism declined and Confucian organizations and Confucianists tended to devote their energies to literary pursuits. By this it is not implied that Confucian ideas lost their influence in the intellectual world, but rather that their position having been established, their supporters were satisfied for the most part simply to maintain it.

This fact is made clear by an analysis of the relations of the Imperial House with Confucianism after 1891. To begin

---

153. *Ibid.*, 166-167. Watanabe suggests that Itō and other councilors and advisors were very hesitant about restricting the Emperor's powers through the constitution. Itō apparently felt that the Imperial institution was the only one in Japan capable of bringing spiritual unity to the extent that Christianity had to nations in the West. Finally, although the Emperor's sovereignty was limited by the constitution, in retrospect one might say that in the Imperial Rescript on Education, Japanese leaders sought to restore some of the spiritual power and aura to the Emperor which the constitution had taken away.

154. The ideal of the unity between the ruler and his subjects is in most Confucian books which mention government and virtuous rule. For example: *Ta-hsüeh* 大學 (*Great Learning*) ch. X, 21; Legge, *op. cit.*, I, 379. *Chung-yung* 中庸 (*Doctrine of the Mean*), ch. XX, 13; Legge, *op. cit.*, I, 409. *Mengtzu* 孟子 (*Mencius*), bk. I, pt. 2, ch. 4, 3; Legge, *op. cit.*, I, 158. Furthermore, the last phrase of the rescript is taken directly from the *Shang-shu* 尚書 (*Book of History*), being also the subtitle of one of its divisions. *Shang-shu* 尚書, Shang-shu 商書, Hsien yo i't'eh 咸有一德; Legge, *op. cit.*, III, 213-219. The last lines of this division tell of how the virtue of the sovereign will serve as an example to lead the people and surely be acknowledged by them. Watanabe, *op. cit.*, 399-402, discusses how the phrase was suggested by the Confucianist Mishima Chūshū 三島中洲 and came to be included in the rescript.

with, lectures on topics found in the Confucian classics were carried out nearly every New Year's day before the Emperor and the Imperial Court.[155] Motoda had inaugurated this custom when he was made Confucian lecturer to the Imperial Household in 1871, and it was continued during the reign of the Emperor Taishō (reigned 1912-26) and the Emperor Shōwa (reigning 1926-present). After 1891, however, there does not seem to have been any regularly appointed Confucian lecturer, and outstanding Confucians were commissioned simply to give the New Year's lecture.[156] The reason for this may have been that government officials and politicians, remembering the influential position which Motoda had held, wished to prevent unofficial advisors from wielding too much power. In any case, among those who lectured most often on New Year's were Mishima Chūshū and Shigeno Yasutsugu, already mentioned as important Confucianists and literary figures during the Meiji period. Neither of these two men, however, was intimately associated with the Emperor Meiji as Motoda has been, nor did they have the influence and prerogatives of the latter in policy making. Shigeno died in 1910, two years before the death of the Emperor Meiji. Mishima then became the chief lecturer, continuing this function during the reign of the Emperor Taishō until 1917, after which Hattori Unokichi 服部宇之吉 (1867-1939) replaced him.[157]

Besides these yearly lectures, however, the Imperial House showed personal interest and favor to Confucian organizations in a number of ways. In 1910, for example, at the fourth year of the celebration of Confucian ceremonies by the Kōshi Saiten Kai 孔子祭典會 (Confucian Ceremony Society), an Imperial prince of the Kuni no Miya 久邇宮 family took part, and from this time

---

155. *Nihon Jugaku nempyō*, 426-448, specifically records the titles of lectures for the years 1892-94, 1899-1900, 1902-14, 1916-20, and 1922, the last year covered by this chronology. It is possible that lectures were delivered in the intervening years, but not recorded. There is also no reason to believe that they did not continue after 1922, since the custom was well established by that time.

156. *Ibid.*, 426-448, lists seven different men as lecturing before the Emperor and the court on New Year's from 1891 to 1922.

157. *Ibid.*, 426-448. The lecturer for each year can be found in the sections outlining events related to Confucianism year by year.

onwards, some member of the Imperial family was always present at these celebrations.[158] The Kōshi Saiten Kai was an organization which had been set up in 1907 by the teachers of the Tōkyō Higher Normal School and others interested in reviving the Confucian ceremonies or *sekiten* 釋奠 which had not been carried out regularly in Japan since the abolition of the Tokugawa and old *han* school system in 1871.[159]

In 1911, one year after the annexation of Korea by Japan, the Korean Government General reorganized the ancient center of Confucian activities in the peninsula known the Sŏnggyun'gwan 成均館, renaming it the Keigakuin 經學院.[160] Toward the upkeep and expenses of this new organization, 250,000 yen were granted by the Emperor from the Imperial Privy Purse to further the spread of benevolence, righteousness, loyalty, and filial piety.[161] Apparently the Korean Government General was seeking ways of assuaging and redirecting the hostile sentiments of the Korean people, and Imperial support for time-honored Korean Confucian institutions was considered a practical method for implementing this.[162]

In 1913 the Tōkyō Ōtsuka Senju Bosho Hozonkai 東京大塚 先儒墓所保存會 was organized for the purpose of caring for the graves of outstanding Confucianists, and the Emperor contributed one thousand yen from the Imperial Privy Purse to support the aims of the organization.[163]

The Kangaku Semmon Nishō Gakusha 漢學專門二松學舍 was referred to earlier as a school founded by Mishima Chūshū for the study of the Chinese classics in 1877. It was an important center for the maintenance and spread of Confucian ideas during the Meiji and Taishō eras, as by 1919, over eight thousand students

---

158. *Ibid.*, 432.
159. *Ibid.*, 430-431. See ch. II, 41-42 of this study.
160. Bureau of Education, *Manual of Education in Chosen*, (Keijō, Korea: The Government General of Chosen, 1920), 113-114.
161. *Ibid.*, 114. *Nihon Jugaku nempyō*, 435.
162. *Manual of Education in Chosen*, 113-115. From reading over these pages in which the purpose of the government's support for the Keigakuin is summarized, one definitely gets this impression, although it is not stated openly.
163. *Nihon Jugaku nempyō*, 436.

were estimated to have graduated from it.[164] The Emperor contributed ten thousand yen in 1915.to help support this school, and again in 1918, he gave five thousand yen to it for the construction of new buildings.[165] From this one can assume that the Emperor and his advisors were in favor of the aims of the school and wished to demonstrate it publicly.

One other important example of how Imperial favor was given indirectly to Confucianism should be mentioned in connection with the raising to court rank of important pre-Meiji Confucianists. The significant point to note in relation to this is that the majority of those chosen for these posthumous honors were Confucianists who had distinguished themselves by their loyalty to the Imperial House or its traditions. Thus in 1908, Kitabatake Chikafusa 北畠親房 (1293-1354), a staunch loyalist who had used Confucian philosophy in his book *Jinnōshōtōki* 神皇正統記 to prove the justice and righteousness of the Imperial succession, was raised to the highest grade possible, senior first rank.[166] Tokugawa Mitsukuni, whose loyalty and devotion to the Imperial tradition were described in the first chapter, similarly had been raised to the senior first rank in 1900.[167] In 1915, when coronation ceremonies were being carried out for the Emperor Taishō, thirty-one former Confucianists were given court rank as part of the ceremonies.[168] Surveying the total number of times this type of honor was bestowed from 1868 to 1935, the following becomes apparent: from 1868 to 1888, only two such cases occurred. This was a period when Confucianism was on the defensive and trying to adapt itself to new conditions. From 1889 to 1918, one hundred and thirteen persons were granted posthumous court rank. This was a period when Confucianism had reestablished its position, and national consciousness was awakening in Japan. Under such

---

164. Shibunkai, *Shibun*, I, 1, (Jan., 1919), 93.
165. *Nihon Jugaku nempyō*, 439, 443.
166. *Ibid.*, 431. For an analysis of Kitabakake's use of Confucianism in the *Jinnō-shōtōki*, see Yamada Yoshio, *Jinnōshōtōki jutsugi* 神皇正統記述義 (*Explanation of the Jinnōshōtōki*), (Tōkyō: Min'yūsha 民友社, 1932). Yamada notes throughout the whole text analogies, comparisons, and quotations made to and taken from the Confucian classics.
167. *Nihon Jugaku nempyō*, 429.
168. *Ibid.*, 440.

circumstances, it was natural that Confucianists who had made outstanding contributions to the nation in times past should be recognized. From 1919 to 1935, only fifty-three such cases occurred. The diminution in numbers is probably due to there not being many important Confucianists remaining who had the proper qualifications to fit into this category, despite the fact that Confucian activity and influence were increasing during this period.[169]

Although as a whole Confucianism and its supporters played a passive role from 1891 to 1918 in the practical political and ideological world, the one strong essay of Confucianists into this field during these years bears scrutiny. The genesis of this activity lay in the growing conflict between the precepts found in the Imperial Rescript on Education and the Christian creed. Christianity had always had its critics in Japan who claimed that its fundamental beliefs were not in harmony with the traditions of the Japanese. Confucianists such as Yasui Sokken, who had bitterly attacked Christianity in his book *Bemmō* 辨妄[170] in the early part of the Meiji period, were among the leaders of this movement. Motoda himself, it will be remembered,[171] had not favored Christian morality, but effective agitation against Christianity did not really begin until after the promulgation of the Imperial Rescript on Education.

With the death of Motoda in 1891, however, Inoue Tetsujirō 井上哲次郎 (1856-1944) became the most ardent public proponent of Confucianism. Inoue was a professor of philosophy at Tōkyō Imperial University whose influence in intellectual and educational circles of the time was quite great.[172] He was best known for a series on Japanese philosophy, the first volume of which appeared in 1900 entitled *Nippon Yōmei gakuha no tetsugaku* 日本陽明學派の哲學 (*The Philosophy of the Japanese Yōmei School*).

169. Nakamura Kyūshirō 中村久四郎, *Nippon bunka to Jukyō* 日本文化と儒教 (*Japanese Culture and Confucianism*), (Tōkyō: Tōkō Shoin 刀江書院, 1935), 144-148, lists all Confucianists granted posthumous court rank year by year from 1868 to 1935, including the court rank received.
170. See ch. II, 54, of this study.
171. See ch. II, 76, of this study.
172. *Shinsen dai jimmei jiten*, VII, 64-65.

In his preface to this book, he spoke of the evil influence which Western ideas of utilitarianism and individualism were having in Japan because they were subverting the traditional ethical standard of the country. In view of the quickening pace of corruption of Japanese moral life, he hoped that by making clear the contributions of Ōyōmei Confucian philosophy to Japanese ethics, people would better appreciate the essence of Oriental morality.[173] These criticisms of the West are similar to those of Motoda, and Inoue in effect succeeded to the latter's position as defender of a nationalistic and conservative Confucianism. It was no wonder, then, that his voice came to the fore in the controversy between Christianity and the Imperial Rescript on Education, and Inoue was the leader of those opposing Christianity.

To understand the rise of this conflict, it is necessary to keep in mind that since 1887 and the failure of treaty revision, the temper of the Japanese was to be more critical of the West and to preserve their own national characteristics.[174] The Imperial Rescript on Education in a very real sense had been drawn up to unite the nation ideologically, with the Emperor representing the unique divinity of the Japanese on the highest level. Because of this, it was natural that as cases of Christians in Japan refusing to bow and do obeisance to pictures of the Emperor increased, people began to criticize Christian doctrines. For example, in the early 1890's a student at an elementary school in Higo 肥後 asserted that he had been taught by a missionary that there were no sacred beings besides God, and then proceeded to knock down a picture of the Emperor, for which he was expelled.[175] In the same period, a Protestant minister, Oshigawa Katayoshi 押川方義, and several others, declared that bowing before the Emperor's picture and the Imperial Rescript on Education was not only use-

173. Inoue Tetsujirō 井上哲次郎, *Nippon Yōmei gakuha no tetsugaku* 日本陽明學派の哲學 (*The Philosophy of the Japanese Yōmei School*), (3rd ed.; Tōkyō: Fusambō 富山房, 1901), first preface, 2-4.

174. See ch. II, 81, of this study.

175. Kiyowara Sadao 清原貞雄, *Kaishū Nippon dōtoku shi* 改修日本道德史 (*History of Japanese Morality, revised edition*), (Tōkyō: Chūbunkan Shoten 中文館書店 1937), 656.

less from an educational standpoint, but also tended to promote the growth of superstition.[176]

In 1893, Inoue launched the first attack on such ideas in an article entitled "Shūkyō to kyōiku no shōtotsu" 宗教と教育の衝突, ("The Collision between Religion and Education"), which appeared in a number of educational magazines in 1893.[177] The kernel of his argument was that Christianity was incompatible with Japanese principles, for "Christianity places its Heavenly Father and its Christ above the Emperor and therein contradicts the principles of loyalty and filial piety of the Imperial Rescript on Education."[178] Furthermore, Christianity, by preaching universal love, failed to make clear the special relationships between parents and children and elders and young. The final result of all this was to eschew the veneration of ancestors which Inoue claimed would subvert the basis of proper respect for the Emperor and hence the nation.[179]

It is easy to see here the role that Confucian thought played, for ideas emphasizing loyalty and filial piety, relationships between parents and children, elders and young, and ancestor worship were among the most fundamental precepts of Confucian social philosophy. What Inoue and others who followed his line were doing was to identify Confucian virtues and ethical principles with the state, a point of view which had been fostered by certain Confucianists in the last years of the Tokugawa period.[180]

The agitation against Christianity continued during the 1890's, supported by Shintoists and Buddhists as well as Confucianists,[181] but the theme running through the attacks of all of these was

---

176. *Ibid.*, 656-657.
177. *Ibid.*, 657.
178. Inoue Tetsujirō 井上哲次郎, "Shūkyō to kyōiku no shōtotsu" 宗教と教育の衝突 ("The Collision between Religion and Education"), cited in Tsukamoto Toraji 塚本寅次, *Gendai Nihon to Kuristokyō* 現代日本と基督教 (*Present-Day Japan and Christianity*), (Tōkyō: 1932), 124, as quoted by Holtom, *op. cit.*, 81.
179. Kiyowara, *op. cit.*, 657-658.
180. See ch. I, section 4, of this study.
181. Kiyowara, *op. cit.*, 660-667.
182. *The Japan Weekly Mail* (Yokohama), July 29, 1899, no. 5, vol. XXXII, 105. In fairness to Confucianism, it should be noted that basically it did not encourage polygamy. But by its reverence for ancestors, degradation of women, and emphasis on filial piety, it indirectly encouraged concubinage in case the regular wife bore no sons.

that Christians had within them the seeds of becoming national traitors. This was taken up by the Confucian scholar Ōtsuki Nyoden 大槻如電 (1845-1931) in an article in the newspaper *Mainichi* 毎日 called, "Christianity brought to bay." There he took pains to show how Christian beliefs on monogamy were incompatible with the preservation of the Imperial line. The continuity of this line could not have been preserved in the past if such principles had been practiced, and therefore to propose such ideas for the future was to suggest a method for the extinction of the Imperial House. Consequently, Ōtsuki concluded that professors and propagandists of the Christian faith in Japan were equivalent to national traitors.[182]

Inoue in 1899 was also still pressing his criticisms of Christianity, saying that Japan was a nation founded on family life and the virtues of loyalty and filial piety. Rome, he pointed out, had been a nation based on family life too, and the Roman Empire became weak and crumbled only when Christian doctrines undermined this unity and substituted individualism for it. This was the great danger of Christianity, for by encouraging individualism, it destroyed loyalty and filial piety. He asserted that only Confucianism properly maintained these virtues so essential to the Japanese family and the Japanese nation.[183]

The upshot of all this anti-Christian agitation of the decade of the 1890's was the Educational Ordinance of August, 1899 which prohibited teaching religion in officially recognized schools, whether private or public.[184] This no doubt pleased the Confucianists, although evidence has been unavailable on whether they had a determining voice in deciding the matter. It is clear, however, that by this time or shortly afterwards, many Confucian ideas had been incorporated into the morals courses in elementary and secondary schools,[185] and significantly, Inoue Tetsujirō was on

---

The *Japan Weekly Mail* transcribes the given name of Ōtsuki Nyoden 大槻如電 as Joden, apparently because the first character of his given name, 如, has the alternate readings *jo* and *nyo*. The reading given in the *Shinsen dai jimmei jiten*, I, 559, is *nyo*.

183. *Ibid.*, Dec. 23, 1899, no. 26, vol. XXXII, 643-644.

184. *The Japan Weekly Mail*, Aug. 19, 1899, no. 8, vol. XXXII, 191.

185. Dairoku Kikuchi, *Japanese Education*, (London: John Murray, 1909), 102-103, 149-163, 217-220. Kikuchi Dairoku 菊池大麓 (1855-1917) had held various high government

the commission which compiled the textbooks for these morals courses.[186] From the following regulations to guide teachers in the proper instruction of morals in elementary schools at this time, it is possible to assess the important role played by Confucian principles in these compulsory courses.

> The teaching of Morals must be based on the Imperial Rescript on Education, and its aim should be to cultivate the moral nature of children and to guide them in the practice of virtues.
>
> In the ordinary elementary course, easy precepts appropriate for practice and concerning such virtues as filial piety and obedience to elders, affection and friendship, frugality and industry, modesty, fidelity, courage, etc., should be given and then some of the duties towards the State and society, with a view to elevate their moral character, strengthen their will, increase their spirit of enterprise, make them value public virtues and foster the spirit of loyalty and patriotism.[187]

Confucian virtues such as those found in the Imperial Rescript on Education of 1890 also continued to appear in later Imperial rescripts. In a rescript issued on October 13, 1908, as part of an effort to combat the laxity of morals, the heavy influx of Western ideas, and the effects of inflation caused by the Russo-Japanese war,[188] the Emperor said:

> ...we desire all classes of Our people to act in unison, to be faithful to their callings, frugal in the management of their households, submissive to the dictates of their conscience and calls of duty, to abide by simplicity and avoid ostentation, and to inure themselves to arduous toils without yielding to any degree of indulgence... [with the] cooperation of our loyal subjects, the noble work of the Restoration may be augmented, and the benevolent virtue of our ancestors exalted.[189]

posts, among them Minister of Education from 1901 to 1903, and was in a good position to know the types of reforms and changes that had occurred in Japanese education. In his book, in the pages above, he gives examples and summaries from the textbooks used in morals courses in elementary and middle schools. The large number of Confucian ethical principles included in these is quite surprising.

186. *Ibid.*, 150-151.
187. *Ibid.*, 150.
188. This interpretation of why the rescript was promulgated is found in: *Dai hyakka jiten*, XXIIV, 516. The rescript is called the *Boshin shōsho* 戊申詔書.
189. *The Japan Weekly Mail*, Oct. 17, 1908, no. 16, vol. I, 460, includes a complete translation of the rescript.

Briefly analyzing the above, it includes ideas of harmonious unified activity by the people, of duty to responsibilities, of loyalty to the throne, and of augmenting the benevolent virtue of one's ancestors. All of these are Confucian in some measure, and their use reflects the fact that certain Confucian ideas were being re-emphasized as an integral part of the Japanese literary and ethical heritage.

This was stressed again in 1915 when the Emperor Taishō reaffirmed the principles in the Imperial Rescript on Education of the Emperor Meiji and commanded his subjects connected with educational affairs to promote the "...gracious teachings bequeathed by Our Imperial Forefathers to consummate the national education."[190]

As part of Japanese tradition, then, many Confucian ideas could be used to appeal to the people, especially when they were presented as essentially Japanese virtues upon which the future and welfare of the nation depended. This in itself shows the success that the leaders of Japan had achieved in creating and fostering a sense of unified, national sentiment throughout the country since 1868.

A striking example of how national sentiments and Confucian concepts had become intertwined by the end of the Meiji period is found in the manner of defining "national polity" or *kokutai* 國體. Articles and studies on the term had appeared before, but a problem related to its definition arose in 1911 when one official textbook editor proposed that both the northern and southern courts during the Nambokuchō period 南北朝 (1336-92) be described as legitimate.[191] Since the northern court was considered as an usurper group, having been declared illegitimate early in the Meiji period, such ideas smacked of treason and undermined the prestige and honor given to national heroes like Kusunoki Masashige 楠木正成 (1294-1336) and Kita-

190. Seventh Biennial Conference of the World Federation of Education Associations, *Education in Japan*, (Tōkyō: The World Conference Committee of the Japanese Education Association, 1938), I, 391.

191. Kiyowara, *op. cit.*, 716-717.

batake Chikafusa. These two men had been supporters of the southern court and epitomized the ideal loyal subject and faithful minister. People began to see a relationship between legitimacy and *kokutai,* and many scholars wrote on the meaning of *kokutai.*

Inoue Tetsujirō was outstanding among these, and he claimed that there were seven special characteristics which set off the *kokutai* of Japan. Four of these were related directly to Confucian ideas of just relationships between men and a proper social order: the unity of the love for one's country and loyalty to one's prince; the veneration of ancestors; emphasis on the family system; the clear division between rulers and subjects.[192]

But although Confucian principles might be found useful for ethics textbooks or for stimulating feelings of loyalty and filial piety, on an organized level for presenting integrated and developed philosophical and social ideas, Confucianism had little appeal. On the contrary, those Confucian organizations which had been set up in the early years of the Meiji period began to decline steadily after 1891, and what activity there was among Confucianists was mainly in literary pursuits and historical analysis.

The Shibun Gakkai had been the largest and most influential Confucian organization before 1890 with a wide membership and diverse activities. It also counted important men as its leaders such as Imperial Prince Taruhito of the Arisugawa no Miya family, Major General Tani Kanjō, and Shigeno Yasutsugu. Prince Taruhito, who had been the head of the society since 1881, died in 1895[193] and he was replaced by Tani Kanjō. The life of the organization seems to have gradually ebbed away, due mainly to fires which gutted its lecture halls in 1891 and 1893. Up to that time, there had been a large popular response to the society's

---

192. *Ibid.,* 721.
193. Shibunkai, *Shibun,* X, 1, (Jan., 1928), 60. The usually accurate *Nihon Jugaku Nempyō* made a serious error in recording the death of Prince Arisugawa, placing it in 1886. The mistake the compilers made was apparently to confuse two princes of the Arisugawa family because the Chinese characters for their names are so similar. Taruhito 熾仁 who died in 1895 was head of the Shibun Gakkai, while Takahito 幟仁, though associated with a number of similar organizations, was never a member of the Shibun Gakkai and died in 1886.

daily lectures, but due to the repeated postponement and cancellation of addresses after this caused by the lack of proper buildings, interest fell off and the lectures finally were stopped entirely in 1910.[194] One may presume that the death of many members was also a contributing factor to the decline of the Shibun Gakkai, since a large part of its support had come from men who were trained in the last years of the Tokugawa period.

Tani Kanjō, as well as other younger members of the society like Kaneko Kentarō 金子堅太郎 (1853-1942) and Shibusawa Eiichi 澁澤榮一 (1840-1931),[195] were aware of this state of affairs, and in 1910 they made an effort to use the society's funds for establishing a chair of Confucian studies at Tōkyō Imperial University. Apparently they felt that redirecting the energies of the society along this line would be more efficacious in promoting Confucianism, but it was found that the society did not even have enough money to carry out this modest proposal.[196]

Kanjō died in 1911, and after that the society was completely inactive for eight years, its buildings and grounds being only an empty shell. Not until 1918, when the Shibun Gakkai was amalgamated with a number of other Confucian organizations to form the Shibunkai 斯文會, did any signs of life appear there.[197]

More significant, though, than the Shibun Gakkai during the last twenty-five years of its existence was the rise of a number of Confucian literary organizations. The appearance of these coincided with the growth of modern historical methods in analyzing Oriental history in Japan about 1895. Many historians and literary men, who in earlier days might have written in Chinese, making abstruse references to the Confucian classics or

194. Shibunkai, *Shibun*, I, 1, (Jan., 1919), 107.

195. Kaneko Kentarō was an important figure in the educational and political world of this time, being a member of the influential Privy Council (*Sūmitsuin* 樞密院), while Shibusawa Eiichi was the millionaire banker-industrialist who headed the famous Dai Ichi Ginkō 第一銀行. Shibusawa had been a member of Shibun Gakkai from at least as early as 1891, for in the preface, p. 2, of the Shibunkai's *Kinsei Nihon no Jugaku* 近世日本の儒學 (*Recent Japanese Confucianism*), (Tōkyō: Iwanami Shoten 岩波書店, 1939), he is spoken of in the activities of the society at that time.

196. Shibunkai, *Kinsei Nihon no Jugaku*, preface 3. Shibunkai, *Shibun*, I, 1 (Jan., 1919), 107.

197. Shibunkai, *Shibun*, I, (Jan., 1919), 107-108.

the orthodox histories, now began to make critical studies of Oriental history and philosophy.[199] In 1895, for the first time, the subject of Oriental history was introduced into middle school education,[199] and from this time on, an ever-increasing number of articles and books explaining and analyzing various aspects of Oriental civilization were published. Because of the important position Confucian ideas and literature held in the past of the Orient, it was natural that much attention was given to subjects like "Legends related to the Origins of Chinese Literature" ("Shina bungaku no kigen ni kan suru densetsu" 支那文學の起源に關する傳說), "Chinese Revolutionary Theory" ("Shina kakumei ron" 支那革命論), and "Confucius and Confucian Teachings" ("Kō-shi oyobi Kōshikyō" 孔子及孔子敎).[200]

The Kenkeikai 研經會, formed in 1899, is a good example of the type of literary organization which arose in the period between 1891 and 1918 and to which Confucianists were attracted. Though it only had twelve members, they gave lectures every month on their respective studies and published a magazine which was outstanding in the field of Chinese studies.[201] The Ibunkai 以文會 was another organization similar to the Kenkeikai that was formed in 1901, primarily for the purpose of stimulating poetry writing. Well-known Confucianists like Yasui Kotarō 安井小太郎 were among its members.[202] More important than these two groups was the Tōa Gakujutsu Kenkyūkai 東亞學術研究會 founded in 1909 at Tōkyō Imperial University. The aims of this society were nearly synonymous with those of the later Shibunkai, although it tended to emphasize literary activities more than the latter. Under its aegis, lectures were held every spring and fall, and a periodical issued called *Kangaku* 漢學 (*Chinese Studies*), whose name was later changed to *Tōa kenkyū* 東亞研究

---

198. Takada Shinji 高田眞治, *Nippon Jugaku shi* 日本儒學史 (*History of Japanese Confucianism*), (Tōkyō: Chijin Shokan 地人書館, 1941), 207-275, lists over twenty-five prominent historians and books and articles they wrote from 1895 to 1912 related to Chinese history and Confucian problems.

199. *Ibid.*, 190.

200. *Ibid.*, 193-195.

201. Shibunkai, *Shibun*, I, 1 (Jan., 1919), 109-110.

202. *Nihon Jugaku nempyō*, 429.

(*Asiatic Studies*). This magazine was published nearly every month and had a wide circulation among intellectual circles. Typical of the kind of subjects found there were: a "Confucius Number" ("Kōshi gō" 孔子號); a "Ssu-ma Ch'ien Number ("Shi-ba Sen gō" 司馬遷號); and a special "Anti-Romaji Number" ("Romaji hantai gō" ロマ字反對號). The membership of the society fluctuated between four hundred and six hundred, and included all the members of the Kenkeikai as councilors.[203] One other organization, the Kambun Gakkai deserves to be mentioned here. It was founded in 1910 at Tōkyō Imperial University, mainly for the purpose of encouraging the spread of *kambun* 漢文 [204] studies in middle schools and among middle school teachers. During its years of activity up to 1918, the group sent various memorials to the Ministry of Education on the necessity of increasing the number of hours of *kambun* instruction in middle schools and opposing the use of *romaji* (romanization).[205]

All of the organizations above, with the exception of the Ibunkai, were amalgamated with the Shibun Gakkai in 1918 to form a new and vigorous Confucian society known as the Shibunkai.[206] The incentive behind this change which ushered in a fresh era of activity for Confucianism in Japan was the anxiety over the trends of the times and the tendencies of popular sentiment. The vice-head of the Shibun Gakkai, Matano Taku 股野琢, discussed plans to reform popular sentiment with important members of the society such as Sakatani Yoshio 阪谷芳郎 (1863-1941), Kiyoura Keigo 清浦奎吾 (1850-1942), Yoshikawa Akimasa 芳川顯正 (1841-1920), and Shibusawa Eiichi,[207] but because of the long period of inactivity of the society, there was hardly any response to these efforts. Therefore it was decided to organize a com-

---

203. Shibunkai, *Shibun*, I, 1 (Jan., 1919), 109-110.
204. *Kambun* is the reading and writing of Chinese in Japanese.
205. *Ibid.*, 110-111.
206. *Ibid.*, 111.
207. *Ibid.*, 107-108. It is significant to note here the types of men who were most interested in the Shibun Gakkai and the later Shibunkai. They were all conservative persons of importance in politics, having each been the head of at least one ministry. Considering this, it is easier to understand their interest in Cofucianism, since it probably appealed to them as a doctrine which would bring harmony and stability in Japan which was wrought with strikes and labor unrest.

pletely new society in which other Confucian organizations could take part as well. Privy Councilor Komatsubara Eitarō 小松原 英太郎 (1852-1919) was chosen to head the new group and showed himself very conscientious in his task. Apparently the reason for this was that he felt that organizations like the Shibunkai were very necessary for the nation at a time when public morality was declining and the intellectual world was in ferment.[208] Through his personal efforts the Mitsui 三井 and the Iwasaki 岩崎 families gave large sums to help support the new organization, and by the time the Shibunkai held its opening ceremonies in December, 1918, in addition to grounds and buildings, the society had over 200,000 yen with which to carry on its work.[209] The Ministry of Education also turned over to the Shibunkai the famous Seidō 聖堂 which had been the center of Confucianism in Tokugawa times.[210] This last action is significant because it shows that the government recognized the Shibunkai as the leading Confucian organization in Japan and wished to give it support and encouragement.

---

208. *Kinsei Nihon no Jugaku*, preface, 4-5. The Confucianist Hattori Unokichi, who wrote this preface, says he learned of Komatsubara's interest in the Shibunkai through Egi Kazuyuki. Egi was the head of the Kōten Kōkyūsho 皇典講究所 at the time, an organization devoted primarily to Shintō studies, and Komatsubara spoke to him of the need for encouraging organizations similar to his own such as the Shibunkai. Hattori heard about this because, although he was a Confucianist, at that time he was heading the Kokugakuin Daigaku 國學院大學, closely affiliated with the Kōten Kōkyūsho. This is an interesting example of the close relation between Confucianists and Shintoists in modern Japan.

209. *Ibid.*, preface, 5.

210. *Ibid.*, preface, 5. Concerning the relationship of the Seidō and Confucianism in Tokugawa times, see ch. I, footnote 38, of this study.

III

THE SHIBUNKAI AND THE CHARACTERISTICS OF
THE CONFUCIAN REVIVAL FROM 1918 - 1933

1. Aims of the Shibunkai and Opening Speeches given at its
   Founding Ceremonies in 1918.

The reorganization and consolidation of various Confucian
societies in late 1918 into the Shibunkai was of momentous importance in the history of Confucianism in modern Japan, for it
ushered in a period of greatly increased Confucian activity in
many fields. Not only did genuine Confucianists take part in
this, but also businessmen, politicians, government officials,
military men, and scholars. Some of these men seem to have
believed sincerely in Confucian ethical and philosophical principles, but others apparently felt that such principles still could
profitably be appealed to for bringing social stability and therefore tried to identify themselves with them.

Perhaps the best exposition of the type of ideas supported by
the Shibunkai can be found in the "Aims of the Shibunkai" which
were drawn up in September 1918, prior to the official founding
ceremonies of the society in December 1918.[1] Because of the
importance of this document in relating the Shibunkai to the
earlier efforts of the Shibun Gakkai and in setting the stage for
Confucian activities after 1918, it has been translated in full in

---

1. The Japanese text of the "Aims of the Shibunkai" (*Shibunkai shuisho* 斯文會
趣意書) is included in nearly every issue of the magazine *Shibun* 斯文 for several years
after it began publication in February 1919. It may also be found in: Shibunkai 斯文會,
Shibun rokujūnen shi 斯文六十年史 (*A History of Sixty Years of Confucian Studies*),
(Tōkyō: Shibunkai, 1923), 317-318.

the appendix. Only an analysis of its main points is given here.

The document began by stressing the uniqueness of Japan among all other nations in the Far East arising from the fact that she had remained free from foreign intrusion. This had been possible because high and low cooperated at the time of the Meiji Restoration to develop the nation and to enhance the peerless Japanese *kokutai* 國體 (national polity).

In the process of development, however, materialism began to have deleterious effects on the time-honored morality of the nation. According to the "Aims of the Shibunkai," this was caused by indiscriminate and excessive borrowing from abroad through which materialistic values were brought to the fore. The effects of this had been evident in the increasing unrest among the people, who were being exposed to revolutionary and radical ideas. This latter reference was probably an allusion to the spread of socialist ideas in Japan, and in particular to the violent peasant and labor disturbances and strikes that began to sweep the country from 1918 onward.[2]

The document then continued by ascribing the formation of the Shibunkai to the perspicacity of public-spirited and patriotic men who saw the dangers of the situation and resolved to restore the good ways and morality inherent in old Japanese customs. In this way they planned to prevent further deterioration of public morals.

The efforts of these men were also spoken of as enhancing the Imperial Rescript on Education of the Emperor Meiji because the essentials of the Confucian Way, which the Shibunkai advocated, corresponded so closely to the principes in the Rescript on Education.

Then reviewing the scope and accomplishments of the Shibun Gakkai, the manifesto deplored the limited scope of the activities of the earlier society and its decline. It was determined that the new Shibunkai, while carrying on the Confucian principles of the Shibun Gakkai, would expand and widen the sphere of

---

2. Chitoshi Yanaga, *Japan Since Perry* (New York: McGraw Hill Book Co., 1949), 390-393.

its activities to meet the problems of the day.

The problems of the day were described primarily as those resulting from the impact of the World War on the intellectual world. This unprecedented example of a great war had stirred men to realize that a need for spiritual culture existed. It was this spiritual need which the Shibunkai planned to fill by the spread of Confucianism. In this manner, the Shibunkai expected that spiritual progress equal to the progress made in the material world could be achieved, and consequently Japan's future would exceed that of other nations.

This finishes the analysis of the "Aims of the Shibunkai." The policy of the society may be summarized as one of attempting to strengthen Japan by doing away with the evils of materialism and by reviving Confucian spiritual culture that was in harmony with traditional Japanese morality. This sounds very much like the position advocated by Motoda Eifu in the first half of the Meiji period when he blamed Western materialism for many of the social and political problems of his day. Confucian philosophy and Confucian ethics had been the *sine qua non* to him for a stable and harmonious society, and to the extent that they were lacking, he believed chaos and discord would ensue. Supporters of this type of ethical interpretation of history in 1918 had the recent example of a horribly destructive World War as *prima facie* evidence of the effects of the decline of morality among men.

In China, outstanding earlier reformers and liberal thinkers such as Liang Ch'i-ch'ao 梁啓超 (1873-1929), who had borrowed much from the West, now began to cast doubts on whether Western materialistic culture could solve the basic moral and social problems of the world. In this state of mind, they advocated a return to China's traditional heritage in which Confucianism had played such an important part.[3] Japanese Confucianists likewise insisted that Confucianism was not simply a doctrine of the past, but could lead men toward universal peace by avoiding the pitfalls of narrow self-interest and materialism.

---

3. Wen-han Kiang, *The Chinese Student Movement.* (New York: King's Crown Press, 1948), 40-42.

In a speech on the "Meaning of Confucianism for the Present," given at the founding ceremonies of the Shibunkai on December 1, 1918, Hattori Unokichi 服部宇之吉 (1867-1939)[4] stressed this point and claimed that it was the responsibility of the Shibunkai to clarify the meaning of Confucianism. Because Hattori was one of the leaders of the Shibunkai, as well as a scholar of standing and probably the most influential Confucianist in Japan after 1920,[5] it is worthwhile noting his ideas. Many of these were not only to be repeated later, but also were the basis for much of the thinking on political, social, and philosophical problems of other Confucianists and advocates of Confucianism.

Discussing the World War, Hattori pointed out how German militarism was similar to the *Pa-tao* 覇道 or "Way of the Usurpers" spoken of by Confucius and Mencius.[6] Professing adherence, on the surface, to principles of humaneness and righteousness, the Germans had in practice used naked force to attain their hegemony, completely disregarding the rights of small nations.

While condemning Germany for such unethical conduct, Hattori did not imply that world peace could be attained by complete disarmament because of the essential nature of man, who had both animal and moral instincts. To depend entirely on the moral instincts of man and overlook his animal ones would be to invite bloodshed and social strife. Confucianism recognized this and did not reject the use of military power, but made it one of the prerequisites of government. In China, where the military had been despised, there was constant strife because this truth had been overlooked.

---

4. Hattori Unokichi, "Meaning of Confucianism for the Present," *Shibun*, I, 1 (Feb., 1919), 19-36.

5. For a list of books and articles by Hattori, as well as a thirty-two page autobiography from which some idea may be gained of his activity in cultural, educational, and political fields, see *Hattori sensei koki shukuga kinen rombunshū* 服部先生 古稀祝賀記念論文集 (*Collection of Commemorative Essays Congratulating Professor Hattori on his Seventieth Year*), (Tōkyō: Fuzambō 富山房, 1936), 1-57.

6. *Mengtzu* 孟子. Gk. II, pt. 1, ch. 3-4. James Legge, *The Confucian Classics*, second edition, revised (Oxford: Clarendon Press, 1893), II, 196-199. *Lun-yü* 論語 XIV, 20. Legge, *op. cit.*, I, 282. While actually neither Confucius or Mencius used the words *Pa-tao*, their use of the word *pa* to indicate someone who gained hegemony by force rather than by the example of virtue and benevolence led later Confucianists to use *Pa-tao* as a generic term.

Hattori next spoke of the trend to discuss world peace as if it were an economic problem involving gain and loss. This made the realization of world peace more difficult because while some might feel war should be abolished since it was unprofitable, the use of force could be justified if only it were profitable. The problems of world peace were matters rather of strengthening man's ethical foundations and spreading the principles of humaneness and righteousness advocated by Confucianism.

Humaneness, while implying a full development of the faculties of individuals, was not a screen for the bald individualism which asserted "every man for himself and the devil take the hindmost." As Hattori put it,

> Individual progress becomes significant as a means to the progress of society. If one understands this well, one realizes that individualism [alone] is never the absolute truth, but beginning as it is mutually amalgamated and reconciled with the principles of the family and humanitarianism, it attains the full breadth of truth.[7]

Righteousness he described as the ultimate form of reason which made it possible for man to recognize duties and responsibilities such as those to his ruler, his father, or his family.

These principles applied on a world-wide scale could bring peace and destroy narrow nationalism and racial discrimination, which were equivalent in the national sphere to excessive individualism in the personal sphere.

Besides Hattori's speech at the opening ceremonies of the Shibunkai, Baron Shibusawa Eiichi. Viscount Kaneko Kentarō, and Privy Councillor Komatsubara Eitarō also delivered addresses. The important political and business connection of these men were spoken of in the last chapter, but their conservative background needs to be mentioned again because it was typical of those who gave their support to the Shibunkai.

Shibusawa, the millionaire industrialist who had started the Dai Ichi Ginkō 第一銀行 and promoted numerous business enter-

---

7. Hattori, "Meaning of Confucianism for the Present," *Shibun*, I, 1 (Feb., 1919), 27 ff.

prises throughout Japan and Korea, spoke on "Morality and Economics."[8] He stressed the fact that in his forty years of business dealings, simply making a profit had never been a satisfactory goal. Only by following the teachings of Confucius and spreading the way of humaneness and righteousness had it been possible to preserve harmony in economic life. This unity of morality and economics, applied to wider areas of social contacts and politics, provided the only hope for achieving world peace and doing away with the "dog eat dog" philosophy of past international relations.

Looking at the recent World War, he said the defeat of Germany was not due to a lack of arms or food, but to the fact that the German government's actions were so lacking in virtue that it had forfeited the faith of the people and united the opposition of the whole world against it. Confucius himself, when questioned by a disciple on the prerequisites for government, had asserted that no government could stand without the confidence of the people, and Shibusawa insisted that a similar lack of confidence between individuals or institutions always brought ruin. This was the reason he felt it was so important to maintain a close relationship between morality and economic activity.

Komatsubara, the head of the Shibunkai and a political figure of some importance at this time, discussed the "Aims of the Shibunkai" in his speech.[9]

The Harvard-trained diplomat and politician Kaneko Kentarō, however, spoke on "The Development of Japan and the Power of Chinese Studies,"[10] pointing out how the Shibunkai, by encouraging Chinese studies (*kangaku* 漢學), was strengthening a force which had been of tremendous importance in moulding Japanese history. For example, the fact that Japanese law from the time of the *Taihōryō* 大寶令 in 701 had been patterned after Chinese law was due to the mastery of *kangaku* that the Japanese

---

8. Shibusawa Eiichi "Morality and Economics," *Shibun*, I, 1 (Feb., 1919), 36 ff.
9. Komatsubara Eitarō, "Purpose of this Organization," *Shibun*, I, 1 (Feb., 1919, 1-4.
10. Kaneko Kentarō, "The Development of Japan and the Power of Chinese Studies," *Shibun*, I, 1 (Feb., 1919), 5-18.

had acquired. Japanese historians also were dependent on *kan-gaku*, beginning with the *Nihongi* 日本紀 down to the *Dainihon shi* 大日本史. Kaneko particularly felt that in morality and government the influence of *kangaku* had been great. Ideas of loyalty, filial piety, and proper service to one's lord, which developed the basis of later devotion and duty to the Imperial House, had received a great impetus through the introduction of the Confucian classics and Sung learning. In government, *kangaku* had been the means for the Japanese to learn of the path of humaneness, righteousness, and virtue whereby they could avoid the extremes of republicanism and despotism prevalent in the West. *Kangaku* could also be of help in cementing friendly relations between Japan and China. But most important of all was that the power of *kangaku* gave added honor and esteem to Imperial government in its relations with its subjects. The most recent example of this was the Imperial Rescript on Education of the Emperor Meiji in which the close and affectionate feelings of the ruler and his people had been displayed in a way that evoked the admiration of the whole world.

From the description of the "Aims of the Shibunkai" and from the excerpts of the speeches of some of its most active supporters, the major trends inherent in the revival of Confucianism in Japan after 1918 can be surmised. Recapitulating these, they would include encouragement of *kangaku*, advocacy of Oriental spiritual and ethical values over Western pragmatic and material ones for the solution of current social and political problems, and the association of Confucianism with the unique *kokutai* 國體 (national polity) and Imperial system of Japan.

2.   Literary and Educational Activities related to Confucianism.

The Shibunkai, as the center of Confucianism in Japan after 1918, published a monthly periodical known as *Shibun* whose first number appeared in February 1919. It is from this journal that the most detailed information on Confucian activities throughout Japan may be found. An analysis of the type of articles included in the *Shibun* indicates that a majority of them dealt with topics of literary interest. It is possible to infer from this that while Japanese Confucianists were worried over the social and moral problems of the day, their main endeavors were directed toward discussions and interpretations of Chinese and Japanese Confucian texts. The following is a rough breakdown of the type of articles in the *Shibun* from volume I in 1919 to volume XV in 1933.

Vol. No.	Number of Articles Related to Present Political, Social, Educational, and Ideological Problems	Number of Articles on Literary Topics and Problems of Interpretation and Exegesis
I (1919)	12	52
II (1920)	14	47
III (1921)	8	54
IV (1922)	7	77
V (1923)	11	42
VI (1924)	6	26
VII (1925)	4	38
VIII (1926)	12	85
IX (1927)	18	135
X (1928)	32	102
XI (1929)	22	119
XII (1930)	23	121
XIII (1931)	42	128
XIV (1932)	52	128
XV (1933)	62	115

In the above, it is significant to note the proportionate increase in the number of articles on present- day topics in relation to literary topics. This followed in the wake of the rise of critical political, economic, and international problems in Japan during the late 1920's and early 1930's. Despite this, the major publications of the Shibunkai in this period were entirely on technical linguistic and educational subjects, or studies, translations, and reprints of Confucian historical and literary works.[11]

Closely related to the literary interests of Confucianists in Japan were the attempts made to influence educational policy by the Shibunkai, for which purpose meetings of teachers were organized, and petitions and reports sent to the Ministry of Education.

In March 1919, a fourteen page study was made by the Department of Research of the Shibunkai on *kambun* 漢文 courses in middle schools.[12] The purpose of middle school education was first discussed and determined to be the giving of necessary general knowledge and moral instruction to those who were to form the backbone of Japan's social structure. In the latter field, *kambun* played an indispensable role by its elucidation of the Japanese *kokutai*, national history, geography, and the ethical foundations of the state. But in addition to this, *kambun* could be the key to building up good relations and an understanding with China. Refuting the arguments against the extension of *kambun* courses in middle schools, the fact that the weakness of Japanese education lay in the field of moral and ethical training rather than in scientific and technical lines was pointed out. *Kambun* courses, especially those related to the Confucian classics, could greatly help in spreading ideas of virtue and right, and thus assist in realizing the principles of the Imperial Rescript on Education.

Only a month after this, on April 27, 1919, Baron Sakatani Yoshio 阪谷芳郎 (1863-1941), prominent in politics and society, and an ardent supporter of the Shibunkai, gave a speech discussing the need for *kangaku* 漢學 (Chinese studies) as a means of settling and reuniting the intellectual world.[13] Recalling that his father, the Confucianist Sakatani Rōro 阪谷朗盧 (1822-81), had

11. A list of the publications of the Shibunkai up to 1927 may be found in *Shibun*, IIX, 9 (Dec., 1926), 627-629. Between 1927 and 1929, the writer knows of only one further publication by the Shibunkai, *Kokuyaku Rongo nishu* 國譯論語二種) (*Two Versions of Japanese Translations of the Analects*), in 1929.

12. Department of Research of the Shibunkai, "Concerning the *kambun* course in Middle Schools," *Shibun*, I, 2 (April, 1919), supplement of fourteen pages. *Kambun* is the reading and writing of Chinese in Japanese.

13. Sakatani Yoshio, "Discussion of the Need for Chinese Studies from the standpoint of the Ideas of the People of the Empire," *Shibun*, I, (May, 1919), 213-227.

advocated the same measures for quieting the people's thoughts early in the Meiji period,[14] he said that the transmission of *kangaku* to Japan had buttressed the foundations of the Japanese state and made the relations between the Imperial House and the people as those of one large family. In this way, the true meaning of the words found in the *Great Learning* (*Ta-hsüeh* 大學) that "the government of the state depends on the regulation of the family" had been realized in Japan.[15] Sakatani recognized that with the necessity of importing European knowledge and adapting it to Japanese civilization, it was impossible for students also to carry a full course in *kangaku*. Nevertheless, because of the influx of so many disturbing thoughts from Germany and Russia, it was necessary to continue inculcating the spirit of *kangaku* in schools and among the people. Only in this way could the essential concomitants of peace and harmony be developed in Japan, and her superior national traditions be preserved.

The common theme in all the appeals for an increased study of *kangaku* discussed so far is that it would clarify the ethical foundations of Japan, help preserve her unique traditions, and serve as a barrier against the adoption of radical or extreme Western ideas. This point of view was not an ephemeral one, but on the contrary continued to be emphasized more and more by members of the Shibunkai and others interested in encouraging Confucianism. These men clearly realized that in order to spread Confucian ideas in a period of increasing popular education, it was necessary to include in the school curriculum courses with a Confucian content and courses in which the students could learn the rudiments of *kambun*, the key to any mastery of the Confucian classics. Therefore they naturally tended to associate such study with pressing social and ideological problems, as well

---

14. Sakatani Rōro had been instrumental in setting up the Tōkyō Shūshin Gakusha 東京修身學社 in 1876 with several other men for the purpose of clarifying the path of loyalty, filial piety, humaneness, and righteousness. See Shibunkai, *Nihon Jugaku nempyō* 日本儒學年表 (*Chronological Table of Japanese Confucianism*), (Tōkyō: Shibunkai, 1923), 422.

15. *Ta-hsüeh* 大學, ch. IX, 5; translated by James Legge, *Confucian Classics*, (Oxford: Clarendon Press, 1893), I, 371.

as with more general cultural purposes, in order to gain the support of educational and other influential government officials. It should be pointed out, nevertheless, that this was not just a policy of opportunism, and many of the advocates of Confucianism probably sincerely believed that it could provide the cohesive force for stabilizing society.

Shionoya On 鹽谷溫 (b. 1878), an ardent Confucianist and nationalist who also was a leader of the Shibunkai and professor at Tōkyō Imperial University, reiterated the above in an article on the need for *kambun* studies in middle schools written in 1928.[16] He spoke of how in the past, during the Sino-Japanese War and the Russo-Japanese War, the Imperial Rescript on Education of the Emperor Meiji had brilliantly supported the nation. Since the World War, Japan once again needed the kind of firm educational foundation provided by the Imperial Rescript on Education. As its elucidation was to be found in the Confucian classics which could only be understood by those who had mastered *kambun*, it was impossible to say that *kambun* was a useless course in present-day schools. Rather, *kambun* courses in middle schools should be reformed and emphasized so that students could understand how the spirit of Confucianism had been amalgamated into the Japanese *kokutai* and formed the basis of the Imperial Rescript on Education.

In 1928 an Educational Department of the Shibunkai was formed mainly for the purpose of encouraging *kambun* courses in schools and making studies on subjects such as character frequency which could assist in the teaching of *kambun*.[17] Soon after this, a proposal was presented by the Shibunkai to the Prime Minister and Minister of Education regarding the extension of *kambun* courses and the diffusion of materials on Con-

16. Shionoya On, *Shibun*, X, 11 (Nov., 1928), 777.
17. The Shibunkai had been organized originally with four departments: Culture, Research, Sacrifices, and Publication. The addition of an Educational Department reflects the fact that the Shibunkai was becoming increasingly active in this field in which it probably had the most contact with the public. For information on the organization of the Shibunkai, see *Shibun*, I, 1 (Feb., 1919), "Abbreviated Regulations of the Shibunkai" inserted at the beginning of the number. Changes in the regulations of the Shibunkai are included in various numbers of *Shibun* throughout the years.

fucianism in the schools.[18] It was suggested that in elementary
schools, more Confucian teachings be incorporated into existing
courses, and in middle schools, that *kambun* courses be raised
in importance. In addition, the introduction of *kambun* courses
to Girls' Higher Schools and vocational schools was urged, and
the wide use of old classics of the Far East in social education
and youth training was proposed.

Beginning with the February 1929 issue, the *Shibun* carried
every month an Educational Column of several pages in which
various educational problems were discussed, especially those
related to ethics and the teaching of *kambun*. A typical example
of one of these was an article by Sera Ryōichi 世良亮一 on *kambun*
textbooks of middle school.[19] Dealing first with what *kambun*
actually was, Sera said it was part and parcel of the Japanese
language and that within it was much of the content of Asiatic
thought, especially Confucianism, on which Japanese morality
was based. Speaking then of the kinds of materials that should
be included in *kambun* textbooks, he suggested that Japanese
works in which there were many Chinese characters and phrases
would make a good beginning, after which the Confucian classics
and outstanding poets and philosophers should be read. Materials
dealing in particular with morality, humaneness, righteousness,
and similar Confucian ideas were suitable.

In keeping with such aims was the Shibunkai's printing of
a Japanese translation of the Confucian *Analects* (*Lun-yü* 論語)
which was sent as a gift in 1929 to every school in Japan. Special
copies also were sent to the Emperor, the Empress, the Empress
Dowager, and all Imperial Princes, and the Imperial Household
acknowledged the receipt of the gift.[20] Probably of more consequence in promoting *kambun* studies and the spread of Confucian
ideas were the specific representations made by the Shibunkai

---

18. Educational Column, *Shibun*, XI, 2 (Feb., 1929). A copy of this proposal was
included in every number of *Shibun* throughout 1929 and 1930, showing the importance
that the Shibunkai placed on the proposal.
19. Sera Ryōichi, "Concerning the *Kambun* Textbooks of Middle School," *Shibun*,
XII, 5 (May, 1930), 36-40.
20. *Shibun*, XI, 5 (May, 1929), 423.

to the educational authorities concerning changes in the regulations for carrying out middle school ordinances. For example, on May 22, 1931, in a petition presented to the Minister of Education, Tanaka Ryūzō 田中隆三, the Shibunkai suggested that beginning with the first year of middle school, a minimum of one hour of *kambun* per week be taught entirely separately from Japanese language or other courses.[21] It maintained that unless this were done, *kambun* texts could never be properly understood by students. Considering the value of such texts in dealing with many of the idealogical problems of the day, the omission of a special *kambun* course would be widely felt.

The Shibunkai also sponsored meetings of middle school *kambun* teachers in an effort to realize its aims. A typical gathering was one in 1933, attended by about two hundred teachers from middle schools all over Japan, for the purpose of determining what measures should be taken in *kambun* instruction in order to stimulate the spirit of the people in a time of crisis.[22] It was decided that a greater stress on understanding the Confucian spirit as part of the Imperial way and in the Imperial Rescript on Education was needed. *Kambun* teachers also were advised to use teaching materials which contained the essentials of Confucian ideas of self-cultivation, regulation of the home, and pacification of the Empire. Textbooks which had a disposition toward encouraging disorder or disunity should be replaced by those encouraging uniformity, and in ethics courses, parts of the *Great Learning*, the *Classic of Filial Piety* (*Hsiao-ching* 孝經), and the *Analects* could be of value used together with the regular textbooks. Finally, the group felt that whenever possible, teachers should make trips to Manchuria and China in order to observe conditions first-hand.

---

21. "Chūgakkōrei shikō kisoku kaisei ni kan shi Mombudaijin e no gushin" 中學校令施行規則改正に關し文部大臣への具申 ("Representation to the Minister of Education Concerning a Reform of the Regulations for Carrying Out the Middle School Law"), *Shibun*, XIII, 7 (July, 1931), 593–594.

22. "Zenkoku chūtō gakkō kambunka kyōin kyōgikai" 全國中等學校漢文科教員協議會 ("Nation-wide Conference of Middle School *Kambun* Teachers"), *Shibun*, XV, 12 (Dec., 1933), 58–59.

It is difficult to tell to what extent the Shibunkai and other supporters of Confucianism succeeded in their efforts to introduce more Confucian ideas into the school curriculum, for ethics textbooks taught in the schools already included a large number of Confucian concepts.[23] The same observations hold true for the teaching of *kambun,* although the latter was combined with compulsory courses in Japanese in the middle schools at this time.[24] By their activities, however, these groups did stimulate greater interest and awareness in Confucianism among educators and government officials. The *Shibun* first begins to record the regular attendance of government officials at the Shibunkai's *sekiten* in 1926. They were not just representatives of one or two ministries, but important men like the Prime Minister, the Home Affairs Minister, the Minister of Education, the Imperial Household Minister, and other cabinet ministers. Ordinarily each would deliver a short address in which the importance of Confucian principles for stabilizing the social situation and warding off the dangers of foreign materialism was emphasized. This is a clear indication that Japan's leaders were becoming aware of present-day social and political uses for Confucian doctrine.[25]

The forerunner of this official interest in Confucianism was the old-line Confucianist Egi Kazuyuki 江木千之 (1853-1932) who had written Confucian texts for the Ministry of Education in the 1880's. When he was Minister of Education in the Kiyoura cabinet in 1924, he personally visited the Seidō where the Shibunkai held its regular *sekiten* 釋奠 or spring and autumn Confucian ceremonies and took part in one of the ceremonies himself.[26] He

---

23. Although four years later than the period under consideration, the tables of contents of elementary school moral education textbooks in 1937 have been translated in the Seventh Biennial Conference of the World Federation of Education Associations, *Education in Japan,* (Tōkyō: The World Conference Committee of the Japanese Education Association, 1938), I, 414-416. It is significant to note that about one-quarter of the material taught was directly related to Confucian concepts of social and human relationships.

24. Hugh Keenleyside and A. F. Thomas, *History of Japanese Education and Present Educational System,* (Tōkyō: Hokuseidō Press, 1937), 194-195. While it is not directly stated that *kambun* courses were part of the compulsory Japanese course in middle schools, this can be inferred from a table and certain statements in the text. Several Japanese who were in school in the early 1930's have also confirmed this.

25. *Shibun,* VIII, 3 (June, 1926), 1-4.

was also responsible for reinstituting the *Taihōryō* 大寶令 system according to which important government officials were meant to be present at these Confucian ceremonies.[27] Up to this time, government officials ordinarily had not attended, but Egi put aside a sum of money in the Ministry of Education's budget expressly for carrying out the *sekiten* under official auspices. Besides this encouragement to Confucianism, Egi wrote moral stories based on Confucianism and the Japanese spirit for elementary school children.[28]

In May 1926, the Shibunkai organized an association for the restoration of the Yushima Seidō, which had been destroyed in the great Tōkyō earthquake and fire in 1923.[29] The Seidō was traditionally the center of Confucian educational and ceremonial activities in Japan, and the task of the Seidō Fukkō Kiseikai 聖堂復興期成會 (Association for the Restoration of the Seidō) was characterized as one of restoring the prestige and influence of Confucianism, as well as reconstructing the burned buildings. The Prime Minister, Wakatsuki Reijirō 若槻禮次郎, the Minister of Education, Okada Ryōhei 岡田良平, and members of the House of Peers, the Diet, the Privy Council, prefectural governors, industrialists, and the heads of schools were invited to be present at the inauguration of the work and to become sponsors of the association.[30] Although the Prime Minister was unable to attend, he agreed to be among the sponsors. The Minister of Education, however, appeared with such prominent figures as Shibusawa Eiichi and Sakatani Yoshio, and they all gave short addresses. In his speech, the Minister of Education described the anxiety he had for the people, but said that to allay such feelings, Confucian principles were most appropriate since they strengthened the spirit of the people. In view of this, the Ministry of Education planned to support as far as possible the restoration of the Seidō.[31]

26. *Shibun*, VIII, 4 (July, 1926), 289-290.
27. *Shibun*, VIII, 3 (June, 1926), 1-4.
28. *Shibun*, XV, 12 (Dec., 1933), 10-15.
29. *Shibun*, VIII, 4 (July, 1926), 289-290, 301-302.
30. *Shibun*, VIII, 4 (July, 1926), 289-290.
31. *Ibid.*, 289.

Similar reasons for encouraging Confucian teachings were given by the new Minister of Education, Mizuno Rentarō 水野 鍊太郎, in a speech delivered at a Confucian celebration in 1927.[32] Stressing the fact that Confucianism should form the basis of the morality of the people, he criticized *kambun* teachers for emphasizing the analysis of sentences while not explaining well the fundamental meaning of the Confucian ideas contained in them. This he claimed was the main reason that Confucianism was considered old-fashioned and unrelated to present-day problems.

In 1930, as progress on the restoration of the Seidō was proceeding, the Shibunkai asked a number of prominent men to express their feelings on the significance of this work. General Hongō Fusatarō 本鄉房太郎 (1860-1931), a military councilor or *gunji sangikan* 軍事參議官 and head of the Dainihon Butokukai 大日本武德會 (Great Japan Military Virtue Society), presented an article demanding a spiritual renaissance.[33] The decline of affairs in China was due, he said, to the fact that the teachings of Confucius and Mencius had not been applied to modern conditions. In Japan a similar tendency was evident among many of the brighter youths who were attracted by anarchistic and radical ideas. Under the circumstances, it was the duty of educators and administrators to bring a practical application of the Confucian spirit to social realities. The significance of the restoration of the Seidō would depend on the extent to which it contributed to this needed spiritual renaissance.

A retired general, Ichinoe Hyōe 一戶兵衛 (1855-1931), known for his courage at the siege of Port Arthur and currently head of the Teikoku Zaigō Gunjinkai 帝國在鄉軍人會 (Imperial Reservists Military Association), also submitted an article to the Shibunkai in which he said that the most urgent problem of the day was the proper guidance of Japan's youth.[34] Fortunately for Japan,

---

32. Mizuno Rentarō, "The Way of Confucius," *Shibun*, IX, 12 (Dec., 1927), 721-727.
33. Hongō Fusatarō, "Seishinteki ni fukkō seyo" 精神的に復興せよ ("Let Us Have a Spiritual Renaissance"), *Shibun*, XII, 10 (Oct., 1930), 3-6.
34. Ichinoe Hyōe, "Arasowazu Seidō o funde susume" 爭はず正道を踏んで進め ("Step Forward on the True Way Without Quarreling"), *Shibun*, XII, 10 (Oct., 1930), 3 ff.

one of her strong points was that she borrowed foreign philosophies without indulging in the quarrels and ruinous disputes
which characterized China, India, and the West. Of all such
philosophies, Confucianism had harmonized most with Japan's
kokutai and helped the nation. Therefore the restoration of the
Seidō as a center of Confucianism would bring with it an awakening of the moral sense and assist in the task of guiding the youth.

A more outspoken statement on the need for developing
Confucian virtues of loyalty and filial piety was made by Shionoya
On in a radio broadcast at Kyōto in June, 1931, to commemorate
the 100th anniversary of Rai Sanyō's 頼山陽 death.[35] He referred
to the fact that a Parent-Teachers Association in the United
States recently had extolled filial piety, obedience, service, and
other virtues of the home, and offered this as evidence that the
material cultures of the West were satiated and finding it necessary to turn toward the superior elements of the spiritual civilization of the East. In such a period, when the world was plagued
with economic disturbances and unrest like that in China and
Russia, the Japanese people should not be deluded by radical
foreign ideas, but should instead develop their own *kokutai* by
laying stress on great duties of loyalty and filial piety. The
heavenly task of the Japanese to bring world peace and happiness
could be accomplished by this process.

The note struck by Shionoya contrasting Western material
civilization with Asiatic spiritual culture was not a new one,
for it had been mentioned in the "Aims of the Shibunkai" in 1918,
and Motoda Eifu had made a special point of it in trying to revive
Confucianism in the Meiji period.[36] The appeal of such a thesis,
however, seems to have been strongest when crises in internal
and external affairs began to weigh heavily on Japan. This had
been true in 1887 and the years immediately following when
Japanese reaction set in against the unwillingness of the Western
powers to revise their treaties with Japan.[37] In 1918, on the other

---

35. Shionoya On, "Nankō to Sanyō Sensei" 楠公と山陽先生 ("Kusunoki Masashige and Rai Sanyō"), *Shibun*, XIII, 7 (July, 1931), 6-7.

36. See ch. II, sec. 4 of this study.

37. *Ibid.*, 82.

hand, although there had been labor troubles and the spectacle of a great war, the country as a whole was prosperous and had received recognition as one of the major world powers. Under these circumstances, it is significant to note that the Confucian appeal of East versus West was not so popular. By 1931, however, Japan's position was once again becoming isolated and economic conditions were badly depressed. After the outbreak of the Manchurian Incident in September, 1931, relations between Japan and the West became more strained, and this provided the necessary undercurrent to give the type of Confucian interpretations above greater prestige.

The Chief of the Social Education Bureau of the Ministry of Education, Sekiya Ryūkichi 關屋龍吉, wrote an article in May, 1931, in which he made essentially the same contrast between Western materialistic ideas and Asiatic spiritual ones.[38] Western ideas of progress and Marxism were capturing the minds of many social leaders and causing confusion in the intellectual world. The spiritual force found in Confucian principles of morality and government could counteract these, but unfortunately, due to the inability of people to read *kambun,* the most appropriate doctrine for the times was being forgotten. Sekiya urged that *kambun* courses be encouraged, and that the moral aspects of Confucianism in them particularly be stressed. This would help develop a wide understanding of Confucianism among the intellectual classes who could then properly lead the nation.

A prominent middle school educator, Abe Munetaka 阿部宗孝 (b. 1875), in a speech before a conference of middle school *kambun* teachers on October 30, 1933, made similar comments on the need for a renaissance of Asiatic spiritual civilization.[39] Japan was in a special position where she could transmit this spiritual culture to Western nations, and in this way alleviate the world-wide spiritual crisis of the times. It was for this reason that

---

38. Sekiya Ryūkichi, "Shakai kyōka no kihon toshite no Jukyō" 社會教化の基本としての儒教 ("Confucianism as the Basis of Social Cultivation"), *Shibun*, XIII, 5 (May, 1931), q. v.

39. Abe Munetaka, "Koten no sonchō" 古典の尊重 (("Reverence for the Classics"), *Shibun*, XV, 12 (Dec., 1933), q.v.

kambun courses and classical learning should be emphasized in schools.

Major General Hayashi Yasakichi 林彌三吉 (b. 1876) also felt that schools ought to provide greater spiritual training for students,[40] as otherwise many of the most talented young men would become adherents of material philosophies like Marxism. Since the Confucian classics could give students the background for rejecting such mistaken and dangerous philosophies, schools should stress the learning of the sages, and organizations like the Shibunkai were to be congratulated for their efforts in this direction.

In reviewing Confucian activities related to educational matters between 1919 and 1933, the most significant feature is the increasing tendency to associate Confucianism with the Japanese spirit and traditional Japanese ways. Confucianists discovered that they were having much greater success in spreading their ideas to schools and society when Confucianism was related to social and political problems. *Kambun* for *kambun*'s sake, or *kangaku* for its cultural benefits alone could not have a wide appeal. With the rising tide of Japanese nationalism, however, in which Japan faced Western nations increasingly hostile to her plans for expansion, Confucianism had a special role to play because one of its major themes was opposition to the West as being materialistic. Combined with this was an ethical interpretation of events that could prove useful in clothing Japan's actions as virtuous and righteous, such as in Manchuria after 1931 where events were described as the spreading of the principles of *Wang-tao* 王道 or "Way of True Kingship."[41] Finally, by an overemphasis on Confucian concepts of loyalty, filial piety, and ideals of service to the sovereign and the state, authoritarian

---

40. Hayashi Yasakichi, "Seiken no gaku o shinki seyo" 聖賢の學を振起せよ ("Let Us Encourage the Learning of the Sages"), *Shibun*, XV, 11 (Nov., 1933), 7-8.

41. The whole of *Shibun*, XIV, 5 (May, 1932) was devoted to articles on Manchuria, describing how the principles of *wang tao* had finally triumphed with Japanese aid. Basically, *Wang-tao* was considered as rule by the example of virtue and benevolence whereby the people would be led naturally to follow the example of the ruler. The term was the opposite of *Pa-tao* 霸道, and can be found in the Confucian classics. *Mengtzu* 孟子, bk. I, pt. 1, ch. 3: Legge, *op. cit.*, II, 131. *Shu-ching* 書經, IV, 14; Legge, *op. cit.*, IV, 331.

elements in Japan increasingly strengthened their hold and made dissension from these standards seem like a particularly heinous aberration.

3. Confucian Views on Political, Economic and Intellectual Problems.

One of the outstanding characteristics of Confucianism in Japan after 1918 was the increasing concern of its followers for present-day problems. Some of the reasons for this already have been noted, along with the growing demand from many quarters that Confucianism prove its worth by offering solutions to current social and political ills.

A major problem in Japan immediately following the first World War was the relations between capital and labor. Many labor unions had come into existence during the years of war-stimulated activity, and in 1919, the number of laborers exceeded two million. By the fall of that year, strikes and labor violence began to occur in many industries.[42] It was under such circumstances that the veteran Confucianist and business leader, Shibusawa Eiichi, conceived of a plan to bring about peace and conciliation between capital and labor. In the winter of 1919, he founded the Kyōchōkai 協調會 or Conciliation Society for the purpose of preventing further acrimonious labor disputes, and was supported in his efforts by such men as Prince Tokugawa Iesato 德川家達, President of the House of Peers, Kiyoura Keigo 清浦奎吾, Vice-President of the Privy Council, and other officials in the government.[43] Both Tokugawa Iesato and Kiyoura Keigo were strong advocates of Confucianism, Kiyoura having been among those responsible for the reorganization of the Shibunkai in 1918,[44] while Prince Tokugawa became the head of the Shibunkai in 1922.[45] With this background, it is not strange to find that

---

42. Yanaga, op. cit., 390-391.
43. Ibid., 392.
44. Shibun, I, 1 (Jan., 1919), 107-108.
45. Shibunkai 斯文會, Kinsei Nihon no Jugaku 近世日本の儒學 (Recent Japanese Confucianism), (Tōkyō: Iwanami Shoten 岩波書店, 1939), preface, has a long description

the principles of the Kyōchōkai were based on Confucian concepts of common interests and mutual responsibilities, rather than cut-and-dried principles of collective bargaining between antagonistic classes. As Shibusawa himself explained:

> We occasionally witness sad events in labor troubles in civilized nations. The trouble begins with a breach of harmony between Capital and Labor. The breach is soon aggravated into ill will and resentment between the two parties. The evil disturbs the good order of society and threatens the peace of the nation....
>
> [A labor] law may be necessary for better management. But its enforcement may serve to emphasize the notion of rights and obligations between Capital and Labor, which would tend to lead both parties to a cold and perfunctory relationship destroying the beautiful relations of affection and loyalty long inculcated in the labor life of Japan.
>
> Instead of the law, *wang tao* should be practiced by Capital and Labor. If Capital deals with Labor according to *wang tao* and vice versa, believing that their interests are common to each other, there will be no strife. True harmony between them can be fully established.[46]

In those periods during which Confucian philosophy was elucidated and developed, there never were highly industrialized centers with many laborers crowded together working for a few large concerns. Such interest as Confucianism had taken in economics dealt almost exclusively with peasants and agricultural problems, but even then, the problems were considered more as ethical than economic ones. Koyanagi Shigeta 小柳司氣太 (1870-1940), a well-known scholar of Chinese studies and a staunch Confucianist, made clear this emphasis of Confucianism on ethics rather than economics in a speech in November, 1919.[47] Discussing the distribution of wealth, he said it was not only a major problem

of how Hattori Unokichi and other members of the Shibunkai were able to persuade Tokugawa Iesato to become head of the Shibunkai. Because of his influence and position in society, Tokugawa's becoming head of the Shibunkai gave the organization added prestige.

46. Kyugoro Obata, *An Interpretation of the Life of Viscount Shibusawa*, (Tōkyō: Tōkyō Printing Co., 1939), 166-167.

47. Koyanagi Shigeta, "Japanese *Kangaku* and the World Situation," *Shibun*, II, 2 (April, 1920), 89-94.

of economics, but inextricably related to ethics. Confucius, Ko-yanagi pointed out, also had spoken of distribution in this way when he stated: "I do not worry over scarcity, but I am anxious over inequality. I do not worry over poverty, but I am anxious about not being at peace."

Confucianism answered the question of the proper position of the proletariat by adjusting traditional Confucian ethical princi-ples so that labor became simply another of the interdependent groups in a corporate society. This solution by Confucianists of the labor problem can readily be compared to that of Catholic social philosophy in the West, for Catholics like Confucianists tended to think of social problems in ethical terms. The unity of morality and economics stressed by Shibusawa in 1918, as well as his ideas on capital-labor harmony, would certainly have conformed to principles of Catholic social philosophy.[48]

Unfortunately, there is little information on how the Kyō-chōkai worked in practice, and on whether it achieved any real success in reconciling labor and capital.[49] There is a question, however, whether conservative businessmen and politicians such as took part in the Kyōchōkai could adequately deal with labor problems simply by appealing to high-sounding moral phrases. On the contrary, these types of ethical pronouncements may well have served as a cover-up for the rejection by capital of justified labor demands, or as a means of encouraging submis-siveness among laborers.

In any case, labor strife continued, evoking comment from Confucianists and others who felt Confucianism could contribute to a solution of the trouble. Count Ōki Tōkichi 大木遠吉 (1871-

---

48. The encyclical of Pope Leo XIII on May 15, 1891, *Rerum Novarum*, and of Pope Pius XI on May 15, 1931, *Quadragesimo Anno*, are generally considered as best reflecting Church views on labor-capital relations. It it significant to notice that the similarity in the proposed Catholic and Confucian solutions to the labor-capital problems probably resulted from the similar backgrounds of the two systems. Both had developed their basic social and ethical concepts in feudal periods when economic principles were considered subordinate to and derived from more basic ethical considerations. Therefore it is natural to find that they both still viewed economic problems as fundamentally ethical.

49. Obata, *op. cit.*, 167-168 states that the efforts of the Kyōchōkai averted many threatening labor disputes. He cites no specific cases, though, and the context of the statements make it seem more like an attempt to praise Shibusawa's work than a description of what actually occurred.

1926), a member of the House of Peers and Minister of Justice in the Hara cabinet of 1920, delivered a speech at the 1920 spring lecture series of the Shibunkai in which he discussed the unrest and labor problems besetting Japan.[50] Emphasizing the value of Confucianism under these circumstances, he said:

> ...And in addition, with sabotage and strikes, conditions are indeed disturbed. Strikes are still understandable, but sabotage is derived from the lowest mental processes. It is in this situation that I speak of the great necessity for Confucianism, and feel that we need to give full scope to the true essentials of Confucian teachings. Such things as sabotage, because they have as their aim not carrying out one's duties faithfully, are outside the realm of discussion.
>
> ...Speaking from the point of view of the social organization of our nation, the development of a sense of responsibility is a basic element of our social structure. Somehow or other we must prevent today the disordering of the ideas of the people; and for that, I think the special mental characteristics of Confucianism should be inculcated well into the minds of the people.[51]

In the corporate view of society that Confucianists held as ideal, everyone carried out his duties and fulfilled his responsibilities, thus bringing mutual peace and prosperity. Rigid classes conceived of in Marxian dialectic were nonexistent because ethical considerations determined the relations of men, rather than economic position. Theoretically, a man could rise in society if he displayed ability, for the examinations were open to all. Hattori Unokichi analyzed these ideas in a speech given at the fall lecture series of the Shibunkai in 1920, and he compared them to Communist ideas.[52] Criticizing the Communist view of history, he claimed its attempts to idealize a classless society were like trying to go back to primitive ages when man did not differentiate between physical and mental labor.

---

50. Ōki Tōkichi, "*Kangaku* and Ideological Problems," *Shibun*, II, (1920), q.v. The exact reference to this speech in the *Shibun* was lost by the writer, but as each volume of *Shibun* includes a table of contents for the numbers of the whole year, the speech can be pin-pointed easily by anyone who has the volume.

51. *Ibid.*

52. Hattori Unokichi, "Radical Thoughts as Seen from the Point of View of Confucianism," *Shibun*, II, 6 (Dec., 1920), 375-386.

In Confucianism, society was made up of both physical and mental workers, the latter being called *chün-tzu* 君子, and the former being called *hsiao-jen* 小人. The *hsiao-jen* produced things necessary for life and supported the *chün-tzu*, while the *chün-tzu* did not labor physically, but used his mind in matters of government and education, governing and instructing the *hsiao-jen*, thus supporting their life in this way. And in education there was general education and higher education. Those who received general education and were outstanding could receive higher education. As a result, the *hsiao-jen* could become a *chün-tzu*, and therefore it was not a rigid class system.

Nowadays those who oppose capitalism assume that there are two classes, workers and capitalists, and assert that classes must be wiped out. Although a true class system is said to be based on blood, and there are examples of such among the capitalists today, this is not the case with all of them. And the same is true for the laborers, for there are many examples of capitalists who became laborers and laborers who became capitalists. It may be that such cases are rare in the West, but in Japan it is not so. Therefore in the strictest sense, capitalists and laborers should not be said to make up classes.[53]

The type of cooperative economy pictured in the foregoing statements of Confucianists, while inadequate to deal with the problems of modern industrial life, did stress the unity of interest of divergent social groups. Japanese leaders did not overlook the value that such attitudes might have in mobilizing the efforts of the people toward particular goals, and they were described as praiseworthy in school ethics textbooks.[54] Especially after 1931, the goal of making the nation strong by cooperative effort was emphasized, and this trend reached a climax in exhortations such as were included in the widely circulated book *Kokutai no hongi* 國體の本義:

> ...Only where the people one and all put heart and soul into their respective occupations, and there is coherence and order in

---

53. *Ibid. Chün-tzu* is usually translated as "superior man," while *hsiao-jen* is literally "small man."

54. Robert King Hall, *Shūshin: the Ethics of a Defeated Nation*, (New York: Columbia University, 1949), 145, 147, 195. It is interesting to note that in the last reference given, Shibusawa Eiichi, the veteran Confucianist mentioned at various points in this chapter, is held up as one who sought to honor the people of Japan and serve the nation.

everyone's activity, with their minds set on guarding and maintaining the prosperity of the Imperial Throne, is it possible to see a healthy development in the people's economic life.[55]

Political thought, however, rather than economics was suitable to Confucian analysis because it dealt more with problems of human nature and human relations that were capable of measurement by Confucian ethical standards. Many new political ideas came to Japan in the years immediately after the first World War, and generally speaking, liberal and democratic thought received a great impetus. This did not go unnoticed by Confucianists who found much to criticize in the new trends.

Hattori Unokichi gave a speech on June 15, 1919 comparing "Democrary and Confucianism."[56] He began by trying to discover elements in democracy besides the political, and decided they were a sense of social justice and equal opportunity. In actual practice, though, these were difficult to realize, and consequently the problem resolved itself into making distinctions according to differences in ability that existed naturally among people, and then allowing each to develop himself to the greatest extent possible. In Confucianism also existed the ideal of allowing each to develop himself to the fullest extent, and this had been practiced in China through the system of examinations for public office open theoretically to everyone. Therefore Hattori claimed that Confucianism had the same concomitants of social justice as "modern" democracy.

Speaking next of the political aspects of democracy, he pointed out that the principle of sovereign power residing finally with the people was entirely contrary to Confucianism in which sovereign power was conceived of as being derived from Heaven, the source of all things in the universe. The people, however, in the sense that man is the highest creation of Heaven, could be said to deserve the most important consideration, and from this

---

55. *Kokutai no hongi* 國體の本義 (*Cardinal Principles of the National Entity of Japan*); translated by John Owen Gauntlett and edited with an introduction by Robert King Hall (Cambridge: Harvard University Press, 1949), 181.

56. Hattori Unokichi, "Democracy and Confucianism," *Shibun*, I, 4 (August, 1919), 327-334.

point of view it was possible for Confucianists to accept the principle of making the people the basis of government. Heaven, nevertheless, always ultimately conferred the supreme power to rule. Looking at democracy from Abraham Lincoln's phrase of "government by the people, for the people, and of the people," Confucianists could say that in Japan there was government by the people, achieved through the organs of representative government; and that government for the people had been the basis of rule in Japan from earliest times; but government of the people would never be possible because supreme power lay in Heaven and not in the people.

While Hattori showed a certain amount of sympathy and insight into Western political theory, there were many men who in praising Confucianism found nothing but radical ideas and threats to Japanese traditions in Western thought. Uzawa Sōmei 鵜澤聰明 (1872-1957), a distinguished lawyer and member of the Diet, could certainly be included in this category on the basis of a speech he made in 1919 at the Kōshi Saiten Kai 孔子祭典會 entitled "On the Way of True Kingship."[57] Surveying Western philosophy, Uzawa said there was a constant struggle between the ideas of freedom and order. This was reflected in the fact that the West lacked any real firm moral code, since neither equality, freedom, or charity could serve as a foundation for family life. In Asia, though, there was a moral standard such that all men, high and low, near and far, were included in a harmonious unity known as *Wang-tao*.

Wang-tao, being based on universal feelings of humaneness and filial piety, could appeal to all men, and Uzawa said that President Wilson would no doubt have used this term in his pronouncements to the world if he had lived in the Orient. Uzawa quoted from the *Analects* to show what the effects would be of following such a policy: "The philosopher Yu said, 'They are few who, being filial and fraternal, are fond of offending against their superiors. There have been none who, not liking to offend

57. Uzawa Sōmei, "On the *Wang-tao*," *Shibun*, I, 4 (Aug., 1919), 313-336; I, 5 (Oct., 1919), 393-402.

their superiors, have been fond of stirring up confusion."[58] Thus Uzawa claimed that the principles of Oriental morality could bring peace and stability to a world foundering in confusion. Fortunately, in Japan these principles had been inculcated from early times, but the nation had to be on guard against radical ideas which threatened her from Russia, England, France, and the United States. In other words, though the League of Nations was trying to realize the ideal of world peace, individual countries might misuse their power for selfish purposes because there was still no common moral code among nations.

Ichimura Sanjirō 市村瓚次郎 (1868-1947), an outstanding professor of Chinese studies at Tōkyō Imperial University and a leader of the Shibunkai, dealt more specfically with political problems at a speech in the spring of 1920 on "Confucianism and General Elections." Defending the views of Confucianism in regard to the importance of public opinion, he stated:

> ...In short, Confucian political principles of course make the welfare of the state and happiness of the people the central fact, and they put great importance on the trend of opinion of the people. Therefore, from the beginning, Confucianism does not recognize despotic governing, but making the people the foundation, values public opinion. And this valuing of public opinion is related to Confucian cosmological views and Confucian views of the state, and is based on the idea that the ruler receives the mandate of Heaven.[59]

But while Ichimura asserted that Confucianism conflicted neither with constitutional government nor with representative government, he felt that in Japan it would be more in keeping with tradition and the social system to make the family rather than the individual the basic voting unit. As he described it:

> ...If it is true that the family is the basic unit of the nation, then it is natural to move according to this truth. And since in Confucianism the family is recognized as the basic unit of the state,

---

58. *Lun-yü* 論語, ch. II, 1; translated by Legge, *op. cit.*, I, 138.
59. Ichimura Sanjirō, "Confucianism and General Elections," *Shibun*, II, 3 (June, 1920), 157.

general elections in which the family is given the fundamental position would agree with the spirit of Confucianism.[60]

In view of the type of corporate society idealized by Confucianism in which social justice, peace, and harmony were achieved when everybody understood their proper positions and fulfilled their commensurate responsibilities, it is natural to find the family and not the individual held up as the foundation of the state. The family was considered the smallest self-sufficient unit in society, and within it, all the important human relations of society were present on a smaller scale. Thus the relations of ruler and subject were analogous to those of father and son, while the relations of superior and inferior were similar to those of elder brother and younger brother. In the Confucian system, the father was responsible for the ultimate well-being of the family, like that of the ruler for the welfare of his subjects. Therefore to have persons, other than those bearing the responsibility for the well-being of the family, making decisions effecting family welfare would logically have been unacceptable.

Uno Tetsuto 宇野哲人 (b. 1875), a professor at Tōkyō Imperial University and an active supporter of the Shibunkai, presented a fuller picture of Confucian social ideals in an essay written in 1920 entitled "Freedom and Equality." He began by critically commenting on the craze for equality, freedom, and democracy that was rampant throughout Japan, for he said that these theories were oblivious of the fact that all men were not equally endowed. Confucianism, however, recognized men's differences. Therefore it could bring a truer form of justice, freedom, and benevolent government to society than foreign importations, because it would not insist upon giving to persons responsibilities and duties beyond their abilities. The way Confucianism resolved the problem of freedom and equality he described as follows:

...In Confucianism, there is the ideal of taking the people of the Empire and giving each his proper place. The realization of this ideal

---

60. *Ibid.*, II, 4 (Aug., 1920), 244-245.

is called the Way of True Kingship and Benevolent Government. When the Way of True Kingship is carried out, differences between wealth and poverty are generally equalized; there are no extremes of wealth or extremes of poverty; education is generally disseminated; morality is put into effect perfectly; ruler and subjects share pleasures together and enjoy equal benefits; and old men, widows, orphans, the physically handicapped and the sick are all cared for at government expense until their death. Therefore from the point of view of government and society, we should call this the most perfect kind of institution. In Mencius, the essentials of the Way of True Kingship are generally written down. Those who study well balanced and moderate political and social institutions, based on true explanations and the spirit of freedom and equality, should follow the examples in Confucianism and especially should read thoroughly the writings of Mencius.[61]

Professor K. Yamada in August, 1924, delivered a lecture in Tōkyō in which he praised the humane object of Confucian ideals of government in a manner similar to Uno Tetsuto. Comparing these ideals with political practice in the West, he made the contrast seem very striking by the use of a few well-chosen adjectives and phrases:

On reading any page of Confucius one always comes across the word benevolence; it is to be noted that whenever Confucius talks of administration or government, every page of his writing abounds with the word subjects. In other words, the main object of government in China was to take care particularly of those who were to be governed; that is, the fundamental creed of government in the East was built on the foundation of all-embracing benevolence. The administrative methods in China according to Confucius's teachings were not handicapped by either insubordination or upper-handed tyranny like those of Western countries.... In Japan, where this unique doctrine has had no less influence, there has been, and will be forever, only one government under one definite God-ordained Ruler. Thus our ideas of government are quite different from those of Europe and America where it is instituted by people whose guiding standard of government is chiefly due to their instinctive sense of right and responsibility which, by the way, not seldom

61. Uno Tetsuto, "Freedom and Equality," *Shibun*, II, 5 (Oct., 1920), 305.

comes into conflict, bringing on cold-blooded slaughter as shown in the recent war of Europe.[62]

This superficial criticism of Western ideas completely ignored the hundreds of years during which government in both Japan and China had been marked by despotism and internecine strife. It does serve to show, nevertheless, how Japanese Confucianists at this time sought to associate superior ethical value judgements with traditional Oriental ways, while putting the burden for such disasters as the World War entirely on Western political ideas. Yamada himself openly said:

> We do not believe that Western ideas of morality have reached the height of our own standard, as was plainly shown by the outbreak of the Great War, which has devastated the whole of Europe mentally and physically, ignoring any sense or conception of "humanity and benevolence," such as Confucius teaches us is the fundamental law for human conduct.[63]

Although most Confucianists no doubt agreed with Yamada's views on the superiority of Confucian ethical and political ideas over Western ones, such diatribes as his were quite ineffective in student and intellectual circles. It is not surprising to find, then, that more sophisticated analyses of Confucianism were offered which approached Western thought moderately, though nonetheless critically. For example, in 1924, Ichimura Sanjirō delivered a speech on "The System of Confucianism as seen from a Cultural Standpoint"[64] in which he discussed the historical background of Confucianism, showing the synthesis that had taken place between the original forms of Confucianism, Buddhism, and Taoism. The result of this synthesis was that modern Confucianism integrated harmoniously elements of ethics, government, and economics. Present-day tendencies,

62. K. Yamada, *Two Lectures*, translated by K. Matsuda (Shanghai: Tung Wen College, 1926), 11-13. The translator's English has been corrected at points where there were simple grammatical errors.

63. *Ibid.*, 47.

64. Ichimura Sanjirō, "The System of Confucianism as seen from a Cultural Standpoint," *Shibun*, VIII, 2 (April, 1925), 82-84.

though, were to isolate these fields, and study or promote activity in only one at a time. This was true for businessmen, politicians, and scholars, and unfortunately it robbed them of the basis for making sound judgements. The emphasis of modern cultural life reflected this type of compartmentalized thinking, for when people talked of free love, living in Western style houses, or scratching and blowing on musical instruments as culture, they had mistaken the true meaning of culture. Only by a proper perspective of the elements of ethics, government, and economics in life could an appreciation of culture be achieved. This was why Confucianism with its synthesis of these three was so important to the present-day world.

Koyanagi Shigeta also gave a speech along these lines in 1926 entitled "Characteristics of Confucianism."[65] He stressed the integration of knowledge attained in Confucianism, and pointed out how through it, watertight divisions between fields of study like ethics, government, and economics, as existed in the West, would be impossible. This type of well-rounded point of view would also prevent persons from advocating extremes of radicalism or conservatism because of its emphasis on the just mean, particularly important at the present due to the spread of dangerous Communist ideas. Finally, Koyanagi spoke of the essential practicality of Confucianism which eschewed falling into theoretical struggles similar to those in the West over such matters as the economic theories of Marx. The Confucian way was to find a method of uniting theory and practice as was being done in Japan.

But increasingly critical times in Japan seem to have brought forth more anti-Western statements again on the part of Confucianists. By 1931, Shionoya On could compare the West to the Mongols in describing the feelings that came over him at a celebration making the 650th year of the latter's attempted invasion of Japan. The present invaders did not attack with warships, he said, but used ideas like Communist ideology to

---

65. Koyanagi Shigeta, "Characteristics of Confucianism," *Shibun*, IX, 3 (March, 1927), 1-23.

weaken the nation. The great Confucian scholar Wang Yang-ming
王陽明 (1473-1529) had aptly described the situation centuries
before with the words: "Destroying the bandits of the mountains
is easy, but destroying the thieves of the heart is difficult."[66]
Although Japan was surrounded by republican nation such as
China, Russia, and the United States where Imperial government
was opposed, Shionoya still felt confident that the nation could
withstand all attacks if every citizen advanced armed with
Yamato damashii 大和魂 (Japanese spirit), and clarified the way
of loyalty and filial piety.

Finally in 1933, Shionoya On, writing on "Critical Times and
Chinese Studies,"[67] made Confucianism play an integral part
in support of Japanese nationalism. Shionoya said that the problems of the day were not political or economic, but moral and
spiritual. To deal with the situation, it was essential to revive
the Japanese spirit. This meant that the people must comprehend
the meaning of the eternal Imperial line, the oneness of ruler
and subjects, the unity of loyalty and filial piety, reverence for
the gods, and veneration for ancestors. The teachings of Confucius were the basis for successfully inculcating such principles
and therefore should be encouraged. Chinese studies (*kangaku*)
with Confucianism as the core would not only strengthen the
country, but also make clear the true meaning of *Wang-tao* on
which Manchuria was founded, and hence bring about greater
contact between Japan and China. Through this, the deleterious
American and European influences on the Chinese could be
abolished.

Reviewing the trends in Confucian attitudes toward economic,
political, and intellectual problems between 1918 and 1933, most
recurrent and significant was the criticism of the West. Often
when it was not openly stated, it was implied in the solutions
offered by Confucianists to particular social problems. For example, while in favor of some sort of arbitration in labor-capital

---

66. Shionoya On, "Kamakura tsūshin" 鎌倉通信 ("News from Kamakura"), *Shibun*,
XIII, 9 (Sept., 1933), 1-19.
67. Shionoya On, "Hijōji to kangaku" 非常時と漢學 ("Critical Times and Chinese
Studies"), *Shibun*, XV, 9 (Sept., 1933), 1-10.

disputes, Confucianists felt that the division of society into separate groups on an economic basis, as had happened in the West, was a mistake. They suggested a return to the type of conditions prevalent in guilds where the master craftsman looked after the apprentice and journeyman, and there was unity of interest in the efforts of all.

Western political thought also had little to recommend itself to Confucianists. For them, Confucianism already included the strong points of such theories as democracy and representative government, while at the same time avoiding their faults. They claimed that such important differentiations as between freedom and license, or responsibility and neglect of duty could only be made properly in Confucianism because it alone clearly conceived of the true nature of man and his basic relationships.

Furthermore, the unity of the ethical and spiritual aspects of life with economics and politics were affirmed solely in Confucianism. In the West, the trend was to consider each separately with the result that social life became chaotic, and people fell into such extremes as the materialistic interpretations of Marxism.

Considering this background of anti-Western thought, it was nearly inevitable that Confucianism would become intimately associated with Japanese nationalism, especially after 1931 when Japan invaded Manchuria and left the League of Nations. In particular, the negative role of Confucianism as primarily a means of criticizing Western institutions and ideas was replaced, Confucianism was given an active part to play in stimulating Japanese national consciousness and awakening the people to the interrelationship of concepts such as loyalty, filial piety, and duty toward the throne.

4. Government Participation in Confucian Ceremonies and the Increasing Association of Confucianism with Japan's *Kokutai*.

Among the most significant developments related to Confucian activities after the establishment of the Shibunkai was the beginning in 1926[68] of official government participation in the society's spring and autumn Confucian sacrifices (*sekiten* 釋奠). Although individuals in high government positions, including members of the Imperial family, had sporadically attended these yearly Confucian sacrifices before this, after 1926, the highest officials such as the Prime Minister, Home Affairs Minister, and other heads of departments personally took part and ordinarily delivered short addresses, praising Confucianism and stressing its importance in stabilizing society and helping develop spiritual discipline.

One of the constant themes reiterated in these addresses was that Confucianism had now become an integral part of the *kokutai* (national polity) of Japan and had an especially important role to play in combatting the excessive materialism and radicalism of the West. The same theme was also taken up in the writings of many Confucianists at this time, and they usually pointed out how the rejection of Confucianism by China had led her to chaos, while in Japan, its amalgamation into the Imperial system had provided the nation with a firm foundation.

The first large-scale participation of government officials at a Confucian ceremony, presaging the regular attendance of officials after 1926, was at the celebration held in 1922 to commemorate the 2400th anniversary of the death of Confucius.[69] It took place on Octover 29, at the Tōkyō Women's Higher Normal School, and was attended by three Imperial Princes,[70] the Prime Minister, the heads of most of the government ministries, representatives from the Governor General of Chōsen and Taiwan, leaders of the Diet and House of Peers, and other dignitaries and socially prominent people.

---

68. See ch. III, p. 118 of this study. *Shibun* VIII, 4 (July, 1926), 238, indicates that from 1926 on, a member of the Imperial family was always present at the Shibunkai's *sekiten.*

69. For the details of this celebration, including the names of all the important people present, speeches given, and pictures of the ceremonies, see *Shibun*, IV, 6 (Dec., 1922), 350-360.

70. The Imperial Princes who took part were: Kotohito 載仁 of the Kanin no Miya 閑院宮 family; Takehiko 武彦 of the Yamashina no Miya 山階宮 family; and Tsunenori 恒憲 of the Kaya no Miya 賀陽宮 family.

Besides the Imperial Princes taking part in these ceremonies, the Imperial House gave the Shibunkai 30,000 yen as a gift in order to further the aims of the society,[71] and there were other signs of official favor as well. After a speech by Prime Minister Katō Tomosaburō 加藤友三郎 praising the work of the Shibunkai in helping preserve good public morals, the Home Affairs Minister, Mizuno Rentarō 水野錬太郎, delivered an address in which he said:

> As to the strong points of Western culture, it is necessary to study and transmit these, but as to morality, the study of the Asiatic sage Confucius is of paramount importance. Especially we in Japan, who have for a thousand and some hundred years encouraged and cultivated public morals according to Confucian teachings, must never forget the virtuous teachings of Confucianism. The duty of our Japan is to create a great civilization by uniting the beauty of the path of virtue of the East with the strong points of Western culture. We do not study Confucianism for the sake of uselessly transmitting the Way of Confucius, but must study Confucianism for the sake of creating a great civilization.[72]

In the above, there is once again discernible the view that Confucian ethics combined with certain elements of Western culture can produce a new civilization. A stand similar to this had been taken in the late Tokugawa period by Sakuma Shōzan 佐久間象山 (1811-64),[73] although a comparison would indicate clearly that in 1922, Confucianism was on the defensive and having to justify its existence, while in 1860, it was still the dominant pattern of thought.

In 1926, when official government participation in the Shibunkai's *sekiten* began, the Prime Minister, Wakatsuki Reijirō 若槻禮次郎, the Minister of Education, Okada Ryōhei 岡田良平, and the Imperial Household Minister, Ichiki Kitokurō 一木喜徳郎, all delivered brief addresses, praising Confucius and speaking of how Confucianism, by becoming fused with the Japanese *kokutai*, had nourished the morality of the people.[74]

---

71. *Shibun*, VII, 2 (April, 1925), 23.
72. *Ibid.*, IV, 6 (Dec., 1922), 350 ff.
73. See ch. I, 26 of this study.
74. *Shibun*, VIII, 3 (June, 1926), 1-4.

As Japan entered the period of the 1930's, however, the role of Confucianism was no longer conceived of in such a narrow way, and this fact is evident from the addresses given by various government officials at the Shibunkai's *sekiten*. For example, in April, 1930, the Prime Minister, Hamaguchi Osachi 濱口雄幸, the Minister of Education, Tanaka Ryūzō 田中隆藏, and the Minister of Home Affairs, Adachi Kenzō 安達謙藏, spoke of the important part the Shibunkai could play in guiding the thoughts of the nation with Confucianism. This was particularly true because Confucian philosophy and ethics could deal effectively with the theories of radical social change that were disturbing the nation. Furthermore, Confucianism was a force for stability and the development of "spiritual culture" as a time when Japan was faced with a flood of Western materialistic innovations.[75]

It is interesting to note that the Shibunkai sent invitations for these ceremonies to about four hundred persons, including all the cabinet ministers, members of the Privy Council, selected members of the Diet and House of Peers, the heads of all public and private schools in Tōkyō, the chief editors of Tōkyō news-papers, and certain businessmen.[76] This is a good cross section of the type of person in modern Japan to whom Confucian thought had an appeal. It is also indicative of the fact that the Shibunkai aimed its appeal at the more conservative leaders of society,[77] apparently expecting in this way to gain the most influence. In view of Confucianism's lack of any general popularity, this was probably the most effective method that the Shibunkai could have used; but it did, of course, tend to make Confucianism, insofar as it became an active political force, a tool of the conservative and later nationalistic elements in the government.

In order clearly to understand, though, how nationalistic elements in the 1930's would preempt and use the force of Confucian ethical values for their own purposes, it is necessary to

---

75. *Shibun*, XII, 6 (June, 1930), 1-6.
76. *Loc. cit.*
77. In the *Shibun*, lists of the members, officers, and advisers of the Shibunkai were published at intervals, and an analysis of the social and economic status of many of these also leads to this conclusion.

examine the increasing association of Confucianism with Japan's *kokutai*.

The roots of this relationship went back at least to the last years of the Tokugawa period when loyalists had sought to re-direct Confucianism so that the Emperor would become the central focus of loyalty and filial piety.[78] Motoda Eifu also had stressed the close relationship between following Confucian moral precepts and being a good Japanese,[79] and in the Imperial Rescript on Education of the Emperor Meiji in whose formulation Motoda had played such an important part, the Imperial line was spoken of as having bequeathed teachings and implanted virtues, most of which were Confucian.[80]

Because the Imperial line was considered as one of the cornerstones of Japan's *kokutai*, to the extent that Confucianism was associated with the Imperial system it also became an integral part of the Japanese *kokutai*. One of the first descriptions of this process of association was made in 1916 by the distinguished historian and linguist Shiratori Kurakichi 白鳥庫吉 (b. 1865) in an address at the Kokugakuin Daigaku 國學院大學 entitled "Kokutai to Jukyō" 國體と儒教 ("The National Polity and Confucianism").[81] Shiratori began by explaining how Japan's *kokutai* differed from that of other countries, pointing out that Japan had never been conquered by foreign peoples; that she had been ruled over by the same house since her origins; and that the Japanese ruling house was of divine ancestry. The particular characteristic of the Japanese people was their willingness to import foreign culture in order to improve themselves, though always remaining aware of their unique *kokutai*.

Confucianism had been one of these importations, representing the essential world view of the Chinese in which man was considered the highest being in the universe. This concept of

---

78. See ch. I, sec. 4 of this study.

79. *Ibid.*, 74.

80. *Ibid.*, 87. Also see the translation of Imperial Rescript on Education in the appendix.

81. Shiratori Kurakichi, "Kokutai to Jukyō" 國體と儒教 ("The National Polity and Confucianism"), *Kokugakuin zasshi* 國學院雑誌, XXIII, 1 (Jan., 1917), 1-16.

existence, however, was only a horizontal one, for even Chinese Confucianism's most revered personages such as Yao 堯 and Shun 舜 were not gods, but simply exemplary human beings.

When Confucianism came to Japan, though, in addition to the horizontal axis comprising human beings and their relations with one another, there was a vertical axis in which gods and spiritual beings were above men. In other words, in Japan, Confucianism which regulated men's relationships in a beautiful and just way was strengthened by making these relationships dependent on Shintō gods and spiritual forces higher than man. Therefore Shiratori concluded that in Japan morality would never decline to a form of utilitarianism as in China because its relationship to the divine would preclude its ever becoming simply an empty form.

The basic postulate of Shiratori's analysis is that Shintō gods being divine, secular Confucianism was strengthened by its association with Shintoism. This is contrary to the opinion of most foreign scholars, who feel rather that Shintoism benefitted from its contact with Confucianism by obtaining the elements of an ethical code. Nevertheless, acceptance of Shiratori's views would make a divine Emperor logically the source of strength for Confucianism in modern Japan.

The same stress on a continuing line of divine rulers as setting off Japan's *kokutai* and giving Confucian precepts special significance was made by Ichimura Sanjirō 市村瓚次郎 in a speech in honor of the Crown Prince on "Kokutai to chūkō" 國體と忠孝 ("The National Polity and Loyalty and Filial Piety").[82] Ichimura claimed that only in Japan was it possible for the ruler to demand both loyalty and filial piety of the people without evoking opposition. This was due to the fact that in Japan an unbroken line of sovereigns had ruled over a homogeneous and unconquered people, giving the state the semblance of a large family. In countries such as China, though, where ruling families had gained control by conquest, loyalty could never be invoked to by the

---

82. Ichimura Sanjrō, "Kukutai to chūkō" 國體と忠孝 ("The National Polity and Loyalty and Filial Piety"), *Kokugakuin zasshi* 國學院雜誌, XXXIII, 1 (Jan., 1917), 17-29.

ruler since a difference would always exist between the conquered and conquerors.

Shintō and Confucianism had also become so closely equated by this time that the Minister of Education, Mizuno Rentarō 水野錬太郎, could say in a speech in 1927 that it was natural to carry out Confucian ceremonies in Shintō fashion. This was possible, he claimed, because Confucianism had been adjusted to the Japanese *kokutai* over many centuries until it completely harmonized with the latter.[83]

Mizuno's words seem to have coincided with actual fact, for in 1926, the Confucian ceremonies at the Kumamoto 熊本 branch of the Shibunkai had been carried out by Shintō priests in a manner ordinarily associated with Shintō ceremonies.[84] There was also a tendency to worship Confucius as a Shintō god in some places, which was noted by Hattori Unokichi when speaking of a visit he had made to Shintō shrines in Saga 佐賀 prefecture and the city of Takamatsu 高松.[85]

Meanwhile, Japanese Confucianists in the late 1920's and early 1930's began to take particular notice of the anti-Confucian and anti-traditional movements sweeping China. They were wont to compare developments in Japan and China by saying that Confucianism in Japan had been completely amalgamated to the *kokutai*, bringing stability and peace, while its rejection in China was leading to chaos.

As Shionoya On 鹽谷溫 pointed out, though, certain aspects of Chinese Confucianism such as the justification for revolution in Mencius were not compatible with the Japanese *kokutai*, and so these elements had been rejected. For proof of this, he said that a Chinese book written during the Ming dynasty, the *Wu-tsa-tsu* 五雜俎, had mentioned of how any ship bringing a copy of *Mencius* to Japan would sink. Shionoya insisted, however, that Confucius had never thought of revolutions as good, and this tendency towards internal strife was simply a characteristic of

83. Mizuno Rentarō, "The Way of Confucius," *Shibun*, IX, 12 (Dec., 1927), 721-726.
84. *Shibun*, VIII, 3 (June, 1926), 216.
85. *Shibun*, IX, 12 (Dec., 1927), 889-892.

the Chinese and not a true element of Confucianism.[86]

In 1928 Shionoya made a trip to China, and on his return to Japan, he emphasized again that the amalgamation of Confucianism into Japan's *kokutai* was a unique feature of Japanese culture which could protect the nation against destructive Communist ideas. In China, the Kuomintang simply spoke of the *San-min-chu-i* 三民主義 (Three Principles of the People), and disregarded Confucianism, bringing disaster to the nation. The only sign of encouragement in this picture had been the efforts of Chang Tso-lin 張作霖 to revive Confucian ceremonies and Confucian studies in North China.[87]

The scholar Iijima Tadao 飯島忠夫 in 1930, noting this tendency in China to cyclical change and revolution, wrote that Japan's own morality was cultivated best by Confucianism. He claimed the reason for this was that Confucius had originally envisaged government in China being carried out by an unchanging ruling house which maintained its virtue, but that the diversity of China, the many invasions from abroad, and the frequent differences between the rulers and the people had made this impossible. In order to rationalize this situation, the Chinese had developed a theory of revolution. In Japan, however, as the *kokutai* was characterized by an eternal Imperial line outstanding for its virtue, the Way of Confucius was most closely realized and appropriate to Japanese concepts of an unchanging, divine moral order.[88]

Representative of the trend in the early 1930's seeking to obtain official support for Confucianism and relate it to the Japanese *kokutai* was the emotional message of Uda Hisashi 宇田 尙 entitled "The Readvocacy of a New Confucian Spirit and the Mission of the Imperial Nation."[89] Uda was an influential busi-

---

86. Shionoya On, "Confucius and the Japanese National Polity," *Shibun*, VIII, 5 (Aug., 1926), 305-308.

87. Shionoya On, "Kōfushi to waga kokutai" 孔夫子と我が國體 ("Confucius and Our National Polity"), *Shibun*, XI, 9 (Sept., 1929), 687-704.

88. Iijima Tadao 飯島忠夫, "Kōshi no michi" 孔子の道 ("The Way of Confucius"), *Shibun*, XII, 9 (Sept., 1930), 631-642.

89. Uda Hisashi, "Kōkoku no shimei to shin Jukyō seishin no saiteishō" 皇國の 使命と新儒教精神の再提唱 ("The Readvocacy of a New Confucian Spirit and the Mission of the Imperial Nation"), *Shibun*, XV, 11 (Nov., 1933), 16-17.

nessman who took an interest in educational matters. He wrote this article in 1933 when a nationalistic spirit was beginning to sweep over Japan, and in it he claimed that a new Confucianism combining the spiritual civilization of Asia with the scientific ideas of the West could sweep the earth and bring peace to the world. Because this new Confucianism was an integral part of the Japanese *kokutai*, he said it would serve to display the brilliance of the Imperial way in its mission throughout Asia.

Although Uda was not a member of the government, his associating the "Mission of the Imperial Nation" and Confucianism was well established by this time. For besides official participation in Confucian ceremonies, there were increasing suggestions that these ceremonies should become a national observance.[90] By 1937, less than four years after this, teachers were instructing students all over Japan with *Kokutai no hongi* 國體の本義, a book in which the Confucian virtues of loyalty and filial piety were described as follows:

> Verily, loyalty and filial piety as one is the flower of our national entity,[91] and is the cardinal point of our people's morals. Hence, national entity forms not only the foundations of morality but of all branches of things as politics, economics, and industry. Accordingly, the great Way of loyalty and filial piety as one must be made manifest in all practical fields of these national activities and the people's lives. We subjects must strive all the more in loyalty and filial piety for the real manifestation of the immense and endless national entity.[92]

The increasingly close ties between Confucian principles and national welfare that have been described in the preceding pages show in a striking manner the extent to which Confucianism

---

90. Egi Kazuyuki 江木千之, 'Kokka toshite no sekiten" 國家としての釋奠 ("The Confucian Ceremony as a National [Ceremony]"), *Shibun* XII, 10 (Oct., 1930), 3-5.

91. In John Gauntlett's translation of *Kokutai no hongi* from which the passage was taken, the word *kokutai* was rendered as "national entity," although in this study it has generally been translated as "national polity." See ch. I, footnote 101.

92. *Kokutai no Hongi, Cardinal Principles of the National Entity of Japan*, translated by John Owen Gauntlett and edited with an introduction by Robert King Hall (Cambridge: Harvard University Press, 1949), 91-92.

from 1918 to 1933 had become associated with Japanese nationalism. This relationship, while certainly not absent during the Meiji and early Taishō periods, had been of less importance to Confucianists and those interested in Confucianism in earlier years. What must be kept in mind is that Confucianism during the Tokugawa period had an appeal as a universal philosophy and cosmology. Supporters of Confucianism in the Meiji period, influenced by Tokugawa thought, espoused Confucianism as a creed for Japan because they felt it offered a true picture of man in the universe and was based on eternally valid principles.

Motoda Eifu 元田永孚 (1819-91), whose beliefs have already been described in chapter two,[93] was typical of this type of Confucianist, for he considered that Confucian moral precepts were essential to all civilized societies. Consequently in his draft of the Imperial Rescript on Education of the Emperor Meiji, Motoda did not feel it was necessary to mention respect for the constitution and observance of the law because these were actions which he was certain would naturally follow if Confucian moral and social principles were observed. Motoda's views on this point, however, were opposed by those who considered that the Imperial Rescript should serve as a means to emphasize national unity and strengthen the state, rather than to stress any particular philosophy or universal code of ethics.

It is significant to note the existence of a similar dichotomy between Confucianism and nationalism in the history of modern China. With the rise of nationalism in China in the first two decades of the twentieth century, Confucianism as a body of unchanging and universally valid principles was challenged by nationalism just as it had been in Japan. By the 1930's, however, the Nationalists in China (Kuomintang 國民黨), having been successful in their struggle to unite the country, began to stress that Confucianism as a part of China's national heritage should not be forgotten.[94]

---

93. See ch. II, sec. 4 of this study.

94. Henri Bernard, *Sagesse Chinoise et Philosophie Chrétienne* (*Chinese Wisdom and Christian Philosophy*), Série Culturelle des Hautes Études de Tientsin (Paris: Cathasia, 1935), 260.

This development bears comparison to the vicissitudes of Confucianism in Japan, for from a condition of general neglect and outright rejection in the Meiji period as unsuitable for dealing with the problems facing Japan, Confucianism came increasingly to be accepted as a basic element of the "Japanese spirit." This was especially so after 1920 when the possibility that radical Western political and social ideas might take hold in Japan appeared as a danger to both nationalists and conservatives. While willing to accept Western technology and industrial methods, such groups were apprehensive of the social, political, and economic changes which were causing traditional Japanese concepts to be replaced by Western ones. Under these circumstances, Confucianism, with its strong anti-Western bias, recommended itself as a means of contrasting the avowedly superior spiritual civilization of the East with the materialism of the West. The sugar coating to this appeal was that since Confucianism was most active in Japan, the Japanese could consider themselves as the leaders of Asiatic spiritual civilization. On the basis of this, it was also possible for Japan to view herself as superior to China and to justify intervention in China for the purpose of restoring traditional spiritual values and redeeming the Chinese from the abyss of Western materialism.

IV

CONFUCIANISM IN JAPAN AFTER 1933 AND ITS CHARACTERISTICS IN JAPANESE OVERSEAS POSSESSIONS AND JAPANESE DOMINATED AREAS

1. The Nationalisation of Confucianism in Japan Proper.

After 1933, the trends apparent in the development of Confucianism in Japan from 1918 to 1933 became accelerated, but the most prominent of these was the growing identification of Confucianism with the Japanese spirit, the Imperial way, and the Japanese *kokutai* 國體 (national polity). The term "Japanese spirit" in particular became a favorite after 1933 for speakers who wished to contrast Japanese civilization and ideals with those of the rest of the world. Often this was done in order to justify the motives of Japanese expansion, for it was claimed that Japan had a mission to perform in protecting and developing spiritual civilization in Asia which was threatened by the egoistical and materialistic culture of the West.

Ever since the Imperial Restoration in 1868, individual Confucianists and Confucian organizations had insisted on the dichotomy between the spiritual civilization of the East and the material civilization of the West. The latter was invariably felt to be inferior, and this point of view followed logically from the premises of Confucian philosophy in which man was considered to have a fundamental moral nature whose development constituted the primary aim of civilization.

Similar in this respect to Catholic philosophy in the West, Confucianism claimed that when preoccupation with material life led man to forget his moral nature, he was no longer fulfilling the purpose of his existence.[1] Closely related to this was the Confucian attitude towards Marxism as basically a product of the materialistic emphasis in the West, already pointed out in the speeches of many prominent Confucianists in the third chapter.

Unfortunately, the magazine *Shibun* has not been available after 1933 for analyzing in detail the attitudes of Confucianists with respect to the increasingly critical problems facing Japan. The Shibunkai did continue as an active organization, nevertheless, until 1945,[2] and from the isolated statements on Confucianism found in popular literature and educational books during the period from 1934 to 1945, it is clear that Confucianism came to have a valuable appeal in the ideological program of Japanese nationalists.

The rise of one new and apparently influential Confucian organization during this period needs to be mentioned, for statements by its members and interested individuals indicate how Confucian attitudes towards spiritual culture could serve to bolster the Japanese spirit.

The founding ceremonies of the Nippon Jukyō Senyōkai 日本儒教宣揚會 (Japanese Society for the Promotion of Confu-

---

1. Among the many passages in the Confucian classics which display this is one by Mencius:

The Minister of Agriculture taught the people to sow and reap, cultivating the five grains. When the five grains were brought to maturity, the people all obtained a subsistence. But men possess a moral nature; and if they are well-fed, warmly clad, and comfortably lodged, without being taught at the same time, they become almost like the beasts. This was a subject of anxious solicitude to the sage Shun, and he appointed Hsieh to be the minister of Instruction to teach the relations of humanity. *Mengtzu* 孟子, Bk. III, pt. 1, ch. 4, 8; as translated by James Legge, *The Confucian Classics*, second edition, revised (Oxford: Clarendon Press, 1895), II, 251.

Some idea of Catholic views on the nature of man and its distortion by the materialism characteristic of both monopoly capitalism and Communism can be found in Fulton J. Sheen, *Communism and the Conscience of the West*, (New York: The Bobbs-Merrill Co., 1948), 48-52. It is interesting to compare the similar Catholic and Confucian criticisms of the evils of capitalism and Communism as being derived from materialistic interpretations of life and the nature of man.

2. The last issue of *Shibun* 斯文 that was published appears to have been in September, 1945. *Shōwa jūkyū-nijū nendo Tōyōshi kenkyū bunken ruimoku* 昭和十九・二十年度東洋史研究文獻類目 (*Bibliography of Oriental Historical Studies for 1944 and 1945*), (Kyōto Daigaku Jimbun Kagaku Kenkyūjo 京都大學人文科學研究所, 1951), 1. From the information in this bibliography, one can infer that the Shibunkai remained actively functioning at least until September, 1945.

cianism) were held in Tōkyō on January 27, 1934 at the Tōkyō Kaikan 東京會館. About seven hundred people participated,[3] including the Prime Minister, Saitō Makoto 齋藤實, the Home Affairs Minister, Yamamoto Tatsuo 山本達雄, the Minister of Education, Hatoyama Ichirō 鳩山一郎, the head of the House of Peers, Prince Konoe Fumimaro 近衛文麿, and the head of the Lower House, Akita Kiyoshi 秋田清.

These men all made congratulatory statements in which they spoke of the value of Confucianism for stabilizing the people's thoughts and restoring traditional morality from the excess of Western materialism.[4] But most significant of all was the address by Katō Masanosuke 加藤政之助 (b. 1854).

Katō, an influential politician and member of the House of Peers, was head of the Daitō Bunka Gakuin 大東文化學院 (Academy of Oriental Culture). This was a cultural and educational institution formed in 1923 as a part of the Daitō Bunka Kyōkai 大東文化協會 (Society of Oriental Culture) for the purpose of combating dangerous thoughts and strengthening Japanese civilization.[5] The Daitō Bunka Gakuin had for over ten years supported Confucianism as part of its own program of reviving the Japanese spirit. Katō and others had finally felt that in view of the times, it was necessary actively to spread Confucian ideas in society, and therefore they had organized the Nippon Jukyō Senyōkai.[6]

With this as a background, Katō's opening address takes on importance as representing the aims and attitudes of the new organization. He spoke in a particularly disparaging way of the materialistic civilization of the West and blamed it for many of Japan's ills.

In the short space of forty or fifty years, threatened by the people of Europe and America, we realized great [material] pro-

---

3. *Nihon no Jukyō* 日本の儒教 (*Japanese Confucianism*), (Tōkyō: Nippon Jukyō Senyōkai 日本儒教宣揚會 1934), foreword.
4. *Ibid.*, 11-24.
5. *Zenkoku kyōka dantai meikan* 全國教化團體名鑑 (*Register of Cultural Organizations throughout the Country*), (Tōkyō: Chūō Kyōka Dantai Rengōkai 中央教化團體聯合會, 1929), 296-98.
6. *Nihon no Jukyō*, foreword.

gress which, needless to say, was felicitous for the nation. But what I feel is most deplorable is that together with the advance of material culture, every type of evil that should have been avoided was introduced. This was so-called individualism and utilitarianism. The result of revering individualism was that our traditional national principles were relegated to a secondary place; and the result of being infatuated with utilitarianism was that fame and profit occupied the foremost position, while justice and humanity were discarded. Without reflection, we have amplified the mad condition in which we have nothing but fame and profit in mind.

Capitalists exploiting the flesh and blood of laborers while laborers unite and strike in opposition; landlords and tenants each wishing their own harvest to be large, with tenant disputes arising constantly; politicians taking advantage of their positions and yearning for unfair profits; the problem of the sale of doctor's degrees at the Nagasaki Medical College; the problem of the buying and selling of Tōkyō school principalships; and the problem of Communist influence at Kyōto University and Nagano elementary school; all these are the poison of following material culture.[7]

Katō then asked his audience to consider how the Emperor Meiji had dealt with a similar situation when materialism was sweeping Japan in 1886. He had published the *Seiyuki* 聖喩記,[8] and ordered the creation of a special course in Japanese and Chinese studies at Tōkyō Imperial University. Katō felt that the Nippon Jukyō Senyōkai in 1934 could play a similar role in strengthening the spiritual culture of Japan, and copies of the *Seiyuki* were distributed to everyone in the audience.[9] The address ended with Katō asserting that any help given to advance the aims of the Nippon Jukyō Senyōkai would be felicitous for Japan.

Many letters of congratulation and encouragement poured into the offices of the Nippon Jukyō Senyōkai, and typical of the kind of messages sent was one by Major General Horiuchi Bunjirō 堀內文次郎 (gō: Shinsui 信水, b. 1861) entitled "Confucianism and Chinese studies, a great critical problem" ("Jukyō to

---

7. *Ibid.*, 7. The whole address by Katō has been translated and included in the appendix of this study.
8. See ch. II, p. 79, of this study.
9. *Nihon no Jukyō*, 9.

The Bakudan Sanyūshi

(School children paying homage to the spirits of the Bakudan Sanyūshi
before a bronze likeness of these war heroes at the Seishō temple, Shiba,
Tōkyō, in February, 1936.)

kangaku, kinkyū dai mondai nari" 儒教と漢學，緊急大問題也) .[10]

General Horiuchi said that Confucianism was the basis of Oriental spiritual culture, which had no equivalent in Western material culture. At the present time, however, Confucianism existed primarily only in Japan, where it was most prominently displayed in the virtues of loyalty and filial piety. The examples of bravery by war heroes such as Commander Hirose Takeo 廣瀬武夫 (1868-1905) [11] in the Russo-Japanese war and the Baku-dan Sanyūshi 爆彈三勇士 [12] in the fighting around Shanghai in 1932 were the result of loyalty and filial piety.

To appreciate Confucianism, though, one had to master *kan-gaku* 漢學 (Chinese studies) which had been used to express the Japanese spirit. Therefore *kangaku* was really a Japanese thing, and General Horiuchi felt it might more accurately be termed *Nihongaku* 日本學 (Japanese studies). In any case, a study of Confucianism was especially needed in Japan in order to help her carry out her mission of cooperating with and guiding China and Manchuria. Japan had the great task of making a peaceful Orient, and the strength of Confucianism and Chinese studies could be re-exported to China for this purpose. This of course meant that in general, English would be unnecessary, and General Horiuchi hoped the Prime Minister and educational authorities would consider this basic problem.

Besides such written messages as the above, the Nippon Jukyō Senyōkai sent speakers to various places throughout Japan to give popular lectures on Confucian topics. Two examples

---

10. *Ibid.*, 157-158.

11. Commander Hirose Takeo was known to all Japanese for his bravery in the Russo-Japanese war during which he was killed while trying to block the entrance of Port Arthur. Ordered to sink his ship, he had all hands leave the ship, but one man was left behind. When he realized this, Commander Hirose returned to save his ship-mate and was blown to pieces by an enemy shell. E. S. Stephenson and W. Asano, *Famous People of Japan*, (Yokohama: Kelly and Walsh Ltd., 1911), 204-205.

12. The Bakudan Sanyūshi were three Japanese soldiers who acted as human torpedoes in storming a Chinese position during the fighting between the Chinese and Japanese at Shanghai in February, 1932. They carried a torpedo into a Chinese barbed-wire entanglement and blew themselves up in accomplishing their mission. This heroic deed had a great effect on Japanese public opinion. For a description of the incident and its repercussions in Japan, see A. Morgan Young, *Imperial Japan, 1926-38*, (London: George Allen and Unwin Ltd., 1938), 141-142.

taken from these lectures can show how attempts were made to relate Confucian principles with modern problems, though a constant theme in nearly every lecture was the criticism of Western materialism.

Professor of political science, Gorai Kinzō 五來欣造, spoke on the "Confucian Principles of *Wang-tao* that have helped Germany" ("Doitsu o sukutta Jukyō no ōdōshugi" 獨逸を救つた儒教の王道主義).[13] He began by saying that Western culture was facing a crisis, largely because of its overemphasis on individualism and egocentrism. This crisis was recurrent in the West, however, as egocentrism had appeared in different forms throughout its history. Confucian principles of *Wang-tao* were especially appropriate to mitigate this tendency in the West, and in the 18th century, the examples of Germany and France clearly illustrated this fact.

At that time, Confucianism had become known to Europe through such men as Leibniz, and the king of Prussia, Frederick the Great, was influenced by ideas of *Wang-tao*. Government, he realized, must bring a measure of harmony and prosperity to all, and so he made plans for the gradual emancipation of the serfs and other measures to help them. This, said Gorai, created stability in Germany and made it possible for her to avoid such internal strife as the French Revolution. In France, however, Louis XVI had ruled like a complete despot, the equivalent to egocentrism, but on the plane of government. With no thought for the welfare of his subjects, Louis dismissed his minister Turgot when the latter suggested land reform to alleviate the misery of the peasants, and thus laid the foundations for the holocaust. Considering this, Gorai felt that Confucian ideas were most appropriate in Japan at the present in order to lessen the tensions caused by the influence of Western egocentric culture, exhibited in such phenomena as the clash between capital and labor.

Koyanagi Shigeta 小柳司氣太, in a lecture at Ōsaka on "The Japanese Spirit and the Basic Characteristics of Confucianism"

---

13. *Nihon no Jukyō*, 218-225.

("Nihon seishin to Jukyō no honshitsu" 日本精神と儒教の本質),[14] was more direct in his criticism of Western civilization. Pointing out first how Confucianism in Japan had become an integral part of the Japanese spirit, as was evident in the Imperial Rescript on Education of the Emperor Meiji, he went on to say that there was no equivalent to this in the ethical, philosophical, or historical concepts of the West. Actual political practice in the West, based on a constitution, implied class struggle that was entirely antithetical to the spirit of Confucianism in which harmony and mutual prosperity were fundamental principles.

In recent times, however, Western education, Western science, and Western culture of all sorts had become predominant in Japan, and traditional values were being rapidly forgotten. This tendency had reached such a point that the Ministry of Education had not included the character *ju* 儒 (Confucian) among those prescribed for common usage, while it had included such characters as *shō* 娼 (prostitute). Oriental spiritual culture, Oriental ethics, Oriental philosophy, and Oriental political science were not to be found taught as the foremost subjects at middle schools and universities, but as the least important. Under these circumstances, despite the fact there were more schools and more students, the latter were only trained along Western lines. The proof of this was in the spread of radical and Communist thoughts among students themselves. This was natural, said Koyanagi, for the students and young people heard of Western things from morning until night, and no longer knew anything about their Japanese heritage. Some even considered the Japanese Imperial House as equivalent to monarchies in the West.

To remedy this situation and bring about an understanding of the Japanese spirit which was represented in the Imperial Rescript on Education, Koyanagi insisted that a study of the Confucian classics was essential. Statesmen of the Meiji period such as Yamagata Aritomo 山縣有朋 and Itō Hirobumi 伊藤博文 had been accomplished masters of Chinese studies, and Koyanagi felt that if the present-day decline of the social and political world

---

14. *Ibid.*, 255-268.

was to be stopped, a knowledge of *kangaku* and Confucian principles would have to be fostered as the basis of the Japanese spirit.

The foregoing criticisms of Western culture as being materialistic and injurious to the Japanese spirit were voiced not only
by Confucianists after 1933, but also became a rallying cry for
nationalists and militarists. Many of the younger army and navy
officers, to whom nationalism seems to have had the most appeal,
had backgrounds of difficult lives on farms or in crowded industrial centers.[15] For them, capitalism represented by such vast
industrial and financial holdings as those of Mitsui or Mitsubishi
was most distasteful.[16] And yet the kinds of activities supported
by Communists were intolerable because they weakned the nation
and implied disloyalty to the Emperor. An anonymous leaflet
circulated in 1932 among prominent Japanese political, industrial,
and military leaders by a group of Nagoya officers shows how
they were opposed to Communism and at the same time wished
to reform capitalism. Decrying the attempts of capitalists to join
forces with socialistic groups in order to allay criticism of themselves, the leaflet nevertheless advised the capitalists to divide
their wealth more equitably.

> The only thing that will save the capitalists is complete renunciation
> of their self-seeking practices and a greater respect by them of
> the principles of law and justice. It is necessary to exploit natural
> resources for the improvement of the public weal, but the wealth
> obtained by such exploitation is not the property of individuals.

---

15. O. Tanin and E. Yohan, *Militarism and Fascism in Japan*, (New York: International Publishers, 1934), 179-180.

16. *Ibid.*, 173-265. The analysis of the relations between the army and Japanese
social, economic, and political life presented by Tanin and Yohan must be accepted with
reservations. They were Soviet writers wishing to prove the validity of Marxian dialectic
with respect to Japan, and therefore often misinterpreted or distorted events. Nevertheless, their book has much useful material in it, including many quotations from Japanese sources.

It is interesting to note that in Manchuria and North China, the preserve of the
young officers and militarists, traditional Japanese industrial firms such as Mitsui were
not encouraged. Instead, inducements were made to attract new firms like the Nissan
Company, whose capital structure was different from that of Mitsui in that Nissan shares
were fairly widely distributed while Mitsui shares were concentrated in a few hands.
See G. C. Allen, *A Short Economic History of Modern Japan*, (London: George Allen and
Unwin Ltd., 1946), 148-149; also Jerome B. Cohen, *Japan's Economy in War and Reconstruction*, (Minneapolis: University of Minnesota Press, 1949), 39 ff.

Araki Sadao

The wealth should be justly distributed among the people. The capitalists of the whole country must understand these principles if they wish to escape destruction.[17]

In this dilemma, it is not surprising that many nationalists and militarists took a stand similar to that of Confucianists in criticizing both capitalism and Communism as being caused by too much concern over Western materialistic values. General Araki Sadao 荒木貞夫 (b. 1877), a vigorous exponent of Japanese expansion and one of the leaders among the so-called "young officers," expressed this attitude in a speech in 1933 on "Problems Facing Japan in the Era of Shōwa."

> From the very beginning of history Japanese superiority consisted in this, that evil and injustice never guided its actions, never took the place of high virtue in its deeds.
> Now there is, however, a basis for disquietude, as there are groups among the people, though few in number, but who taken in by foreign radical ideology and following Marxian theories sometimes forget the honor of Japan, its aim and their duty. There are also people that are conducting themselves in a way which leads to ruin, as they give themselves over to slothfulness and rest while lacking ideals and consciousness.
> It is unnecessary to speak here of the fact that the theory of materialism that does not recognize the spiritual functions of man, transforming him into a machine, robbing him of his ideals and freedom, transforming him into a public slave is harmful for a healthy society.[18]

Having flayed Communism, Araki next excoriated capitalism and egoism in society.

> To give support to the greatness of the Emperor means to realize the great ideal of Great Japan. For as it burned with the great self-realization as the Japanese people.
> However, lately, this strong national enthusiasm is gradually waning; it can even be said it is in a severely fallen state.
> As an example, we shall take the spread of frivolous ideology in society. Capitalists are concerned only with their own interests and

---

17. As quoted by Tanin and Yohan, *op. cit.*, 269.
18. *Japan Chronicle*, Mar. 22, 1933, as quoted by Tanin and Yohan, *op. cit.*, 302.

pay no attention to public life; politicians often forget the general situation in the country while absorbed in their party interest; clerks and students forget their duty giving themselves over to merriment and pleasures.[19]

Finally finishing his exposition, Araki lashed out against borrowing from the West and condemned materialism in an emotional climax.

> The Japanese people must not adopt uncritically American and European culture and weaken the traditional spirit of Japan. Developing its great spirit that has defined itself for 3,000 years, the Japanese people must strive to spread Imperial virtue. In this lies its eternal life and fame as an apostle of peace.
> Down with the heretical doctrine of materialism! Destroy vicious tendencies! One must not rely on matter.[20]

The characterization of Confucianism after 1933 as nationalized however, is not based simply on the similarity of certain attitudes taken by both Confucianists and supporters of ultranationalism. In a number of books and articles dealing with Confucianism between 1934 and 1945, it is clear that Confucianism was encouraged by the authorities as an integral part of the Japanese *kokutai* and spoken of by Confucianists and others in this manner.

For example, the veteran Confucianist, Nakamura Kyūshirō 中村久四郎 wrote in 1935 how Confucianism had influenced every phase of Japanese life. In his book entitled *Nippon bunka to Jukyō* 日本文化と儒教 (*Japanese Culture and Confucianism*),[21] he compared Confucianism to a beam which was buttressing Japanese culture. He justified the changes and deletions made to Confucianism in Japan, as for example the discarding of Mencius' theories of revolution, by quoting a passage from the *Doctrine of the Mean* (*Chung-yung* 中庸) which spoke of adjustment to environment:

---

19. *Ibid.*, 303.
20. *Ibid.*, 308-309.
21. Nakamura Kyūshirō 中村久四郎 *Nippon bunka to Jukyō* 日本文化と儒教 (*Japanese Culture and Confucianism*), (Tōkyō: Tōkō Shoin 刀江書院, 1935), 1-7.

Chungni handed down the doctrines of Yao and Shun, as if they had
been his ancestors, and elegantly displayed the regulations of Wen
and Wu taking them as his model. Above he harmonized with
the times of heaven, and below he conformed to the water and
land.[22]

Iijima Tadao 飯島忠夫 (1875-1954), author veteran Confucianist, explained the relationship of Confucianism to the *kokutai*
of Japan more in detail in a book authorized and published
in 1938 and 1940 by the Bureau of Instruction of the Ministry
of Education.[23] In the introduction to *Nippon no Jukyō; kokutai
no hongi kaisetsu sōsho* 日本の儒教，國體の本義解說叢書 (*Japanese
Confucianism; Explanatory Series on the Meaning of the National
Polity*), he spoke of the eclectic nature of Japanese Confucianism.

...[from the time Confucianism was transmitted to our country]
up to the present is a period of 1653 years. During this long period,
Confucianism has passed through numerous ups and downs, and
having been divorced from impure ideas of revolution and individualism which were mixed in it, it has finally been possible to adapt
it to our nation.[24]

In his conclusions, he stressed the same point and explained
how Confucianism could support the Imperial way.

Today, in order to give new life to Confucianism, just as Sung
learning in the past critically borrowed Buddhist philosophy and
developed a new Confucianism, so now by critically borrowing
Western philosophy, ethics, political science, and economics, and

---

22. *Chung-yung* 中庸, ch. **XXX**, 1; as translated by Legge, *Confucian Classics*, I,
427. Wan and Wu refer to Wen Wang and his son Wu Wang who became the first king
of the Chou dynasty (1122-1221 B.C.). They were revered by Confucianists and as having
opposed and overthrown the last evil ruler of the Shang dynasty, displaying virtue in
all their actions.
   The "times of heaven" refers to the seasons of the year and the regular cycles of
nature.
   23. The Bureau of Instruction (Kyōgakukyoku 教學局) is spoken of by Robert
King Hall, *Shūshin: The Ethics of a Defeated Nation*, (New York: Columbia University,
1949), 39, as the former Bureau of Thought Control (Shisōkyoku 思想局). The name of
the latter was apparently changed on July 21, 1937, but its functions of thought control
continued.
   24. Iijima Tadao, *Nippon no Jukyō; kokutai no hongi kaisetsu sōsho* 日本の儒教,
國體の本義解說叢書 (*Japanese Confucianism: Explanatory Series on the Meaning of
the Japanese Polity*), 5th edition, (Tōkyō: Kyōgakukyoku 教學局, 1941), introduction.

embellishing Confucianism with them, Confucianism can become a supporting wing of the Imperial way. And impure ideas of revolution and individualism having been put aside, Japan alone will be the country in which the pure essence [of Confucianism] is cultivated.[25]

The ultranationalist Ōkawa Shūmei 大川周明, in his very popular book *Shintei Nippon nisen roppyakunen shi* 新訂日本二千六百年史 (*The Two Thousand Six Hundred Year History of Japan, Newly Revised*), also praised Japan as the only country in which Confucian doctrines were still alive. Ōkawa said this was due to the Japanese spirit giving new life to Confucianism, which had thus become part of Japanese culture.

We Japanese first had contact with Chinese thought and culture, and we made it our own; and then we had contact with Indian thought and culture which we also made our own. These fields of thought and culture, which may be termed the two extremes of Asian mentality, due to having been given direction by the Japanese spirit, have continued to exist and develop up to the present... And isn't the quintessence of Chinese thought and the basis of Chinese civilization the teachings of Confucius and Mencius? These teachings remain alive in Japan, but have died in China. Confucianism, as moral and disciplinary knowledge, and finally as virtue, has been unable to elevate the Chinese people, nor has it politically been able to make them progress.... But only in Japan from the first introduction of Confucianism, with such sad evidence as the suicide of Prince Wakiiratsuko as proof, we have strictly carried out the teaching of Confucius and Mencius. Therefore Confucianism has raised the level of virtue of the Japanese people.[26]

---

25. *Ibid.*, 102.

26. Ōkawa Shūmei, *Shintei Nippon nissen roppyakunen shi* 新訂日本二千六百年史 (*The Two Thousand Six Hundred Year History of Japan, Newly Revised*), 21st ed. (Tōkyō: Daiichi Shobō 第一書房, 1940), 22-23. Prince Uji no Wakiiratsuko 菟道稚郎子 was the son of Emperor Ōjin 應仁 (ca. 390-409) and the heir apparent. The traditional story of Wakiiratsuko's death was that influenced by Confucianism, he felt that he was unworthy to become Emperor and wished to give up his succession to his brother. When the latter refused, Wakiiratsuko committed suicide. The concept of having the most virtuous man rule was idealized by Confucianists who held up the example of Yao 堯 passing over his own son as unworthy and instead choosing Shun 舜 as his successor. It is most unlikely, however, that such concepts actually had anything to do with Wakiiratsuko's death, as Confucianism had only been introduced into Japan about a decade before the prince's suicide in 410. It is more probable that later historians used such ideas to give a vicious succession struggle the aura of virtue. See John Joseph Spae,

In 1944, the well-known scholar Kiyowara Sadao wrote on "The Japanization of Oriental Thoughts" in the English language magazine *Contemporary Japan*. Kiyowara stressed the fact that Confucianism had become entirely assimilated into the Japanese *kokutai*, and he laid down a basic postulate for such assimilation.

> In order to digest both Oriental and Occidental civilizations and combine and unify their various elements upon the basis of our characteristic culture, there must be an unshakable guiding principle. Needless to say, our guiding principle is the genius of our national polity. It consists in the unity of our nation with the Imperial Family as the sole nucleus, around which all national activities are carried on.... Therefore in nationalizing foreign thoughts and cultures, we take in only those elements and features which, after due modification, are found to fit into our Emperor-centric way of life.[27]

Kiyowara then discussed the history of Confucianism and other philosophies in Japan and showed how Confucianism had been united with the Japanese *kokutai*.

> The theory of national constitution or polity developed by Mito scholars denotes the true Japanization of Confucian doctrine. By taking advantage of the Chinese ideas of the "Middle Kingdom," they demonstrated that Japan is the true "Middle Empire" on the ground of facts about the founding of the Empire and events in our national history. They recognized the importance of the precepts of the "three ties of humanity" and the "five cardinal virtues" in the Confucian doctrine, and argued that "these are manifested in the benevolent administration of the successive Emperors and in the loyalty of the subjects to their sovereigns of unbroken lineage."[28]

But the extent to which the ideas of Japanese Confucianists became generally used by the Japanese for indoctrinating youth in loyalty to the state and for disparaging the so-called materi-

---

Itō Jinsai, Monumenta Serica Monograph Series, XII, (Peiping: Catholic University of Peking, 1948), 16-17. One should note that Spae mistakenly refers to Uji no Wakiiratsuko as the elder brother in this apparent succession dispute, although the crown prince, Wakiiratsuko, was the younger brother.

27. Kiyowara Sadao, "Japanization of Oriental Thoughts," *Contemporary Japan*, XIII, 7-9 (July-Sept., 1944), 726.

28. *Ibid.*, 735. For a description of the use of Confucianism by the Mito school, see ch. I, sec. 4 of this study.

alistic concepts of the West can only be appreciated through an analysis of the contents of official school textbooks. In these books, however, criticism of the West as materialistic was no longer held up as a Confucian idea, nor were loyalty and filial piety to the Emperor spoken of as Confucian. These ideas had come to be part and parcel of Japanese thinking and were apparently considered valuable for giving the individual Japanese emotional security and faith in the justice of Japan's world mission. Although it is difficult to assess such intangible psychological factors, nevertheless it seems undeniable that without some such faith, the Japanese could not have fought so stubbornly or endured the hardships they did during the second World War.[29]

Ethics textbooks used in compulsory morals courses[30] in elementary and middle schools provide the first example of how certain Confucian precepts had become a basic part of desired patterns of behavior.[31] Loyalty and filial piety were constantly extolled as basic to family life, harmony in society, and the carrying out of one's duties to the Emperor. In describing a type to be admired, the ethics textbooks said:

> In our homes, our parents are always devoting their strength to family occupations, the education of their children, and the prosperity of their homes and country. We their children must obey our

---

29. The writer himself has heard of cases in which diaries picked up from dead Japanese soldiers in the field spoke of how the material superiority of the enemy could be overcome by the greater spiritual strength of the Japanese.

30. In Hugh Keenleyside and A. F. Thomas, *History of Japanese Education and Present Educational System*, (Tōkyō: Hokuseidō Press, 1937), 186-194, the number of hours of morals instruction required per week in 1933 in elementary, higher elementary, and middle schools is indicated. The ratio of hours of instruction in morals to the total number of hours of instruction was as follows: 1st grade—2/21; 2nd—2/23; 3rd—2/25; 4th—2/29 for girls and 2/27 for boys; 5th—2/30 for girls and 2/28 for boys; 6th—2/30 for girls and 2/29 for boys. In higher elementary school the ratio was: 1st grade—2/30 for girls and 2/29 for boys; 2nd—2/30 for girls and 2/29 for boys; 3rd—2/31 for girls and 2/30 for boys. In middle school the ratio was: 1st grade—1/30; 2nd—1/30; 3rd—1/32: 4th—1/30-35; 5th—1/30-35.

31. In the Seventh Biennial Conference of the World Federation of Education Associations, *Education in Japan*, (Tōkyō: The World Conference Committee of the Japanese Education Association, 1937) I, 390, the titles of the chapters of the ethics textbooks used in elementary school in 1937 are translated, and the ratio of the number of titles related to Confucian subjects to the total number of titles for each year is as follows: 1st year, 4/27; 2nd, 6/27; 3rd, 7/27; 4th, 7/27; 5th, 10/27; 6th, 7/27.

parents' instructions, be filial to them, and, by keeping harmony among our brothers and sisters, set our parents mind at ease.

We must be sincere in everything we do. Our personal conduct will then naturally become just and we shall become men of virtue.

All these reminders are consistent with the aim and purpose of the Imperial Rescript on Education. We must keep this Imperial Will deep in our hearts and practice these instructions with sincerity —and thus become good Japanese.[32]

This passage praised Confucian virtues of harmony, and filial piety, as well as the Imperial Rescript on Education, whose relationship to Confucianism already has been discussed.[33] It also emphasizes sincerity as a means of attaining virtue. This is significant because Confucianists considered that sincerity had almost mystical power wherewith man could transform himself. The *Doctrine of the Mean* explained it by saying:

Sincerity is that whereby self-completion is effected, and its way is that by which man must direct himself. Sincerity is the end and beginning of things; without sincerity, there would be nothing. On this account, the superior man regards the attainment of sincerity as the most excellent thing. The possessor of sincerity does not merely accomplish the self-completion of himself. With this quality he completes other men and things also. The completing of himself shows his perfect virtue.[34]

The ethics textbooks did not, however, mention these types of Confucian virtues merely abstractly or theoretically. Stirring examples of loyalty, filial piety, and sincere devotion to duty were taken from Japanese history. For example, in the section describing the loyalty of Kusunoki Masashige 楠木正成 to the Emperor Go-Daigo 後醍醐 (1287-1338), the teacher's manual explained that, "The purpose of this chapter is to strengthen [the children's] determination to exert full devotion and faith towards their Sovereign...."[35] When dealing with filial piety, the ethics

---

32. Hall, *op. cit.*, 231.

33. See ch. II, sec. 4, of this study.

34. *Chung-yung*, ch. XXV, 1-3; as translated by Legge, *Confucian Classics*, I, 418-419.

35. Hall, *op. cit.*, 114-115. See ch. I, p. 33 of this study for a description of Masashige's loyal service to the Emperor Go-Daigo.

textbook gave the example of Yoshida Shōin 吉田松陰 (1830-59) who said in a letter:

> We have splendid traditions in our family. These are: to worship Gods, to respect our ancestors, to be harmonious with our relatives, to pursue knowledge diligently, and to cultivate our own fields. These things our parents do and we must do likewise. It is what we call filial piety.[36]

In addition to ethics textbooks for compulsory courses on morals in elementary and middle school, the *Kokutai no hongi* 國體の本義 (*Cardinal Principles of the National Polity*) was officially published and disseminated after 1937.[37] This book, characterized as defining the official Japanese theory of the state immediately before the second World War, was required reading in all schools above the secondary school level and required inservice study for all elementary and middle school teachers.[38] The purpose of *Kokutai no hongi* was overtly nationalistic,..."to clarify our national entity and to cultivate and awaken national sentiment and consciousness."[39] In view of the increasing nationalization of Confucianism after 1933, it is not surprising to find many Confucian ideas in the text, although as in the case of the ethics textbooks, these ideas were not labeled as Confucian.

Describing loyalty and filial piety in Japan, *Kokutai no hongi* explained:

> Filial piety in our country has its true characteristics in its perfect conformity with our national entity by heightening still further the relationship between morality and nature. Our country is a great family nation, and the Imperial Household is the head family of the subjects and the nucleus of national life. The subjects revere the Imperial Household which is the head family, with the tender

---

36. Hall, *op. cit.*, 135.
37. The *Kokutai no hongi* is reported to have had a tremendous circulation. There were 1,900,000 official copies distributed in the first 6 years following its first publication, and many more were privately printed. See Hall, *op. cit.*, 56.
38. *Ibid.*, 56-57.
39. *Kokutai no hongi* 國體の本義, as translated by John Owen Gauntlett, *Kokutai No Hongi: Cardinal Principles of the National Entity of Japan*, edited with an introduction by Robert King Hall (Cambridge: Harvard University Press, 1949), 50.

esteem [they have] for their ancestors; and the Emperor loves his subjects as his very own.... In our country there is no filial piety apart from loyalty, and filial piety has loyalty for its basis.⁴⁰

The emphasis in the above passage on the relations between subject and ruler and father and son is probably the most recurrent theme in the whole of *Kokutai no hongi*. Despite the fact that these relations are spoken of as pristine Japanese ones, their debt to Confucianism is implied at various points. For example, in describing the reforms of the Taika 大化 era (645 A.D.), the spirit of the reforms was said to have its origin in the clarification of the meaning of the moral obligations between sovereign and subject,⁴¹ as set forth in Prince Shōtoku's so-called "Seventeen Article Constitution."⁴² In discussing "The Life of the People," these relationships were also mentioned.

> In short, a characteristic of our national life lies in the merging into one, under the Emperor. This is the reason for the existence of the Way in which the relationship between the Sovereign and his subjects should lie in righteousness, and in which the relationship between father and child should lie in feelings of attachment, and this is also why there runs through family life and national life a beautiful sentiment, with the Sovereign and his subjects united as one and with parents and their children living in concord.⁴³

When speaking of morality in Japan, the assimilation of Confucian elements was acknowledged in the *Kokutai no hongi*, but once again, particular stress was put on the relations of sovereign and subject and father and son.

> Our national morality is founded on reverence for the deities and our ancestors, and has brought forth the fruits of the great principles of loyalty and filial piety; and filial piety becomes loyalty. Herein do loyalty and filial piety join in one and become the source of all good.⁴⁴

---

40. *Ibid.*, 89-90.
41. *Ibid.*, 110.
42. *Ibid.*, 110. See Spae, *op. cit.*, 18-20. for an analysis of the Confucian elements in the "Seventeen Article Constitution."
43. Gauntlett, *Kokutai No Hongi*, 126-127.
44. *Ibid.*, 144.

The value of stressing these relationships was that it made the Emperor and the state symbols closely associated with a traditional ethical standard still strong in Japan. The divinity of the Emperor and Shintō mythology further increased the appeal of these secular Confucian moral principles to the extent that they could become a source of emotional and fanatical action in a time of crisis.

In view of the importance of Confucian ethical values for realizing the kind of Japanese society pictured in *Kokutai no hongi*, it is natural to find that the book made attacks on forces considered subversive of these traditional values. It recommended the principles in the book *Yōgaku kōyō* 幼學綱要 (*Fundamentals of Education for the Young*) for teaching how properly to assimilate the knowledge of science and material things to the spirit of the Japanese *kokutai*.[45] The *Yōgaku kōyō*, largely Confucian in content, already has been described as an attempt to restore traditional morality in the face of Western influences in the early Meiji period.[46] This recommendation to use the *Yōgaku kōyō* is significant because it shows the similarity, by the 1930's, between the ideas of Confucianists on how to sublimate Western civilization to spiritual values, and the avowed beliefs of many Japanese nationalists and militarists on how to deal with the influence of Western civilization. As the *Kokutai no hongi* expressed it:

> To put it in a nutshell, while the strong points of Occidental learning and concepts lie in their analytical and intellectual qualities, the characteristics of Oriental learning and concepts lie in their intuitive and ascetic qualities. Our nation has in the past imported, assimilated, and sublimated Chinese and Indian ideologies, and has therewith supported the Imperial Way, making possible the establishment of an original culture based on her national entity. Following the Meiji Restoration Occidental cultures poured in with a rush and contributed immensely towards our national prosperity; but their individualistic qualities soon brought about various difficulties in all the phases of the lives of our people, causing their thoughts to

45. *Ibid.*, 155-157.
46. See ch. II, 72-73, of this study.

fluctuate. However, now is the time for us to sublimate and assimilate these Occidental ideologies in keeping with our national entity, to set up a vast new Japanese culture, and, by taking advantage of these things, to bring about a great national development.[47]

An even more forceful description of the official views concerning Western culture and its proper position relative to Japan can be found in the booklet *Shimmin no michi* 臣民の道 (*The Way of the Subject*).

> In retrospection, this country has been widely seeking knowledge in the world since the Meiji Restoration thereby fostering and maintaining the prosperity of the same. With the influx of European and American culture into this country, however, individualism, liberalism, utilitarianism, and materialism began to assert themselves, with the result that the traditional character of the country was much impaired and the virtuous habits and customs bequeathed by our ancestors were affected unfavorably.
>
> If this situation is left unremedied, it will be difficult to eradicate the evils of European and American thought that are deeply penetrating various strata of the national life of Japan, and to achieve the unprecedentedly great tasks by establishing a structure of material solidarity of guarding and maintaining the prosperity of the Imperial throne. Herein lies an urgent need of discarding the self-centered and utilitarian ideas and elevating and practicing the way of the subjects of the Emperor based on state service as the primary requisite.[48]

Shimmin no michi was first published by the Kyōgakukyoku 教學局 of the Ministry of Education in 1937 and subsequently distributed by the millions of copies.[49] It not only criticized Western utilitarianism and individualism, but also stressed the importance of a subject's loyal service to the Emperor as being a reflection of filial piety in the home.

This same criticism of Western civilization and emphasis on loyalty and filial piety had characterized Japanese Confucianism since the Meiji Restoration. It was not really until the

---

47. Gauntlett, *Kokutai No Hongi*, 178.
48. *Shimmin no michi* 臣民の道 (*Way of the Subject*), as translated by Otto D. Tolischus, *Tokyo Record*, (New York: Reynal and Hitchcock, 1943), 405-406.
49. Hall, *op. cit.*, 68-69.

1930's, however, that the adoption of these elements into an active political and educational program by the government took place. This marks the nationalization of Confucianism, and sets off the 1934 to 1945 period from earlier ones when Confucianism was struggling to maintain itself on at least a semi-independent basis.

To fully appreciate this amalgamation of Confucian ideas into the increasingly nationalistic ideology of Japan during these years, one must keep in mind that it was not an experience unique to Confucianism alone. As D. C. Holtom so ably points out in his book, *Modern Japan and Shinto Nationalism,* universal religions like Christianity and Buddhism also were made to play a part in fostering Japanese nationalism and ideas of loyal, selfless service to the state.[50] Confucian principles, however, much more than those of these other universal creeds, came to be characterized as purely Japanese, although in propaganda and political activities on the Asiatic continent, Japanese leaders continued to emphasize the common heritage provided by Confucianism for uniting all Asia.

2. Japanese Support for Confucianism in Korea.

One of the earliest examples of how the Japanese attempted to take advantage of the universal appeal of Confucianism in their political activities in Asia was in Korea. With the annexation of Korea in 1910, the Japanese were faced with the serious problem of dealing with the political unrest caused by the hostility of the Koreans. Military force, of course, constituted the primary measure used by the Japanese for enforcing their will during the first decade or so of their rule in Korea,[51] but

---

50. D. C. Holtom, *Modern Japan and Shinto Nationalism,* revised edition, (Chicago: University of Chicago Press, 1947); see chapters IV and V dealing respectively with "Japanese Christianity and Shinto Nationalism," and "Buddhism and Japanese Nationalism."

51. See Hatada Takashi 旗田巍, *Chōsen shi* 朝鮮史 (*History of Korea*), Iwanami series 154 (Tōkyō: Iwanami Shoten 岩波書店, 1951), ch. VII, sec. 1, for a good description by a Japanese himself on this subject. He refers to Japanese rule in Korea from 1910 to 1919 as *budan seiji* 武斷政治 (military rule).

The Main building of the former Sŏnggyun'gwan.

apparently some effort was also made at trying to identify Japanese rule with traditional Korean ways.

Confucianism was foremost among traditional Korean ways, for it had dominated all aspects of life in the peninsula since 1392,[52] to an extent unknown in either China or Japan. After the opening up of Korea to Western nations in 1882, Western ideas began to challenge Confucianism, but the knell that really augured the end of Confucian dominance was the abolishment of the kwagŏ 科擧 (national examinations) in 1894.[53] The kwagŏ was a system of national examinations whereby candidates were chosen for government service, patterned after the old examination system in China. Because it was primarily a literary examination, based on a knowledge of the Confucian classics, it had served to perpetuate Confucian thought. Once the kwagŏ was abolished, however, the raison-d'être for acquiring the detailed knowledge of the Confucian classics needed to qualify as a Confucian scholar disappeared.

Despite this, the number of recognized Confucian scholars teaching throughout Korea as late as 1928 numbered over 15,000.[54] Furthermore, in 1918 the Government-General of Chōsen was induced officially to recognize local Confucian village schools known as sŏdang 書堂. The reason for this was that the sŏdang were so numerous that the Japanese felt they could not be abolished. Therefore the yhoped that by controlling the sŏdang instead, these might help to provide educational opportunities in areas where there were still no government schools.[55]

Considering this background, it is not strange that the Japanese attempted to associate their rule with traditional Confucian elements, for they were no doubt aware that they might thereby obtain the support of an important group in the population. In

---

52. For a trenchant analysis of the over-all influence of Confucianism on Korean life from 1392-1910, see *Yun Munhaksa yuko* 尹文學士遺藁 (*Posthumous Works of Mr. Yun, M.A.*), (Keijō: Chōsen Insatsu Kabushiki Kaisha 朝鮮印刷株式會社, 1933), 139-146.
53. The *kwagŏ* and its history are described in detail by Homer Hulbert, "National Examination in Korea," *T.A.K.B.R.A.S.*, XIV (1923), 9-32.
54. *Chōsen no shūraku (zen-pen)* 朝鮮の聚落（前篇）(*Korean Villages, first vol.*), research series No. 38 (Keijō Chōsen Sōtokufu 朝鮮總督府, 1933), 69.
55. *Ibid.*, 68-69.

1911, the Emperor had given 250,000 yen for restoring the Sŏng-gyun'gwan 成均館,[56] the institution which had been the center of Confucian activities in Korea until 1894. The Government-General of Chōsen at the same time changed the name of the old institution to Keigakuin 經學院, reinstituted Confucian spring and autumn ceremonies, made provisions for local Confucian temples to be reactivated with the Keigakuin as a model, and arranged for Confucianists to travel throughout the provinces on lecture tours.

At the ceremonies held in 1911 on the occasion of the establishment of the Keigakuin, Governor General Terauchi Masatake 寺內正毅 (1852-1919) made an address to clarify the purpose of the new organization.

> As shown by the regulations, the Keigakuin has been established with a view to studying the Chinese classics, and conducting services at the Confucian shrine in Seoul, thereby to help forward improvement in the culture of the people. By so doing, the government intends not only to show respect to old men of virtue and high character, and thereby encourage the good custom of holding in high esteem Confucian literati and men of learning, but also to go a step further and contribute to the promotion of virtues and the cultivation of morals. The duties expected of it are indeed big and heavy....
>
> His Majesty has now graciously been pleased to grant a sum of 250,000 yen to provide the fund of the Keigakuin, and there is certainly nobody who is not impressed with the gracious behest of His Majesty. It is sincerely required of functionaries and lecturers of the institution not to be satisfied with merely reading books and conducting Confucian festivals, but to endeavor to make themselves models for their neighbors to rectify their evils, and promote their good habits and thus promote the culture of the public at large.[57]

Such attempts to revive Confucianism in Korea do not seem

---

56. Bureau of Education, *Manual of Education in Chōsen*, (Seoul: Government-General of Chosen, 1920), 112.

57. *Ibid.*, 113-114. The regulations of the Keigakuin spoken of by Terauchi may be found in Oda Shōgo 小田省吾 and Ŏ Yun-jŏk 魚允迪, *Chōsen bunbyō oyobi shōbu Juken* 朝鮮文廟及陞廡儒賢 (*Korean Confucian Temples and Canonized Confucian Sages*), (Keijō: Chōsen Shi Gakkai 朝鮮史學會, 1924), supplement. The Keigakuin published a monthly periodical known as the *Keigakuin zasshi* 經學院雜誌.

to have met with much response on the part of young people,[58] but among older Koreans, especially the more conservative, landowning gentry, some Confucian revival groups were formed and contact made with the Shibunkai in Japan.[59]

At the celebration held in 1922 by the Shibunkai in Tōkyō commemorating the 2400th anniversary of Confucius' death, a number of Koreans were present, including Baron Pak Ki-yang 朴箕陽 representing the Keigakuin, Ŏ Yun-jŏk 魚允迪 representing the Advisory Council (Chungj'uwŏn 中樞院) of the Governor-General of Chōsen, and Chang Sang-j'ŏl 張相轍 representing a Confucian organization from North Kyŏngsang Province.[60] The significance of this participation of Korean Confucianists in a Confucian celebration in Japan can probably best be understood by noting a speech made during these ceremonies by Mizuno Rentarō 水野錬太郎. Mizuno was Minister of Home Affairs (*Naimu*

---

58. Takahashi Tōru 高橋亨, "Chōsen ni okeru Jukyō" 朝鮮に於ける儒教 ("Confucianism in Korea") *Shibun* 斯文, V, 1 (Jan. 1923), 88-89. Takahashi, who was a professor of Chinese literature and philosophy in Korea, delivered a lecture on Korean Confucianism at Tōkyō 東京 Imperial University as part of a program sponsored by the Shibunkai. He said that Korean Confucianism of the future would need Japanese support to be revived because of the tendency among young people in Korea to consider it old-fashioned and valueless. Takahashi himself had been sent by the Government-General in 1911 to Chŏlla Province 全羅道, Ch'ungch'ŏng Province 忠清道, and Kyŏngsang Province 慶尙道 in south Korea to investigate the condition of Cofucianism there. Takahashi Tōru 高橋亨, *Richō Bukkyō* 李朝佛教 (*Buddhism of the Yi dynasty*), Chōsen shisōshi taikei series no. 1 朝鮮思想史大系第一 (Tōkyō and Ōsaka: Hōbunkan 寶文館, 1929), 3.

59. A sightseeing trip of Korean Confucianists came to Japan for the first time in 1920, led by the Korean vice-governor of North Kyŏngsang Province 慶尙北道, Sin Yang-lin 申錫麟. They were met by Hattori Unokichi 服部宇之吉 and Sakatani Yoshio 阪谷芳郎, both important members of the Shibunkai, and the Koreans and Japanese exchanged speeches on how Confucianism could contribute to world peace by strengthening the morality of people everywhere and encouraging moderation. *Shibun*, II, 6 (Dec., 1920), 454. These kinds of trips by Korean Confucianists to Japan seem to have continued, for in November 1924, the *Shibun* noted that the fifth inspection trip sponsored by North Kyŏngsang Province Confucianists visited the temporary buildings of the Shibunkai at Yushima 湯島 in Tōkyō; *Shibun*, VI, 6 (Dec., 1924), 319. The only member of this group that the writer has been able to identify is Yu Man-gyŏm 俞萬兼 a pro-Japanese Korean from a respected old Korean noble family. Yu Man-gyŏm 俞萬兼 later became governor of South Ch'ungch'ŏng province 忠清南道 under the Japanese, and his younger brother, Yu Ŏk-kyŏm 俞億兼, delivered speeches during the second World War denouncing the United States. It is interesting to note, however, that the latter was made Korean head of the Department of Education from 1945-47 under the United States Military Government. The "Purpose and Objectives of Korean Education" drawn up under his direction in 1945-46 were Confucian in character, seeking the cultivation of the "man of benevolence" as the ideal citizen.

60. *Shibun*, IV, 6 (Dec., 1922), 350-360.

daijin 內務大臣) in 1922, but he had been the Chief Civil Administrator (*Seimu sōkan* 政務総監) under the Governor-General of
Chōsen from 1919 to 1922. His comments concerning Korean
Confucianism therefore refer to efforts in Korea made during
his administration to revive Confucianism.

> Up until recently, for the sake of the Korean people I have been
> connected with the Korean government, and I think that the en-
> couragement of the Confucian spring and autumn sacrificial cere-
> monies for the sake of the customs, teaching and morality of the
> people has been most profitable. And like this Shibunkai in Japan,
> influential organizations in Korea have become institutions of en-
> lightment based on Confucian teachings both for the sake of the
> Japanese, and of course for the sake of the Koreans. I also feel
> confident that they have exerted a beneficient influence, and further-
> more cannot restrain my joy at the fact that this has been of value
> in the rapprochment between Japan and Korea.[61]

After the outbreak of the independence movement in Korea
on March 1, 1919, the Japanese realized that an administration
based purely on military strength was impractical, for besides
arousing the opposition of Koreans of all classes, it led the rest
of the world to condemn the Japanese for their brutality. Even
the famous Korean Confucianist Kim Yun-sik 金允植(1835-1920),
who had favored the Japanese and had been raised to the peerage
and appointed by them as first head of the Keigakuin in 1911,
took part in the independence movement.[62] In a petition written
by him and another titled Korean to the Governor-General,
Hasegawa Yoshimichi 長谷川好道 (1850-1924), they returned the
honors given to them by the Japanese, declaring:

> A man's life is not something to be dealt with as the grass that
> grows. In ancient times Mencius said to king Sun of the Che
> kingdom, "If by taking possession of the state you can make the
> people of Yun happy, take possession; but if taking possession will
> render them miserable, forbear to do it."

---

    61. *Ibid.*, 54.
    62. *Chōsen jimmei jisho* 朝鮮人名辞書 (*Korean Biographical Dictionary*), 2nd
edition (Keijō: Chōsen Sōtokufu Chūsūin 朝鮮總督府中樞院, 1938), 1999.

Kim Yun-sik

Though Mencius spoke, the King paid no attention, and as a result, came to a place where he finally said that he was greatly ashamed. This is, indeed, a mirror from history worthy to be looked into. Even the sage cannot run counter to the times in which he lives. We read the mind of God in the attitude of the people. If the people are not made happy, history tells us that there is no way by which their land can be held in possession.

We your seervants have come to these times of danger and difficulty. Old and shameless are we, for when our country was annexed, we accepted the rank of nobility, held office, and lived in disgrace, till, seeing these innocent people of ours in the fire and water, are unable to endure the sight longer. Thus we too in privacy have shouted for independence just like the others.[63]

In order to remedy this situation, the Japanese tried to liberalize their administration, choosing a relatively progressive man, Saitō Makoto 齋藤實 (1858-1936), as the new Governor-General in August 1919. Reforms were instituted to make the government less militaristic, and in particular, a measure of participation in the administration by certain Koreans was invited. Such participation, however, was limited to propertied classes and was further restricted because Koreans could usually only give advice and not determine policy.[64] Nevertheless, this effort by the Japanese to enlist the support of powerful and wealthy Koreans is significant and helps make clear some of the reasons why the Japanese may have considered it worthwhile openly to back Confucianism in Korea. One should also note that the Government-General felt that Christian groups were implicated in the Korean independence movement of 1919. From this point of view, the increasing support for Confucianism by the Government-General can be interpreted as an attempt to encourage groups which were unsympathetic and opposed to the spread of Christianity.

63. Elizabeth Keith and E. K. Robertson Scott, *Old Korea, the Land of Morning Calm*, (London and New York: Hutchinson and Co., 1946), 40-41.

64. Hatada, *op. cit.*, 210-211. George M. McCune, with the collaboration of Arthur L. Grey Jr., *Korea Today*, (Cambridge: Harvard University Press, 1950), 24-25. Andrew J. Grajdanzev, *Modern Korea*, (New York: Institute of Pacific Relations, 1944), 46-47, 243-249.

In Korea, much as in China, a particular relationship between the landed gentry and the bureaucracy had existed in which paths to advancement depended on passing examinations based on the Confucian classics. This examination system, theoretically open to all, had become rigid and circumscribed through the formation of a hereditary upper class known as *yangban* 兩班 who virtually monopolized all government positions in the latter part of the Yi dynasty (1392-1910). The *yangban* class itself considered it degrading to engage in any kind of physical labor and extolled literary pursuits as the only proper concern for superior men. Although the national examination system had come to an end in 1894, and the privileges of the *yangban* had been nominally abolished in the Japanese inspired reforms of 1894-95,[65] the *yangban* retained their power because most of the land was still in their hands. Due to this, even in the 1920's and 1930's Confucianism probably still had an appeal to the landowning groups as being a stabilizing force in society. Therefore, when Japanese administrators such as Mizuno Rentarō spoke of the rapprochment which a revival of Confucianism was bringing between Koreans and Japanese, his reference was most applicable to the Korean hereditary landowning classes for whom Confucianism naturally recommended itself.

The membership and make-up of a Korean Confucian organization formed in the early 1930's, the Taedong Samunhoe 大東斯文會, confirms this relationship, for the president and chairman of the organization were members of the Korean royal family,[66] and among the advisors to the Taedong Samunhoe were many representatives of the best old Korean *yangban* families.[67] It is

65. Oda Shōgo 小田省吾 and Sugimoto Tadasuke 杉本正介, *Chōsen shi taikei; saikinsei shi* 朝鮮史大系最近世史 (*Outline History of Korea; History of the Modern Period*), 3rd edition (Keijō: Chōsen Shi Gakkai 朝鮮史學會, 1929), 130-131. For more details on the economic and social ramifications of the reforms of 1894-95, see: Chōsen Shi Henshūkai 朝鮮史編修會, *Kindai Chōsen shi kenkyū* 近代朝鮮史研究 (*Study of Recent Korean History*), (Keijō: Chōsen Sōtokufu 朝鮮總督府, 1944), 78 ff.

66. They were respectively: Viscount Min Yŏng-hwi 閔泳徽, and Viscount Min Pyŏng-sok 閔丙奭. *Chosŏn sŭngmu Yunhyŏn nyŏnp'yo* 朝鮮陞廡儒賢年表 (*Chronological Table of the Canonized Korean Confucian Sages*), (Keijō: Taedong Samunhoe 大東斯文會, 1928), 8 (Taedong Samunhoe chikwŏn 大東斯文會職員). Both were considered pro-Japanese.

67. Some of the better known were: Yun Yong-gu 尹用求, Yi Chae-gon 李載崐,

significant to note that the Governor-General, Saitō Makoto, the former Chief Civil Administrator, Mizuno Rentarō, as well as other notable Japanese such as Prince Tokugawa Iesato 德川家達, Shibusawa Eiichi 澁澤榮一, Hattori Unokichi 服部宇之吉, and Sakatani Yoshio 阪谷芳郎 were also advisors to the Taedong Samunhoe. One may deduce from this that it was mainly among conservative, wealthy groups in both countries that Confucianism had value for bringing together Koreans and Japanese.

It would be a mistake, however, to interpret this rapprochment entirely from the point of view of economic determinism, for Korean Confucianists seem to have held many beliefs which were the same as those of supporters of Confucianism in Japan simply because both had the same Confucian frame of reference for social and philosophical problems. This is evident from statements made by individual Korean Confucianists discussing the value of Confucianism and Oriental culture. Ŏ Yunjŏk 魚允迪 (1868-1935), for example, in a speech given on March 9, 1924 dealing with Korea's eighteen canonized Confucian sages and the future of Confucianism, concluded by saying:

> Now when the Way [of Confucius] exists in the world, morality always becomes clear; instruction is greatly carried out; and both man and things respectively attain peace. But when Confucianism is lacking in the world, order becomes confused; the weak become the food of the strong; and the whole world is transformed into birds and beasts. This is an unchanging principle.
>
> What is called Confucianism, that is to say its learning, originally was neither a special matter, nor was it lofty or remote or hard to carry out. Therefore Yulgok[68] always said: "Of old there was no

---

Baron Yi Yun-yong 李允用, Marquis Pak Yŏng-hyo 朴泳孝, Yu Sŏng-jun 兪星濬, and Chang Hŏn-sik 張憲植. *Ibid.*, 8-9 (Taedong Samunhoe chikwŏn). All these men were wealthy and collaborated openly with the Japanese. The writer knew Chang Hŏn-sik personally. The latter was governor of South Chŏlla Province 全羅南道, North Ch'ungchŏng Province 忠清北道, and South P'yŏngan Province 平安南道 under the Japanese, and he described his administration as one of "carrying out benevolent government." Chang lived in Seoul until 1950, but he was taken into north Korea by the retreating Communist armies in September of that year. His grandson, Chang Nam-gi 張南基, from whom the above information was obtained, is at present teaching Korean at the Army Language School in Monterey, California.

68. Yi I 李珥 (1536-84; gō: Yulgok 栗谷) was one of Korea's most famous Neo-Confucian scholars. His interpretations of the Confucian classics were particularly

special purpose for names. There was simply a daily use of the social relationships, each being carried out as it ought to be and that was all. In later times, Confucian learning was not understood. Social relationships were followed blindly, so [people] took that which ought to be done and named it Confucian learning. But even though the name of Confucian learning had been established, it was pointed at and looked [down on] by the people. This was the great lament of later generations."

How true these words are! Now, besides this, [Confucianism] is also given the name of conservative and looked upon as reactionary, so that those wearing Confucian caps and gowns can hardly avoid being called thus. Yet the division of those who stick to the past and those who flock to the modern arose due to this, and it has brought about the evil of mutual antagonism. Indeed, it is an extreme misfortune for Confucianism in the world. However, so-called Confucianism, that is the daily carrying out of that which ought to be done, no matter what the period or what kind of world [exists], is above the existence of mankind. Therefore, not only need there be no worry over [Confucianism] being extinguished, but the latter is tending to have great [prospects] for development and advance in the future.

This is not only my shallow viewpoint; it already is the established theory of a precursor. He was Sakuma Shōzan,[69] one of the great men [just] before the Meiji Restoration. Someone asked him: "If the new learning of the West comes in more and more, will the Way of Confucius, so-called Confucianism, be swept away? What do you think?" Shōzan said: "Up to now, the tendency has been to view the greatness of the Confucian Way. At present, Confucius is the sage only of the East. From the mutual contact of East and West, he will certainly become a world-wide Confucius. This fact is to be greatly rejoiced at."

Among Ch'ing dynasty Confucianists was Li Hsuan-lu.[70] It was at the time of the disorders of the Taokuang period (1821-51).

---

valued, although they were opposed by the school of Yi Hwang 李滉 (1501-70; gō: T'oege 退溪). For details on the philosophical beliefs of Yi I, as well as of his great opponent Yi Hwang, see the study by Takahashi Tōru 高橋亨, "Richō Jugakushi ni okeru shuriha shukiha no hattatsu" 李朝儒學史に於ける主理派主氣派の發達 ("Development of the Schools of Form and Matter in the History of Confucianism in the Yi dynasty") included in the collection, Chōsen Shina bunka no kenkyū 朝鮮支那文化の研究 (Studies of Korean and Chinese Culture), edited by the Keijō Teikoku Daigaku Hōbun Gakkai 京城帝國大學法文學會 (Tōkyō: Tōkō Shoin 刀江書院, 1929), 141-281.

69. Sakuma Shōzan 佐久間象山 (1811-64) was a Japanese Confucianist of the last years of the Tokugawa period who was in favor of a synthesis of elements of Western civilization with Confucianism. See ch. I, p. 26-27 of this study.

70. Li Hsuan-lu 李玄呂 was neither listed in Arthur W. Hummel, Eminent Chinese

English and French allied armies had taken Peking.[71] Someone also
asked him whether due to the eastward movement of Western
power, Confucianism would die out. Hsuan-lu said: "Confucianism
will necessarily flourish from this. The East and the West mutually
conciliating and sharing ideas together, then the latter will certainly
greatly revere Confucianism. Indeed, this is to be felicitated."

Furthermore, these are not just the words of Asiatic Confucianists. Such German scholars as Wilhelm[72] said: "The spirit of
Confucian teachings will conquer the whole world." The American
scholar Babbitt[73] said: "The idealism of the East is much superior
to Western culture." If we take these [words] and extend them,
then the brilliance of Confucianism will certainly spread wherever
the sun and the moon shine. There is no doubt of it. Last
year, after the great European war, the various Western nations
were acutely aware of the harm of overemphasizing materialism.
They wished to take the strong points of Asiatic classical learning
in ordeer to supplement their own shortcomings. The results of this
were unsurpassed in the educational [fields], for there was vying
to set up Confucian lectureships at every university.[74]

In the above quotation, Ŏ Yun-jŏk clearly shows how Confucianism in Korea in the 1920's was considered part of a heritage of
universal principles which linked Korea with China and Japan.
Ŏ Yun-jŏk, however, did not believe these principles were limited

---

of the Ch'ing Period, (Washington: Government Printing Office, 1943-44), nor in any of
the better Chinese biographical dictionaries for the Ch'ing period. It is probable that
Hsuan-lu was the *gō* 號 or *ji* 字 of Li, who may well have been included in the
biographical dictionaries above under his regular name.

71. Ŏ Yun-jŏk appears to have been careless in his reference here, for the
British-French occupation and capture of Peking did not occur until 1860 in the Hsienfeng
period 咸豊 (1851-52).

72. The reference here is apparently to the German Sinologist Richard Wilhelm who
originally went to China in the early 1900's as a Lutheran minister. He was greatly
impressed with Chinese civilization, particularly Confucianism, and after the first World
War, spoke of the decline of the mechanical civilization of the West. For some of
Wilhelm's attitudes relative to these questions, see Richard Wilhelm, *The Soul of China,*
translated by John H. Reece and Arthur Waley (New York: Harcourt Brace and Co.,
1928), especially the chapter entitled "East and West," p. 353-373.

73. This reference seems to be to Irving Babbitt, the professor, author, and critic
who became the leader of the so-called "New Humanism" of the 1920's, a conservative
and reactionary movement in which the materialism and disorderliness of modern life
were deplored. For details on this movement, see: Alfred Kazin, *On Native Grounds,*
(New York: Reynal & Hitchcock, 1942), 291-311. From these pages one can get an
insight into why Confucianism with its classical ideals of a stable, orderly society appealed to Babbitt.

74. *Chosŏn sŭngmu Yuhyŏn nyŏnp'yo,* 6-7 (Sŭngmu sipp'al hyŏn kŭp Yudo chi
changnae 陞廡十八賢及儒道之將來).

in scope to Asia alone, but felt they were also becoming influential in the West, particularly since the first World War had focused attention on the harm of over-emphasizing materialism.

These statements are evidence that the Japanese policy of supporting Confucianism in Korea as a means of emphasizing the common cultural heritage of Japan and Korea had a basis in the beliefs of Korean Confucianists. Furthermore, Ŏ Yun-jŏk's views on the need for a world-wide Confucius to lessen the harm of Western materialism were the same as those of many Japanese and Chinese Confucianists of this period. Professor K. Yamada, for example, lectured in 1924 on how Confucianism alone could save the world from the materialism and chaos that had characterized it since the first World War.[75] This had also been a point stressed in the "Aims of the Shibunkai" published in 1918,[76] and Liang Ch'i-ch'ao 梁啓超 (1873-1929) too in the 1920's spoke of how the materialism of the West had to be modified by Asiatic spiritual culture.[77]

In 1927, the "Aims of the Taedong Samunhoe" were first published, and it is significant to note that they included all the points made in Ŏ Yun-jŏk's speech. In particular, the growing recognition of the superiority of Eastern civilization over Western civilization was described, and a statement made of the duty of the Taedong Samunhoe to spread Confucianism to the whole world.

> Confucianism arose in Eastern Asia, and therefore it forms the basis of Eastern culture, extending from the individual and the home to society and the state. There are none of these which do not rely on it for their establishment. Therefore Confucianism is not the exclusive property of the people of Eastern Asia alone, but should be shared together with the whole world, for Confucianism originally was not limited by the boundaries of national frontiers. Furthermore, it does not differentiate between the races of nations.
>
> Today we are not alone reviving the withered and the decayed [Confucianism] of Eastern Asia, for we are also planning to propa-

---

75. See ch. III, 131-132 of this study.
76. *Ibid.*, p. 147.
77. Wen-han Kiang, *The Chinese Student Movement*, (New York: King's Crown Press, 1948), 40-45.

gate it in the West. For the sake of Confucianism, no matter what the exertions, we dare not shirk any toil. The recent European Great War really had its genesis in the overemphasis on materialism, and the fact was that [people] did not understand the great principle that [declared], "Why is it necessary to speak of profit? There is righteousness and humaneness which are sufficient."[78] Consequently, after the war, the various countries reacted by reforming and reawakening, and they directly took the Confucianism of Eastern Asia as a means of succour for future sorrowful calamities.

Some persons established [Confucian] lectureships at universities for teaching; some formed [Confucian] organizations in society for study; some said that the civilization of East Asia was superior to that of the West; and some said that the spirit of Confucianism would conquer the earth. Therefore the elevation of Confucianism as the main trend of the world may be generally recognized.[79]

While it is difficult to tell what influence Confucian organizations like the Taedong Samunhoe actually had in Korea,[80] official Japanese interest in Confucianism continued. In 1924, in honor of the marriage of the Japanese Crown Prince, the the Imperial Household gave 1800 yen to the Governor-General for the encouragement of Confucianism. The money was to be used to help carry out ceremonies honoring the eighteen canonized Korean Confucian sages.[81] In 1928, the Japanese Emperor officially ascended the throne and was crowned. As a gesture of his good will and magnanimity, he repeated the earlier gift of 1800 yen for helping carry out ceremonies honoring the eighteen canonized Korean Confucian sages. The Governor-General, Yamanashi Hanzō 山梨半造 (1868-1944), acknowledged receipt of the gift and spoke of the good influence which the exemplary

---

78. The phrase concerning profit, righteousness, and humaneness is taken from *Mengtsu* 孟子 *(Mencius)*, Liang Hui Wang 梁惠王, pt. I, ch. I, 3.

79. *Chosŏn Sŭngmu Yuhyŏn nyŏnp'yo*, 1 (Taedong Samunhoe ch'uji 大東斯文會趣旨).

80. Besides the officially sponsored ceremonies of the Keigakuin and the official provincial Confucian temples, there seems to have been little popular interest in Confucianism. *Chōsen no ruiji shūkyō* 朝鮮の類似宗教 *(Korean Quasi-religions)*, chōsa shiryō 調査資料 No. 34 (Keijō: Chōsen Sōtokufu, 1935), 463-471, 951. This book gives a plausible explanation for it, pointing out that Confucianism had been the creed *par excellence* of the ruling hierarchy in Korea, but with little appeal to the people. For them, shamanistic cults more directly related to the problems of their daily lives had the greatest attraction.

81. *Chōsen bunbyō oyobi shōbu Juken*, 1-2.

lives of these eighteen Korean Confucian sages could have on public morality.[82] At the same time, a book dealing with the lives of these Korean Confucian sages, *Chosŏn sŭngmu Yuhyŏn nyŏnp'yo, pu shipp'al sŏnsaeng nyŏnpo* 朝鮮陞廡儒賢年表附十八先生年譜 (*Chronological Table of Canonized Korean Confucian Sages, supplement: Chronological Biographies of the Eighteen Masters*), was published by the Taedong Samunhoe to commemorate the Emperor's ascending the throne.[83]

These moves to associate the Japanese Emperor with Confucianism in Korea may have aimed at making the Emperor appear in the role of protector of Korean traditional values. But the activities of the Government-General in support of Confucianism were more important among the attempts made to relate Japanese rule to Korean traditions. For example, the Governor-General seems to have regularly attended the spring and fall Confucian ceremonies (*sekiten* 釋奠) held at the Keigakuin in Seoul, and at such ceremonies, he was always accompanied by important Korean and Japanese officials and civilians. The Governor-General and his party actually took part in the ceremonies, adding incense to various containers at the time of the incense burning ritual. There was also a definite order of entrance and exit for them at the ceremonies, which indicates that the presence of the Governor-General and other officials was not just a chance occurrence, but an integral part of the ceremonies themselves.[84] Basically the same ceremonies were carried out in the 329 officially recognized local Confucian temples in Korea, and ordinarily, the *gun* 郡 (district) chiefs, district officials, teachers, and local Confucianists assisted at them.[85]

---

82. *Chosŏn sŭngmu Yuhyŏn nyŏnp'yo pu shipp'al sŏnsaeng nyŏnpo* 朝鮮陞廡儒賢年表附十八先生年譜 (*Chronological Table of Canonized Korean Confucian Sages, supplement: Chronological Biographies of the Eighteen Masters*), (Keijō: Taedong Samunhoe, 1928), 1-4.

83. *Ibid.*, 4 (Chsŏn sŭngmu Yuhyŏn nyŏnp'yo sŏ 朝鮮陞廡儒賢年表序).

84. *Chōsen no kyōdo jinshi, dai nibu: sekiten, kiu, antaku; fu, kyōdo jinshi bunken* 朝鮮の郷土神祀第二部：釋奠, 祈雨, 安宅, 附郷土神祀文獻. (*Local Korean Temples, part two: Confucian Ceremonies, Prayers for Rain, and Safeguarding the Home; supplement, Records of Local Temples*), chōsa chiryō 調査資料 No. 45 (Keijō: Chōsen Sōtokufu, 1938), 13-17.

85. *Ibid.*, 25. 30-31. A list of the local temples with their locations may be found on pages 33-42.

In 1937, statistics were kept of the persons attending the spring ceremonies at local Confucian temples and at the Keigakuin, and they numbered over 100,000.[86]

This large attendance can only be understood by noting the earlier pattern of encouragement given to Confucianism by the Japanese authorities. In 1930, for example, a Confucian Institute (Meirin Gakuin 明倫學院) was established in Seoul by the Government-General, "with the object of preserving the ideals and spirit of Confucius and for the cultivation of characteristic Oriental morals."[87] The Confucian Institute was to give a two year course in Confucian classics and Confucian doctrines, besides Japanese language and civics. Graduates would be privileged to teach Chinese classics at secondary schools.[88] Further attention was focused on Confucianism by a regulation in the 1930's according to which new students first entering school would attend the Confucian spring ceremonies held on April 15 at the Keigakuin and local Confucian temples. The new students would then ostensibly receive the beneficient influence of the virtue of past sages at an important period in their lives.[89]

In 1928, Confucian organizations in Korea had been officially listed as having 227,547 members,[90] so that with the kind of encouragement described above, the attendance by over 100,000 persons at the Confucian spring ceremonies throughout Korea in 1937 is not surprising. That year, however, marked the re-opening of full-scale hostilities between the Japanese and the Chinese, and this event caused a most interesting addition to be made to the regular Confucian ceremonies. From August 15, 1938 onward, on the first and fifteenth day of each month, the following vow was to be made as part of an incense burning ceremony in order to bring military success to the Japanese.

Universal harmony, great peace, the humaneness of Confucius,

---

86. *Ibid.*, 32.

87. *Annual Report on Administration of Tyosen, 1936-37*, (Keijō: Government-General of Tyosen, 1937), 79.

88. *Loc. cit.*

89. *Chōsen no kyōdo jinshi, dai nibu: sekiten, kiu, antaku; fu, kyōdo jinshi bunken,* 7.

90. *Ibid.*, 31.

and the peace of the Far East are the spirit of our country. But in the Chinese Republic, the Great Way [of Confucius] is [fallen] on thorny ground. Propriety and righteousness have all disappeared, and ethics and human relationships have been lost. They are of the same race and same culture [as we], but they do not consider these close ties. They have turned their back on sincerity and destroyed righteousness. They have continuously been unyielding and insulting. They have acted without any intention of improving neighborly relations. Consequently, under the circumstances, there has been no other recourse [for us] but to marshal our battalions. High and low have united their strength, and the whole country is as one.

[There is reason] to be angry with the [Chinese], but what is there [to be angry over] with us? [Nothing]. If they do not stop their various attacks, we will put an end to it by beating and punishing them. Heaven bearing witness, we conclude our oath.[91]

The most striking aspect of this vow is the way in which it criticizes and condemns the Chinese. Confucian virtues of humaneness, propriety, righteousness, and sincerity are pictured as being trampled under by the wayward Chinese, while only the long-suffering Japanese cultivate the principles of the universal moral code of Confucius. Finally, with the insults and wickedness of the Chinese reaching a peak, the Japanese become morally justified in seeking to punish the wrong-doers.

The tendency of the Japanese to seek moral justification for their actions has been one of the most persistent features of their political pronouncements in modern times. In Korea, the Imperial Rescript on annexation in 1910, the Korean Emperor's Rescript on cession of sovereignty dictated by the Japanese, and the Imperial Rescript dealing with the reorganization of the Government-General in 1919 were filled with phrases descrying concern for the well-being of the people, the peace of the Far East, and enlightened and humane government.[92] In Manchuria in 1931-32, Japanese intervention was similarly described and proclaimed as a direct answer to the prayers of the peoples of Manchuria and Mongolia for justice and freedom from oppres-

---

91. *Chōsen no kyōdo jinshi, dai nibu: sekiten, kiu, antaku; fu, kyōdo jinshi bunken,* 24-25.

92. *Annual Report on Administration of Chosen, 1930* (Keijō: Government-General of Chosen, 1931), 175-178.

sion.[93] Therefore it is in keeping with this background that in 1937, Japanese military action in China should be spoken of as a righteous move to punish the Chinese for their unethical and evil conduct.

By associating the expansion of Japan with the defence of Confucian morality, the Japanese may have hoped to convince people in Korea that their cause had true universal spiritual aims. Even later on, after the outbreak of the second World War, a special Imperial Confucian Association was established in Korea to further this point of view.[94] But this policy of the Japanese in Korea ran counter to other efforts they were making to carry out the "Japan and Korea as one" (*Naisen ittai* 內鮮一體) movement. The latter had been increasingly fostered during the 1930's, and its aims were clearly expressed by Governor-General Minami in 1937 when he said: "It must be the main principle of the government of this peninsula to have the people, without a single exception, believe absolutely in our incomparable, august national polity, and burn with thankfulness for its glory."[95] As a part of the movement, Koreans were forced to change their names to Japanese names, and the use of Japanese in schools became mandatory. In this connection, the inclusion of Japanese in the curriculum of the Confucian Institute already described is significant, for it indicates that although the Japanese authorities wished to encourage Korea's traditional system of ethics, they wanted it done in Japanese. Implicit in this is a contradiction, since Korean traditions in the final analysis could not be preserved without the Korean language, and yet the Japanese were insisting that all teaching be done in Japanese. Therefore even

---

93. *A General Outline of Manchoukuo*, (Hsinking: Department of Foreign Affairs of Manchoukuo, 1932), 14 ff.

94. This information was obtained in a letter from Mr. Hŏ Hyŏn 鉉許, a Korean educator with whom the writer was acquainted during his stay in Korea, 1947-48. As an indication of the significance of "Imperial" for Korean Confucianism, one may note the purpose of the North Kyŏgsang Province United Confucian Society (Kyŏngsang Pukto Yudo Yŏnhaphoe 慶尙北道儒道聯合會) which was, "on the basis of the Imperial Way, to stimulate Confucianism and regulate the contact of Confucianists throughout the province." The concept of the Imperial Way (*Kōdō* 皇道) is Japanese and not basically Confucian. Arai Tsuneyasu 新井恒易, *Nippon chihō bunka dantai sōran* 日本地方文化團體綜覽 (*General View of Japanese Local Cultural Organizations*), (Tōkyō: Nippon Bunka Chūō Remmei 日本文化中央聯盟, 1942), 308.

though the Government-General might support Korean traditional ways such as Confucianism, their attempts to Japanize
the Koreans belied their devotion to the Korean traditions they
were supporting.

One might summarize the situation by saying that Japanese
encouragement of Confucianism in Korea was one of a number
of measures made primarily to indicate the devotion of the
Japanese to certain Korean traditions. By choosing traditions
such as Confucianism which had existed in both countries, it
was possible to appeal to a common background which served
to minimize the attraction of Korean nationalism. But at the
same time, the Japanese were attempting to make over the young
Korean into a loyal Japanese subject for whom Emperor worship
and the Shintō shrine would have as much appeal as to a Japanese
himself.

The violent destruction of nearly every Shintō shrine in
Korea after the defeat of Japan in 1945 shows the extent to which
this policy failed. Instead, Korean nationalism burst into full
bloom. The position of organized Confucianism under the
circumstances is an interesting one, for with the establishment
of an independent Korea (Republic of Korea),[96] the claims of
nationalism became paramount. Confucianism in Korea could
no longer be primarily a set of universally valid principles uniting
the moral concepts of Korea with those of China and Japan.
Confucianism and Confucian institutions now had value as part
of the national heritage, and as such, the new government contributed to the maintenance of the Sŏnggyun'gwan 成均館.[97] This

95. *Annual Report on Administration of Tyosen, 1936-37*, 221.

96. This statement does not imply that a divided Korea such as has existed since
1945 is satisfactory to Korean nationalist aspirations, but rather that the existence of an
independent Korea is fully recognized as fundamental for any political settlement in
the Far East.

97. The appointment of Chŏng In-bo 鄭寅普 as head of the Sŏnggyun'gwan College
serves to emphasize the fact that even among Confucian scholars, nationalism is the
primary consideration. Chŏng was an ardent nationalist who had remained aloof from the
Japanese during their period of control in Korea by teaching at Chōsen Christian college.
After 1945, he left Chōsen Christian College and became chairman of the committee
investigating Japanese collaborators. As a Confucianist, he supported the Silhakp'a 實學派
or School of Practical Learning which held that Confucianism must not simply indulge
itself in empty theorizing, but encourage useful knowledge that could help Korea. Chŏng
was among those taken north by the Communist armies in their retreat in 1950.

was the former Keigakuin of the period of Japanese control of Korea, but as a symbol of the national heritage, the old pre-1910 name was restored.

An ironical epilogue to this nationalistic phase in the development of Korean Confucianism after 1945 was a prophetic warning by the Confucianist Kim Kyŏng-t'ak 金敬琢. He declared that Koreans must reject foreign ideologies such as Russian Communism and American democracy or risk annihilation. Kim's motive for writing thus was the spectacle of carnage and destruction caused by the Communist uprisings in 1948 at Yŏsu 麗水 and Sunch'ŏn 順天 on Korea's southwest coast, and the measures taken to subdue them. He believed that the basic cause for these uprisings had been the clash between the ideologies of America and Russia. To avoid a repetition of this kind of tragic episode, he urged that Korea strengthen her own culture which was based on a heritage of Confucian, Buddhist, and Taoist ideas.

> Our Korean youth and our students must return to the Oriental spirit. Before we read either the explanations of American democracy, Russian Communism, historical materialism, or Marx's theory of capitalism, we must become acquainted with Buddhist sutras, the *Tao-te-ching* of Laotzu, the Confucian classics, and the complete works of T'oege and Yulgok.[98] Once understanding reality, there will be superior doctrines in East Asia rather than American democracy or Russian Communism.... What I am trying to say is, do our young Korean intellectuals, poisoned with American democracy and Russian Communism, look on the incidents which occurred last year at Yŏsu and Sunch'ŏn as a rebellion or a revolution? I implore them not to wander in such ideological mazes, and without a moment's delay to take the spirit of Korea and return to the ideologies of East Asia. My firm belief is that only in this way can our fatherland attain complete independence, and furthermore,

---

98. See ch. IV, footnote 68, for references on T'oege 退溪 and Yulgok 栗谷. Although these two men were Korea's most brilliant confucian scholars, they differed radically in their interpretations of human nature and its relationship to form and matter. Nevertheless, Kim Kyŏng-t'ak includes them together here, as well as mutually associating Confucianism, Buddhism, and Taoism that had for many centuries been antagonistic creeds. This is a significant point, however, because it shows how when faced with the greater threat of Western ideologies, the differences in Oriental ideologies could be reconciled to each other.

protect itself against the chaos and disaster of a third World War.[99]

This plea of Kim Kyŏng-t'ak was included in the preface of a book he wrote on Confucianism, *Yugyo chŏlhak sasang kaeyo* 儒教哲學思想槪要 (*Outline of Confucian Philosophical Ideas*), which was published on June 20, 1950. Five days later Kim's fears became a reality, when North Korean Communist armies launched the brutal attack that embroiled Korea in a struggle between foreign ideologies.

3. The *Wang-tao* in Manchuria.

Manchuria offers the second example of how the Japanese took advantage of the appeal of Confucianism in attempting to rationalize their expansion on the Asiatic continent and to maintain social and political control. Japanese support of Confucianism in Manchuria, however, was to have greater significance than Japanese support of Confucianism in Korea, for in Manchuria, an ostensibly independent state was created, based on principles which were meant to attract traditional and conservative groups throughout China.

The background to the establishment of the state of Manchoukuo in 1932 lies in the increasing Japanese economic and political penetration of Manchuria after the defeat of Russia in the Russo-Japanese war of 1904-05. By 1931, the concept had become fixed in Japanese thinking that Manchuria was economically indispensable to the well-being and very existence of Japan.[100] At the same time, though, the unification of China had taken place under the Kuomintang, and together with it came a wave of nationalism which was spreading to Manchuria

---

99. Kim *Kyŏng-t'ak* 金敬琢, *Yugyo chŏlhak sasang kaeyo* 儒教哲學思想槪要 (*Outline of Confucian Philosophical Ideas*), (Seoul: Sŏnggyun'gwan 成均館, 1950), 4, 9-10.
100. Shigemitsu Mamoru 重光葵, *Shōwa no dōran* 昭和の動亂 (*The Upheavals of the Shōwa Period*), (Tōkyō: Chūō Kōronsha 中央公論社, 1952) I, 50. Writing in 1952, Shigemitsu, one of the pre-war moulders of Japanese foreign policy, still felt that Japan's interests in Manchuria in 1931 were a matter of vital concern to the livelihood of the nation.

and engendering anti-Japanese agitation.[101] Chinese economic penetration of Manchuria also was proceeding apace by 1931,[102] and a possible basis of agreement between Chiang Kai-shek 蔣介石 (b. 1888) and the Chinese war-lord of Manchuria, Chang Hsüeh-liang 張學良 (b. 1898) loomed as a further threat to Japanese interests.[103] In this atmosphere, Japan's determination to maintain its position in Manchuria was fanned by the dissatisfaction of certain elements in the army with what the latter considered to be a weak foreign policy on the part of corrupt party governments.[104] Tension in Manchuria between the Japanese and Chinese mounted in 1930 and 1931 following the occurrence of a number of serious incidents. These finally culminated in the destruction of a portion of the Japanese-controlled South Manchuria railroad on September 18, 1931.[105] This was blamed by the Japanese on the Chinese and led to the occupation of Mukden by Japanese troops, who by late 1932 had eliminated Chinese military and civil authority from all of Manchuria.

The military and political details of this expansion into Manchuria are of less interest here than the justification given for the moves and the ideological principles sponsored by the new state of Manchoukuo. From the first, Confucian principles of justice and morality were appealed to and compared with the tyranny, republicanism, race prejudice, and Communism ram-

---

101. *Manchuria, Report of the Commission of Enquiry Appointed by the League of Nations*, (Washington: United States Government Printing Office, 1932), 30.

102. *Ibid.*, 47-49; also see F. C. Jones, *Manchuria Since 1931*, (London: Royal Institute of International Affairs, 1949), 104-106.

103. Horiuchi Tateki 堀内干城, *Chūgoku no arashi no naka de* 中國の嵐の中で (*In the Midst of the Maelstrom of China*), (Tōkyō: Kangensha 乾元社, 1950), 72. Horiuchi was in the Japanese consular service in China at the time and had an opportunity to assess first hand the background causes of many of the events he describes in his book.

104. Chitoshi Yanaga, *Japan since Perry*, (New York: McGraw-Hill Book Co., 1949), 498-499. Also see Paul S. Dull, "The Assassination of Chang Tso-lin," *F.E.Q.*, XI, 4 (August, 1952), 453-463, for an example of how the dissatisfied elements in the Army could apply direct action to gain their aims. The assassination of Chang Tso-lin deserves particular attention since it was the Kwantung Army which engineered this and the later September 18, 1931 incident to similar to it.

105. The Lytton Commission of the League of Nations reported in 1932 that there were over three hundred unsettled cases and disputes between the Japanese and Chinese in Manchuria. For a detailed description of the major points of friction, including the incidents immediately preceding September 18, 1931, see *Manchuria Report, of the Commission of Enquiry Appointed by the League of Nations*, 37-66.

pant in China proper. This line of reasoning was already evident in the "Declaration of Independence" issued by the Administrative Committee of the Northeastern Provinces on February 18, 1932,[106] but it is most clearly stated in the proclamation made at the establishment of Manchoukuo on March 1, 1932.

The proclamation first described the chaos and tyranny of war-lord rule which had characterized the Chinese Republic since the revolution of 1911, and spoke of Japanese intervention in Manchuria as an act of Heaven.

> Happily through the aid of the army of a neighbor Power, it has been possible to expel these corrupt elements from the area where they had entrenched themselves for many years past. The home of misrule and corruption is thus being given a thorough cleaning. This we believe is a Heaven-sent opportunity to the people of Manchuria and Mongolia to shake off their shackles.[107]

The proclamation then went on to show how the Kuomintang, under the guise of republicanism and the *San-min-chu-i* 三民主義 (Three Principles of the People), had ruled despotically, put people to death, and indulged its own greed. Internal strife caused by such misrule now threatened the very existence of the Kuomintang, and yet Communism with its pernicious doctrines was arising to replace the former. Therefore, people tended to look back longingly to the golden ages of the past, particularly of the Confucian Sage-kings Yao 堯 and Shun 舜.[108] This background was contrasted with the avowed fundamental aims of Manchoukuo which were to bring harmony, peace and prosperity to all people on the basis of universal moral principles.

> We believe that statecraft should be founded upon the principle of *Tao* or Way, and *Tao* founded upon *T'ien* or Heaven. The principle on which this new State is based is to follow *T'ien* or Heaven that

---

106. *Proclamations, Statements and Communications of the Manchoukuo Government,* Publications of the Department of Foreign Affairs, series 1, (Hsinking; Manchoukuo Government, 1932), 1-2.

107. *Ibid.,* 4.

108. *Loc cit.*

the people may have peace and security.... In internal affairs the
new state will reject the policies adopted in the dark days of the
past. It will...promote and popularize education, respect *Li-chao,*
the teachings of Confucianism, and apply the principle of *Wang-tao,*
the Way of [the] Benevolent Ruler, and practice its teachings. These,
we believe will enlighten the people to maintain the honour of
perpetuating the peace of the Far East and thus set an example of
model government to the world.[109]

The keynote of the above statement is the achieving of an
ideal state through the aegis of Confucian principles. The first
idea, that the people will attain peace and security when the state
follows heaven, is a basic Confucian concept, already discussed
by Hattori Unokichi 服部宇之吉 when he spoke of the theory of
sovereign power in comparing Confucianism and democracy.[110]
Confucianism, while making the welfare of the people the aim of
government, could never accede to a doctrine of popular sovereignty, since heaven and not the people was the ultimate regulator
and stadard. In regard to the popularization of education mentioned in the proclamation, events were to prove that it was
closely related to the teaching of the Confucian classics, for by
April, 1932, all old textbooks in Manchoukuo were abolished and
replaced by the Confucian *Ssu-shu* 四書 *(Four Books)* and *Wu-
ching* 五經 *(Five Classics).*[111]

But undoubtedly the most important principle spoken of
in the proclamation was that of the *Wang-tao.* Japanese Confucianists and those interested in Confucianism in Japan had
appealed to it before as an ideal which would bring harmony
to labor troubles, cooperation in society, and world peace.[112]
Basically, the *Wang-tao* was the ideal of rule by the example of
virtue and benevolence whereby the people were led naturally to follow the example of their ruler. It was a concept that
appeared in the Confucian classics and which was contrasted

---

109. *Ibid.,* 5.
110. See ch. III, p. 128-129 of this study.
111. *An Outline of the Manchoukuo Empire,* edited by the Bureau of Information,
Manchoukuo State Council (Dairen: Manchuria Daily News, 1939), 119. For an enumeration of the *Ssu-shu* and *Wu-ching,* see ch. I, footnote 6, of this study.
112. See ch. III, p. 121-123, 128-129 of this study.

with the *Pa-tao* 覇道 or "Way of the Usurper," by which men gained hegemony and maintained their power through force rather than the example of virtue.[113] It is easy to see how the Japanese, by making *Wang-tao* Manchoukuo's fundamental principle of government, could lay claim to the highest ethical aims for the new state. In fact, however, such claims were ironical to an extreme, since the very foundation and preservation of Manchoukuo was based on the superior force of Japanese arms. Yet in 1932, the Japanese were able to make this appeal to traditional values sufficiently attractive that a number of outstanding Chinese traditionalists were induced to take part in the Manchoukuo government.[114] The Japanese hoped that by using such members of the official class who were men of standing in the community, a basis for political control independent of Japanese coercion could be established.

Foremost among these Chinese traditionalists was Cheng Hsiao-hsu 鄭孝胥 (1859-1938). Cheng, whose reputation as a scholar was widespread,[115] became active in behalf of the deposed

---

113. See ch. III, footnotes 6 and 41, of this study.

114. Besides Cheng Hsiao-hsu 鄭孝胥 (1859-1938) whose career is described in the following pages, a number of other prominent traditionalists joined the Manchoukuo government such as: Lo Chen-yu 羅振玉 (1866-1940), well known for his work on Chinese literature and the "oracle bones;" see the index to Arthur W. Hummel, *Eminent Chinese of the Ch'ing Period*, (Washington: United States Government Printing Office, 1943-44), 2 vols., for information on Lo scattered throughout these books. Yuan Chin-kai 袁金鎧 (b. 1870); see *Manchoukuo Year Book, 1934*, (Tōkyō: Tōa Keizai Chōsakyoku 東亞經濟調查局 1934), 777-778, for a brief biography. Ting Chien-hsiu 丁鑑修 (b. 1876); see *Manchoukuo Year Book, 1934*, 772 for a brief biography. Hu Tzu-yüan 胡嗣瑗 (b. 1869); see *Manchoukuo Year Book, 1934*, 772 for a brief biography. Yu Ch'ung-han 干沖漢(1872-1932); see *Tōyō rekishi daijiten* 東洋歷史大辭典 *Historical Dictionary of East Asia*, 2nd printing (Tōkyō: Heibonsha 平凡社, 1941), I, 215, for a brief biography. Chen Pao-shen 陳寶琛 (b. 1847); see *Manchoukuo Year Book, 1934*, 752 for a brief biography.

115. Many details concerning Cheng's life may be found in Reginald F. Johnston's two books, *Confucianism and Modern China*, (London: Victor Gollancz Ltd., 1934), and *Twilight in the Forbidden City*, (London: Victor Gollancz Ltd., 1934). Johnston was a personal friend of Cheng whom he greatly admired.

Cheng himself had been educated along Confucian lines, passing the examination for *chin-shi* 進士 in his youth. After this he held various official positions under the Manchus, and in the decade from 1900-10, established the Constitution Preparatory Society together with such men as Chang Chien 張謇 (1853-1926). Just before the revolution in 1911, Cheng had submitted plans for the nationalization of the railroads, but he persistently remained outside the government of the Republic, in spite of requests made by Li Yüan-hung 黎元洪 and others for him to take various positions. The reason for this appears to have been Cheng's loyalty to the Manchus and his increasing disillusionment with Western learning and republican forms of government.

人類必重道德然後有種族
之見則抑人揚己而道德薄
矣人類必重仁愛然後有國際
之爭則損人利己而仁愛薄
矣今立吾國以道德仁愛為
主除去種族之見國際之爭
王道樂土當可見諸實事
凡我國人望共勉之
執政即位宣言　李肯敬書

Cheng Hsiao-hsu and his calligraphy.

Manchu Emperor Pu Yi 溥儀 (b. 1906) after the latter fled to Tientsin in 1925. As one of Pu Yi's principal tutors, Cheng came into almost daily contact with him, and among Cheng's most cherished desires was to restore the deposed Emperor to the throne. In his efforts, he was assisted by his Japanese trained son, Cheng Ch'ui 鄭垂 (1888-1933). Both Chengs had contacted various Chinese war-lords over the matter, but none of these were willing or able to assist. About a month before the outbreak of the Manchoukuo incident of September 18, 1931, however, Japanese Colonel Doihara Kenji 土肥原賢次 (1885-1948) secretly visited Cheng Hsiao-hsu and his son several times to discuss the possibility of Pu Yi going to Manchuria to become head of a new state. Cheng Hsiao-hsu was overjoyed at this news and soon contacted Pu Yi, who apparently also was pleased over the prospects.[116]

It is important at this point to try and assess the reasons why so distinguished a scholar as Cheng Hsiao-hsu was willing to cooperate with the Japanese and act as intermediary in persuading Pu Yi to go to Manchuria. Cheng knew that the Japanese would be in control, and yet he apparently felt that past Chinese history taught how many Chinese sovereigns had used "barbarians" to establish and maintain legitimate Chinese dynasties. As a traditionalist and Confucianist, Cheng was repelled by the

---

116. Pu Yi escaped from Tientsin to Manchuria in 1931 with Cheng Hsiao-hsu and Cheng Ch'ui. William Wong has made a detailed study of this incident, based on contemporary sources and evidence from statements at the International Military Tribunal for the Far East in Tōkyō, 1946-48, in his *Henry Pu Yi and the Japanese, 1924-45: a Study in Puppetry,* (M.A. thesis, University of California in Berkeley, 1951), 26-46. Before the International Military Tribunal for the Far East, Pu Yi declared the Japanese had forced him to go to Manchuria, but this does not appear to be the case. The writer had the opportunity of discussing this matter with a granddaughter of Cheng Hsiao-hsu. She was acquainted with the personal papers and diary of Cheng Ch'ui, a copy of which is at the Hoover Library of War and Revolution, Stanford University. On the basis of recollection of this diary, it has been possible to reconstruct the backround of Pu Yi's escape to Manchuria and the motives involved. It is significant to note that Cheng Ch'ui, a graduate of Waseda University in Japan, was a personal friend of Colonel (later General) Itagaki Seishirō 板垣征四郎 (1885-1948), at the time head of the Second Section of the Army General Staff for intelligence. Colonel (later General) Doihara was working under Itagaki in this period as Chief of the Army's Special Service Organization. Unfortunately, Cheng Ch'ui's diary was not available for inspection because of having been misplaced at the Hoover Library. Therefore it has been necessary to rely on re-collections of the diary.

type of education then prevalent in Nationalist China in which the Confucian classics had been discarded. He also had become disillusioned with Western learning and seems to have believed sincerely that only by restoring the Confucian classics to the central part of the curriculum could the spiritual and consequent physical decline of China be reversed.[117] With this as a background, one can understand how Cheng viewed cooperating with the Japanese as no more traitorous than seeking the aid of Chinese war-lords for obtaining legitimate aims. And in this case, there was the high purpose of restoring the ex-Emperor to the throne and the attraction of Japanese support for Confucian principles to which Cheng was devoted.

Cheng became the first Prime Minister of Manchoukuo in March, 1932, and concurrently held the position of Minister of Education.[118] Although theoretically such positions would have given him great executive and administrative power, in fact he could do little more than approve legislation and sign agreements drawn up by the Japanese "advisors" to the Manchoukuo government.[119] Cheng in other words was a figurehead, but even so, his ideas concerning the *Wang-tao* and the need for a Confucian basis in the educational system were important to the Japanese because they offered the latter a Chinese interpretation of society and government which could be used to counter the claims of nationalism being fostered by both the Kuomintang and the Chinese Communists.

The *Wang-tao* was declared to be the official theory upon which the internal and external policies of Manchoukuo were based. Pu Yi, as Chief Executive, made the following proclamation on March 9, 1932, attesting to this.

> Mankind should respect Morality. Since there exists racial discrimination, one race attempts to exalt itself by oppressing the others; thus comes the weakness of Morality.

---

117. Based on personal observations of Cheng Hsiao-hsu's granddaughter and her recollections from the diary of Cheng Ch'ui.

118. *Manchoukuo Year Book, 1934*, 735. 738.

119. Jones, *op. cit.*, 25: also see comments of Lytton Commission, *Manchuria, Report of the Commission of Enquiry Appointed by the League of Nation*, 106.

Benevolence should be highly esteemed by mankind. But on account of international strife, one nation strives to benefit herself at the expense of others, which causes Benevolence to lose its value.

Our new State is established on Morality and Benevolence. As a result of the removal of racial discrimination and the termination of international strife, this State will, as a matter of course, become a land of peace and happiness under *Wang-tao*, the Way of Benevolent Rule.

Endeavour, therefore, all people for the attainment of these noble objectives.[120]

Cheng naturally was allowed great leeway in the promotion of Confucian doctrines such as *Wang-tao*, and in the *Manchoukuo Handbook of Information*, published by the Manchoukuo Government in 1933, his views on the application of principles of *Wang-tao* to internal and external affairs were quoted at length. Cheng chose a passage from the Confucian *Li-chi* 禮記 (*Record of Rites*) to summarize the effects of following *Wang-tao* on the internal affairs of the state.

When the great doctrine prevails, all under heaven will work for the common good. The virtuous will be elected to office, and the able will be given responsibility. Faithfulness will be in constant practice and harmony will rule. Consequently, mankind will not only love their own parents and give care to their own children; all the aged will be provided for, and all the young employed in work. Infants will be fathered, widows and widowers, the fatherless and the unmarried, the disabled and the sick, will all be cared for. The men will have their rights and the women their home. No goods will go to waste, nor need they be stored for private possession. No energy should be used for personal gain. Self-interest ceases, and theft and disorder are unknown. Therefore the gates of the houses are never closed.[121]

---

120. *The Chief Executive's Proclamation, the Organic Law of Manchoukuo and other Laws Governing Various Government Offices,* Publications of the Department of Foreign Affairs, series 2 (Hsinking: Manchoukuo Government, 1932), 1. Although this is the official translation, it is rather free and sometimes departs from the Chinese text.

121. *Li-chi* 禮記 (*Record of Rites*), *Li-yun* 禮運; included in the *Shih-san-ching chu shu* 十三經注疏. Chi Ku-ke 汲古閣 edition (1631), XXI chuan 卷, p. 36b ff.; as translated in *Manchoukuo, Handbook of Information,* (Hsinking: Manchoukuo Government, 1933), 17-18. The succeeding phrase to the passage quoted from the *Li-chi*, Li-yun, reads: "Such will be the age of *Ta-t'ung.*" This is significant because *Ta-t'ung,* translated variously as "Great Harmony" or "Universal Brotherhood," was used to "style" the

The ideal society pictured in the above passage represents the epitomy of the Confucian type of corporate, regeulated social order in which everyone has duties and responsibilities commensurate with his age and station in life. Peace and harmony result when each person attends to these duties and responsibilities. The basic assumption in the reasoning of the passage is that there are characteristics common to human nature and human relations which will manifest themselves when the universal ethical law is understood. The universal ethical law would of course be Confucianism, while the characteristics common to human nature and human relations would be the virtues associated with conduct according to the five Confucian social relationships.[122]

Japanese politicians, as well as Confucianists, appreciated the value of inculcating the people with a belief in Confucianism because it could so easily serve to train them in strict obedience and devotion to duty as described in the passage from the *Li-chi*. They may indeed have also believed that the resulting stability in society was in harmony with natural laws, yet for practical men of affairs, the maintenance of social order was of prime consideration, and Confucianism lent itself perfectly to this. In Manchoukuo, an appeal to Confucianism, if successful, would not only lessen the possibility of social disorder, but restore a belief in universal values which would transcend the nationalist aims of the Kuomintang.

There is no doubt that leading Chinese traditionalists such as Cheng Hsiao-hsu desired a return to what they considered universal values as opposed to the narrow, debasing, and amoral

---

new era of government in Manchoukuo from 1932, implying that the new state would achieve the ideal of *Ta-t'ung*. K'ang Yu-wei 康有爲 (1857-1927) had popularized the term in the 1890's in a book called the *Ta-t'ung shu* 大同書 where he described the development toward "universal brotherhood" and a world community. When Pu Yi became Emperor of Manchuria in 1934, he adopted the reign title of *K'ang-te* 康德 which replaced *Ta-t'ung*. Nevertheless, even this new reign title was related to the earlier ideal of "universal brotherhood," for in K'ang Yu-wei's teachings, the stage of *Ta-t'ung* was preceded by that of "advancing peace' styled as *Hsiao-k'ang* 小康. The character for *k'ang* in both cases is the same.

122. See ch. I, footnote 44, of this study for an enumeration of the five Confucian social relationships and virtures.

claims of nationalism and Communism. Cheng himself seems to have blamed nationalism and reliance on militarism and force for the plight of China, and he proposed that Manchoukuo take the lead in being a state based on benevolence and *Wang-tao*.

> ...whose weakness will be its strength, for unjustifiable force used against it by any power would excite the rest of the powers to come to its assistance and prevent invasion. As a result of surfeit of war the world is sick of war. If *Wang-tao* is adopted, the outlook of the whole world will be changed. The development of such an attitude should contribute to the solution of naval and military armament reduction problems. But the most serious menace which confronts us is Communism, because its aim is to overthrow world morality. Communism is our chief enemy, as its very use of the principles of force is contrary to the teachings of *Wang-tao*.[123]

The encouragement of Confucianism in Manchoukuo was not limited to statements and pious wishes, however, for the government made a sustained effort to spread Confucian ideas. First of all, the Confucian *Four Books* and *Five Classics* were adopted in 1932 as school textbooks to replace the earlier ones put out by the Chinese Nationalist government which were described as having "had an alarmingly dangerous effect upon popular education."[124] By dangerous was meant inimical to Japan and over-emphasizing radicalism, recovery of national rights, and anti-foreignism.[125] With Manchoukuo adopting Confucian teachings as the fundamental principles of education, both Chinese traditionists and the Japanese simultaneously achieved their goals of abolishing radicalism and anti-foreignism.[126] Anti-foreignism in China was part of the nationalist movement and was most strongly directed against the Japanese, while radicalism usually

---

123. *Manchoukuo, Handbook of Information*, 19. Another statement made by Cheng on the *Wang-tao* in 1937 may be found in Cheng Hsiao-hsu, "*Wang-tao* or the Kingly Way," *Manchuria*, II, 24 (Dec., 1937), 843. Cheng had resigned from the government in 1935, reportedly being disillusioned with the excessive Japanese control of the Manchoukuo administration. But in spite of this, he remained devoted sincerely to Confucian ideals, as shown in the above article.

124. *An Outline of the Manchoukuo Empire*, 119.

125. *Third Report on Progress in Manchuria to 1932*, (Dairen: South Manchuria Railway, 1932), 176.

126. *Ibid.*, 177.

referred to another aspect of the same movement which sought to destroy and replace ethnocentric Confucian values with more modern, pragmatic, and nationalist ones. Therefore, a tenuous unity of interest between Chinese traditionalists and the Japanese was established, and this relationship was fostered by the Japanese during the 1930's in their claims of being the true supporters of Asiatic spiritual culture and civilization.

Besides activity in the field of education, the Manchoukuo authorities sponsored Confucian cultural organizations and followed a policy of publically rewarding outstanding examples of conduct in keeping with Confucian standards. The two largest organizations conducting social and cultural work were the Manchuria Morality Association and the Confucian Association, both of which aimed at encouraging morality within the family and popularizing the teachings of Confucius. They each had branches in the various districts of the provinces and gave lectures and worked with local education officials.[127] In regard to publically rewarding the virtuous, the policy was outlined in a government publication as follows:

> With a view to popularizing the traditional virtues of filial piety and righteousness, which are famous in Oriental history, the Government has been conferring official commendation upon dutiful children and virtuous women ever since the foundation of the State, by giving awards and in other ways.[128]

Confucianism was also promoted for spiritual and ceremonial observances, since "Manchoukuo, being based on the *Wang-tao*, sought naturally to revive the *Wen-miao* ceremony as a means of cultivating national spirit." The *Wen-miao* 文廟 (Confucian temple) ceremonies referred primarily to the Confucian spring and autumn sacrifices. The day of their observances was made a national holiday, and by 1939, eighty-eight *Wen-miao* had been restored.[129]

---

127. *An Outline of the Manchoukuo Empire,* 124.
128. *Ibid.*, 125.
129. *Loc. cit.*

To understand the general pattern of encouragement of Confucianism in Manchuria, however, it is necessary to keep in mind the increasing awareness to Confucianism in Japan itself during the 1930's by important political and educational leaders. As was already pointed out, many Confucian values such as loyalty, filial piety, devotion to duty, and harmony in social relations were consciously integrated into the Japanese tradition at this time. The whole was characterized as Oriental spiritual culture which was declared to be superior to Western material culture.[130] But Japan, while maintaining her devotion to Oriental spiritual culture, had also learned the Western techniques of mastering nature. Therefore Japan had a special mission to fulfill since she had been able to synthesize and properly balance Oriental and Western values. K. Kawakami, a Japanese newspaper correspondent, aptly summarized this attitude with respect to Manchuria when he wrote:

> The ancient doctrine of *Wang-tao,* as the ideal of government, is perhaps sound enough even today. But modern administration requires modern technique which *Wang-tao* does not supply.... It is here, perhaps, that Japan can be of service to Manchoukuo. Herself a worshipper of Confucius up to some sixty years ago, she has since made feverish efforts to catch up with Europe and America in the study of the sciences and the arts which are the causes of Occidental progress. For some years to come Japanese administrators, Japanese jurists, Japanese educators, and Japanese experts will have to work in the government of Manchoukuo. They enjoy a certain advantage in that they, too, have the background of the Chinese classics, as no Westerners have. Their modern knowledge and technique, combined with classic *Wang-tao* cherished by the leaders of Manchoukuo, may yet bring peace, order, and happiness out of the land of banditry and official "squeeze" that has been Manchuria for unnumbered ages.[131]

Kawakami's moderate statement was meant primarily for Western readers, but similar and often less restrained rationali-

---

130. See ch. IV, section 1 of this study.
131. K. K. Kawakami, *Manchoukuo, Child of Conflict,* (New York: Macmillan Co., 1933), 116-117.

zations of Japan's actions in Manchuria were made for the
Japanese public. Many of these attempted to show how Japan
was devoted to the highest ideals of Oriental culture and ethics
in helping support a sister nation, Manchoukuo, similarly dedicated.[132] In 1932, for example, the veteran Japanese Confucianist,
Inoue Tetsujirō 井上哲次郎, discussed the *Wang-tao* in relation to
Chinese and Japanese history and declared that it was only a
theory in China, but had been practiced from remote antiquity
in Japan. To prove this, he used the statement from the *Analects*
in which Confucius expressed a desire to live in the East, inter-
preting the East as meaning Japan. "The Master was wishing to
go and live among the nine tribes of the East. Someone said,
'They are rude. How can you do such a thing?' The Master
said, 'If a superior man dwells among them, what rudeness is
there?' "[133] Inoue felt this background had to be understood in
order to appreciate the significance of Manchoukuo's attempts
to develop a new state based on the *Wang-tao*.[134]

In 1933, Nakamura Kyūshirō 中村久四郎 wrote on "Manchoukuo
and the New Mission of Confucianism" in which he said that
Manchoukuo's devotion to the *Wang-tao* made it natural for her
to be closely associated with Japan where there was also a special
emphasis on the Confucian spirit. The leaders of both countries
recognized the mission Confucianism must play in promoting
spiritual culture and training those who would put Confucian

---

132. Although many magazines in Japan at the time carried articles of this tenor,
a specific example is *Shibun* 斯文, XIV, 5 (May, 1932). The whole issue was devoted to
discussing Manchuria, and besides articles by Confucianists such as Hattori Unokichi
服部宇之吉, Shionoya On 鹽谷溫. Koyanagi Shigeta 小柳司氣太, and Uno Tetsuto 宇野
哲人, there were two articles by Admirals, two articles by Generals, and one each by
a member of the House of Peers, the head of the Peers School, the head of the Tōkyō
Women's Dental College, and a Foreign Office Section chief.
133. *Lun-yü* 論語 (*Analects*), Tzu-han 子罕, 13; as translated by Legge, *Confucian
Classics*, I, 221.
134. Inoue Tetsujirō 井上哲次郎, "ōdō shugi ni tsuite" 王道主義に就いて ("Concerning the Doctrine of the Kingly Way"), *Shibun*, XIV, 4 (April, 1932), 1-10. It is
interesting to note that the very same interpretation of the "East" in the *Analects* as
referring to Japan appears in the writings of a fifteenth-century Japanese Confucianist,
Kiyowara Naritada 清原業忠 (1408-67), *Shōun seizanhen Rongo shōshoin* 笑雲清三編論語
抄所引, as quoted by Ashikaga Enjutsu 足利衍述, *Kamakura Muromachi jidai no Jukyō*
鎌倉室町時代之儒教 (*Confucianism of the Kamakura and Muromachi Periods*), (Tōkyō:
Nihon Koten Zenshū Kankōkai 日本古典全集刊行會, 1932), 469. It is indicative of the
recurrent strain of nationalism in Japanese Confucianism.

political and ethical ideals into practice.[135]

The Japanese Sinologist Koyanagi Shigeta　小柳司氣太 even more closely identified Japanese ideals with the Confucian ones forming the basis of government in Manchoukuo in a speech on Confucian political thought in 1936. After comparing the Japanese "Imperial way" (Kōdō 皇道) with the Wang-tao, he declared that they embodied basically the same concepts, though on the surface, reverence for heaven in Confucianism and esteem for the gods in Shintoism might appear different. Actually, however, once the Sung dynasty metaphysical interpretations of heaven were dispensed with and Confucius' basic concept reexamined, it was clear that the Confucian heaven included anthropomorphic characteristics corresponding to those of Shintō gods. Therefore Koyanagi reasoned that the Japanese "Imperial way" was really the materialization of the ideals of Wang-tao, making it possible for Manchoukuo to approach Japan on the basis of their common ideals.[136]

Official Japanese school textbooks also took up this line of presenting Japan as the spiritual and moral leader of Asia in descriptions about Manchoukuo and Japan's relations with her.[137] A typical passage in one of these stated that, "...at present, Imperial Japan is leading and helping her neighbor Manchoukuo, and has become her comrade in pressing for the achievement of Manchoukuo's ideals of the Wang-tao and national happiness."[138]

A Japanese art critics, Yamada Chisaburō 山田智三郎, similarly described Japan's role vis-a-vis Manchoukuo and Asia in an article reviewing currents in modern Japanese art.

---

135. Nakamura Kyūshirō 中村久四郎, "Manshūkoku to Kōshikyō no shinshimei" 滿洲國と孔子敎の新使命 ("Manchoukuo and the New Mission of Confucianism"), Shibun XV, 8 (August, 1933), 1-12.

136. Koyanagi Shigeta 小柳司氣太 "Jukyō no seiji shisō" 儒敎の政治思想 ("The Political Thought of Confucianism"), Tōhō gakuhō 東方學報, VI (Feb., 1936), 830-831.

137. Toriyama Kiichi 鳥山喜一, Joshi shingaikoku rekishi, Tōyō no bu 女子新外國歷史,東洋の部 (New History of Foreign Nations for Women, Section on Asia), third revised edition (Tōkyō: Teikoku Shoin 帝國書院, 1939), 91-92; Shotō Kokushi 初等國史 (Elementary National History), fifth grade, fourth printing (Keijō: Chōsen Sōtokufu 朝鮮總督府, 1942), 198-199; Katō Seiichi 加藤盛一 and Takahashi Shunjō 高橋俊乘, Shitei Dai Nihon rekishi teiyō 四訂大日本歷史提要 (Summary of the History of Great Japan, Fourth Revision), approved by the Korean Government-General, fifth printing (Tōkyō: Fuzambō 富山房, 1936), 207-208.

138. Toriyama, op. cit., 94-95.

The Shōwa era, the reign of the present Emperor, which began in
1926, may be called the period of nationalism or the revival of the
national spirit. The Manchurian conflict is not a result of any militarism or imperialism. It is a manifestation of Japanese spirit and
ideals, which advocates that every nation and every race should
maintain themselves for their own sake and at the same time for
humanity, and that in Asia Japan should help Asiatic races to accomplish this ideal.[139]

Surveying Japanese support for Confucianism in Manchuria,
it is possible to distinguish a number of separate uses to which
such support adapted itself. Foremost among these was that of
countering Chinese nationalist propaganda with a time-honored
Chinese creed, and thus encouraging the defection of dissatisfied
and conservative elements in China to the Japanese. This was an
important consideration in 1932, but it became even more so after
the renewal of hostilities between Japan and China in 1937 when
the Japanese desperately needed to bring Chinese of influence
and standing into their puppet governments in northern and
central China. Another aspect of this appeal to traditional and
conservative elements in China was the growing emphasis on the
anti-Communist character of Manchoukuo's ideal of *Wang-tao*.
One pamphlet in 1940 described the difference between *Wang-tao*
and Communism as a contrast of good and evil.

In brief, it may be said that *Wang-tao* is a politico-moral code based
on humanitarianism and unselfishness. Under the system of *Wang-
tao* a man pledges himself to mutual love and help. He undertakes
to serve his fellow men without hope of reward other than the
satisfaction that comes from work well done.... Communism has
been the cause of strife among people of different social strata and
it has fanned up hatred and destructive wars both civil and international. It seeks to bring about the destruction of civilization
through a universal Red revolution. It is evident that such a doctrine
is absolutely inconsistent with the fundamental spirit of benevolence
and morality of *Wang-tao*.[140]

---

139. Yamada Chisaburo 山田智三郎, "Japanese Modern Art," *Monumenta Nipponica*,
V, 2 (Dec., 1942), 123.
140. *The Comintern's Activity in Manchuria*, (Hsinking: Manchuria Daily News,
1940), 39.

Japanese encouragement of Confucianism in Manchoukuo not only proved her devotion to Asiatic morality and spiritual traditions, but put her in the forefront of those nations fighting Communism, the cancer which had sprung from Western materialism. This emphasis on Japan's position of moral leadership in Asia was particularly played up in Japan proper. It can be interpreted as an attempt both to justify Japanese policy to her citizens and to obtain their support on the basis of ethically high motives. It also fits the pattern which one would expect in Japan after 1933 when universal creeds such as Confucianism were nationalized. The interest of the Japanese in expansion on the Asiatic continent, however, made it necessary for Confucianism in Manchuria and later in China to be more than just a phase of Japanese nationalism. But while Confucianism in Manchuria could be sponsored as the leading universal tradition of Asia to which the Japanese were devoted in their efforts at Asiatic revival, in China proper, Chinese nationalism was too strongly entrenched to be displaced. After unsuccessfully attempting to copy the Manchurian pattern in North China, the Japanese subordinated Confucianism to Chinese nationalism, although Confucian ethical standards were still spoken of as a common bond binding the two nations. This particular development in China proper is described in the following section.

4. The Position of Confucianism in the Provisional Government of China and in the Central Government of China.

The Provisional Government of China is the name given to the regime set up by the Japanese North China Army on December 14, 1937, after the campaign of conquest following the Lukouchiao 蘆溝橋 incident of July 7, 1937. Without going into the background of this incident, it is sufficient to indicate that it provided the Japanese North China Army with the pretext for detaching from China her northern provinces.[141] The authority

---

141. The background to Lukouchiao, as well as a description of the events immediately before and after the incident, may be found in T. A. Bisson, *Japan in China*, (New York: The Macmillan Co., 1938).

of the Provisional Government theoretically extended over the four provinces of Hopei 河北, Shantung 山東, Honan 河南, and Shansi 山西,[142] and both Japanese and foreign observers expected that once initial Chinese resistance was broken down, no spontaneous organized opposition to the new government would arise among the traditionally passive peasant population of the hinterlands.[143]

The fact that Chinese nationalism never had more than a tenuous hold in North China was the principal reason for giving credence to this view.[144] The Japanese hoped to replace Chinese nationalist symbols and ideology with traditional Confucian ones that would make the Provisional Government acceptable to the people and lessen the need for Japanese bayonets to prop up the puppet regime. Confucianism, in other words, was looked on as a means of extending the political and social control of the Provisional Government, especially in areas not directly controlled by the Japanese Army.[145]

The character of the men who became the leaders of the Provisional Government throws a great deal of light on these aims of the Japanese and is indicative of where the Japanese expected to draw their greatest support. Wang Keh-min 王克敏 (1875-1945), chairman of the new government, was an old style bureaucrat of the last years of the Manchu dynasty. He had never been particularly sympathetic with the aims of the nationalist revolution in China, although he had taken part in various capacities in diplomatic negotiations between China and Japan during the early 1930's.[146] Wang I-t'ang 王揖唐 (1889-1944), another important member of the Provisional Government, had passed the old literary examinations in 1904, and later had legal training in Japan. A supporter of Yuan Shih-k'ai 袁世凱 (1859-1916) and other northern war-lords, Wang's political fortunes were nearly always opposed to those of the Chinese nationalists, and

---

142. George E. Taylor, *The Struggle for North China*, Institute of Pacific Relations Enquiry Series, (New York: Institute of Pacific Relations, 1940), 33.
143. *Ibid.*, 29, 42.
144. *Ibid.*, 28-29.
145. *Ibid.*, 75-76.
146. *Ibid.*, 22; see also *Tōyō rekishi daijiten*, I, 339.

on a number of occasions he found it necessary to retire or flee the country.[147] Kao Ling-wei 高陵霨 (1868-1940) was another typical member of the Provisional Government. Brought up in the old literary tradition and passing the literary examination, Kao became a follower of Chang Chih-tung 張之洞 (1837-1909) in the last years of the Ch'ing dynasty. After the revolution of 1911, he served in the war-lord governments at Peking, holding at one time or other nearly every major government office. The Nationalist revolution from 1925-27 brought this phase of his political career to an end.[148]

Other examples could be given of high officials in the Provisional Government, but for the most part they would have characteristics similar to those of the men described above. George E. Taylor, who made a special study of the Provisional Government from personal observation in China at the time, has described the common background of this officialdom as follows:

> The most important figures were officials in the former Peking government, which stood in opposition to the Kuomintang and was for many years an obstacle to national unification by that party. These men received their classical education in China and then went to Japan to study political science and law, the favorite subjects of scholars at that time. Some became prominent, most of them had been ministers at one time or another, and one or two rose to the rank of premier. They followed the old Chinese tradition in giving more or less disinterested service to whomsoever happened to be in power at any given time. It must be said of such men that they have been consistent in their opposition to the Kuomintang; they regretted the passing of the Empire and deplored the establishment of the National Government in 1928. When the Northern Expedition reached Peking in 1927 and the Peking government fell, they lost their positions and some of them went to prison for their opinions.[149]

From this description, one can easily see that the leaders to whom the Japanese turned were opposed to the self-conscious nationalism that increasingly characterized China after the revo-

---

147. Taylor, op. cit., 23-24; see also Tōyō rekishi daijiten, I, 371.
148. Taylor, op. cit.. 24; see also Tōyō rekishi daijiten, III, 182.
149. Taylor, op. cit., 21.

lution of 1911. Their background was rather one appealed to by the universal Confucian values of old China. A forceful expression of their faith in the enduring value of traditional Chinese culture can be found in the writings of Ku Hung-ming 辜鴻銘 (1854-1929), an early representative of this school of thought. Ku had nothing but contempt for the current popular movements arising in the West, distinguished by their appeal to the mob and devoid of any ethical standard or aesthetic taste.[150] Nationalism was especially pernicious in this regard because of its lack of any ethical norm other than utility to judge the value of social, economic, or political ideas and institutions.

It is worthwhile briefly to outline the position of Japan relative to this conflict between traditionalism and nationalism in China. Before the Japanese presented China with the "Twenty-one Demands" in 1915, Japan had been considered by many Chinese nationalists as a model of progress.[151] She had quickly achieved industrialization; successfully modernized her institutions of government; and attained a level of national power and prestige such that she was able to challenge Western encroachments. Chinese nationalist leaders, including Sun Yat-sen 孫逸仙 (1866-1925) and Wang Ching-wei 汪精衛 (1885-1944), lived in Japan for extended periods before 1911, and took hope from the example of Japan and the aid received from many Japanese.[152] Under these circumstances, it is not surprising to find that there was hesitancy at the time among Confucian trained officials and traditionalists over the role which Japan might play. A manifestation of this is found in a statement of Ku Hung-ming, made

---

150. Ku Hung-ming, *The Spirit of the Chinese People*, (Peking: The Peking Daily News, 1915), 7-8. For a good summary of Ku's ideas, see T'ang Leang-li, *The Foundations of Modern China*, (London: Noel Douglas, 1923), 109-112.

151. T'ang Leang-li, *China in Revolt*, (London: Noel Douglas, 1927), 100-101. See also, Sun Yat-sen, *Memoirs of a Chinese Revolutionary*, (London: Hutchinson and Co., 1919), 103-105, 114-115.

152. The best biography of Sun Yat-sen in English in Lyon Sharman, *Sun Yat-sen, His Life and Its Meaning*, (New York: The John Day Company, 1934). See the index for the numerous references to the activities of Sun and the other Chinese revolutionaries in Japan. An excellent Japanese source for studying the relationship of Japanese groups with the early Chinese revolutionaries in Kuzū Yoshihisa 葛生能久 *Tōa sengaku shishi kiden* 東亞先覺志士記傳 (*Biography of Pioneer-patriots in East Asia*), (Tōkyō: Kokuryū-kai 黑龍會, 1933-36), especially volumes I and II.

Ku Hung-ming

in 1901 when he was interpreter-secretary to viceroy Chang Chih-tung.

> With her present armament alone, Japan can dictate a policy to the foreigners in dealing with China. But in order to do that Japan must not study the Chinese Question with foreign spectacles. As soon as Japan gets a right and clear view of the real issues in the Chinese Question, Japan will perhaps be the mark-graf [Jōi-shōgun 攘夷将軍] of the civilization of the Far East.[153]

The significant point in the above passage is that even while Ku showed apprehension over the role of Japan *vis-a-vis* China if she followed Western examples, he was hopeful Japan might become the protector of traditional Far Eastern civilization.

By the 1920's, conditions had changed so that Ku's words seem to have been prophetic. In the eyes of many Chinese nationalists, Japan, due to her growing economic and political encroachment on China, had been transformed from a model to China's principal exploiter and foe. Hu Shih 胡適 (b. 1891), commenting in the 1930's on the relative development of China and Japan in modern times, declared that Japan, far from being progressive, was behind China in espousing real fundamental reform.[154] On the other hand, Chinese traditionalists found they were more and more in the same camp with the Japanese who now spoke of themselves as the defenders of Asiatic morality and spiritual culture. Ku Hung-ming himself was in Japan during the fateful years of the Nationalist unification of China, 1924-27, lecturing at the Daitō Bunka Gakuin 大東文化學院 in Tōkyō. This was an institute attached to the Daitō Bunka Kyōkai 大東文化協會, an organization dedicated to the revival of traditional Oriental

---

153. Ku Hung-ming, *Papers from a Viceroy's Yamen*, (Shanghai: Shanghai Mercury, 1901), 78.

154. Hu Shih, "China is more Modern than Japan," *People's Tribune*, as cited by Inoue Tetsujirō 井上哲次郎、*Tōyō bunka to Shina no shōrai* 東洋文化と支那の將來 (*Asiatic Culture and the Future of China*), (Tōkyō: Risōsha 理想社, 1939), 42. Also see Hu Shih, *The Chinese Renaissance*, (Chicago: University of Chicago Press, 1933), 24 ff. where the "conservative" nature of Japan's modernization is analyzed.

155. Meng Ch'i 孟祁, "Chi Ku Hung-ming weng" 記辜鴻銘翁 ("Recollections of the Venerable Ku Hung-ming"), *Jenshien-shih* 人間世, I, 12 (June, 1934), 45. For information on the Daitō Bunka Gakuin and the Daitō Bunka Kyōkai, see ch. IV, footnote 5, of this study.

culture.[155] He is reported to have said that Japan's destiny lay in maintaining and spreading this traditional culture since it was dying out in China.[156] Even Ts'ai Yüan-pei 蔡元培 (1867-1940), chancellor of the National University in Peking, a nationalist and ardent opponent of Confucianism in China, tacitly admitted in 1925 that Japanese civilization was the most similar and most suited to China because of its common basis in ancient Chinese culture.[157] It is also significant, in assessing the position of Confucianism during this period of the nationalist unification of China, that Confucian ceremonies were supported most by the anti-Kuomintang administrations in North China.[158] For example, Chang Tso-lin 張作霖 (1873-1928), the war-lord of Manchuria and North China who had the backing of the Japanese, was assiduous in promoting Confucianism,[159] and it is interesting that he had as his advisor in 1927 no less a person than the redoubtable old Confucianist Ku Hung-ming.[160]

With this background and the advocacy of the *Wang-tao* in Manchuria after 1932, which committed Japan to a policy of supporting Confucianism on the Asiatic continent, it was a natural step for the Japanese sponsored Provisional Government of China also to give its support to Confucian ideals and traditions. And indeed, the Provisional Government made a concerted effort to replace the nationalistic concepts of the Kuomintang with Confucian ones stressing the traditional virtues and social relationships.[161]

The determination to eliminate the Kuomintang and its political slogan of *San-min-chu-i* 三民主義 (Three Principles of the People) involved the creation of a new party with a different political theory. The new organization was called the Hsin-min-hui 新民會 and its program was dubbed the *Hsin-min-chu-i* 新民

---

156. Meng, *op. cit.*, I, 12 (June, 1934), 45.

157. Léon Wieger, *Chaos*, Chine moderne series, VIII, (Sienhsien, Hopei province, China: Hienhien 獻縣 press, 1931), 96.

158. *China Illustrated Review*, (Tientsin), (Feb. and March 10, 1938), as cited by Reginald F. Johnston, *Confucianism and Modern China*, 171.

159. See ch. III, footnote 37, of this study.

160. *Tōyō rekishi daijiten*, III, 234.

161. For an enumeration of the traditional Confucian social relationships and virtues, see ch. I, footnote 44, of this study.

主義, or Principles for Renovating the People.[162] These so-called "principles" deserve to be analyzed because of their similarity with those advocated by Confucianists and nationalists in Japan during the 1930's.

As in Manchuria, the *Wang-tao* was given an important role in legitimizing the new regime and in discrediting the alleged rule by force that had characterized government under the Kuomintang. The *San-min-chu-i* was attacked as the "rubbish of Western thought,"[163] unsuited to China, and the principle of livelihood declared to be sheer Communism.[164] It is notable that Western ideas and Communism were also being strongly attacked in Japan at this time, and in the propaganda of the *Hsin-min-chu-i*, the establishment of a common Sino-Japanese front against the agressive and materialistic Western powers was often proposed. How the *Hsin-min-chu-i* incorporated all these elements is made clear in a statement by a Chinese member of the Hsin-min-hui to primary school teachers in North China.

> Western methods of progress are not natural, as are oriental. The West uses scientific methods to correct and control natural development. This is the method of conflict. The Kuomintang adopted this and destroyed the old family and the old religion. The Japanese are shedding their blood in order to help restore Chinese civilization which was dying because the revolution destroyed Confucianism. China did not have the strength to resist the West one hundred years ago because men had forgotten Confucius and the Great Way. School masters must change the thinking of the students, tell them that the coming of Japan means the regeneration of China. If the two countries cooperate, the Yellow race will assume a big position in the world. China must not forget the five relations and the three bonds. Hu Shih wanted to change to Western methods. Wu Chih-huei said that Chinese methods of making books should be put into the lavatory and Ku Chieh-kang said that Chinese history is all bad. Because China did not like her own culture, Marxism came in;

---

162. Taylor, *op. cit.*, 70-71.
163. *Ibid.*, 210.
164. *Ibid.*, 73. In comparing the attitudes of Confucianists in China to those of Confucianists in Japan, it is significant that both condemned communism, but at the same time criticized the evils of monopoly capitalism and theoretically advocated a system in which profits would be shared more equitably.

Marx is entirely wrong and in fundamental conflct with oriental culture. Psychology says that if you teach children the right way, they will follow it. The Hsin-min-hui exists to correct people's thoughts and put them in the right way. Teachers have a great responsibility, for if we do not change the children, we cannot attain our object and build up China into a strong state.[165]

In other words, the revival of Confucianism as the basis of Chinese civilization was one of the principal aims of the Hsin-min-hui. It provided the Japanese a hope for creating a movement with some popular support, though they must have realized that to many Western trained Chinese, genuflections at Confucian ceremonies would be most distasteful. Nevertheless, it was not these groups that the Japanese had in mind when they sponsored a return to the old ways, but the gentry of the villages and towns through whom they expected to maintain control in the hinterland areas not directly occupied by Japanese troops.[166]

The work of the Hsin-min-hui and related Confucian organizations was widespread, extending to nearly every sphere of political and social action of the Provisional Government.[167] Thus every district (*hsien* 縣) had its local Hsin-min-hui which set up cooperatives, ran schools, distributed relief in distressed areas, spread propaganda, conducted Confucian ceremonies, engaged in censorship, printed textbooks, or even organized model villages. In a sense, the Hsin-min-hui seems to have competed with the Provisional Government, but in any case, its

---

165. *Ibid.*, 73-74. For information on Wu Chih-huei 吳稚暉, see *Tōyō rekishi daijiten*, III, 227. Wu (b. 1864; *gō* Ching-heng 敬恒) is one of the early Chinese revolutionary figures who became a follower of Sun Yat-sen while studying in Japan. He remained actively associated with the Kuomintang and held various positions of importance in it. Wu was known as an advocate of radical change and at one point joined an anarchist group.

Ku Chieh-kang 顧頡剛 (b. 1893), is a prominent historian who has greatly contributed to the study of Chinese history along modern, critical lines, and who was associated with the cultural revolution in China during the 1920's known as the "renaissance movement." A translation of his autobiography with notes and commentaries is available; Ku Chieh-kang, *The Autobiography of a Chinese Historian*, translated and annotated by Arthur W. Hummel (Leyden: E. J. Brill, 1931); the original Chinese was included as the preface to the first volume of Ku's work, *Ku-shih-pien* 古史辨 (*Symposium on Ancient Chinese Culture*), (Peiping: P'u-she 樸社, 1926).

166. Taylor, *op. cit.*, 76, 80-81.

167. Taylor, *op. cit.*, 70 ff. gives a detailed description of the Hsin-min-hui organization and activities.

efforts were closely integrated with the overall ideological purpose of reviving Confucianism; namely, to bring about a change
in loyalties such that the Chinese and Japanese could espouse
devotion to the same cause. This is what made the universal
values of Confucianism useful to the Japanese, for although these
values were originally indigenous to China, they were supra-
national in scope. That is to say, if a man accepted the Confucian
ethical code, lived according to its rules of propriety, and observed
the proper ceremonies, he theoretically could become a Confucian
"superior man" (*chün-tzu* 君子), irrespective of nationality.

Confucianism also offered to the Japanese in North China an
avenue for long-term thought control which the propaganda and
short-term programs of the Hsin-min-hui could not. This avenue
of thought control was mainly dependent on the encouragement
of Confucianism in the educational system to the exclusion of
other ideas which might develop a critical attitude or endanger
Sino-Japanese cooperation. Therefore the rewriting and reprint-
ing of elementary and middle school textbooks became a major
task of this Confucian revival, and by 1938, the authorization of
the *Hsiao-ching* 孝經 (*Classic of Filial Piety*) and *Lun-yü* 論語
(*Analects*) for primary schools; the *Ta-hsüeh* 大學 (*Great Learning*) and *Chung-yung* 中庸 (*Doctrine of the Mean*) for junior
middle schools; and the *Li-chi* 禮記 (*Record of Rites*) and *Tso-
chuan* 左傳 for senior middle schools, gave proof of the materialization of this program.[168]

A Classics Institute was set up too, and temples were restored
in an effort to preserve the visible symbols of Confucianism
throughout North China.[169] The type of preservation work done
is shown in a handsome book of plates of Confucian temples,
ceremonial objects, and other relics, *K'ung Meng cheng-chi t'u-
chien* 孔孟聖蹟圖鑑 (*Album of Plates of Sacred Remains of Confucius and Mencius*), published in 1940 by the Shantung Cultural
Research Society. In an epilogue to this book, the Society was
praised for working to save Confucianism in China after Western

---

168. *Ibid.*, 90-91
169. *Ibid.*, 83.

ideas had nearly destroyed it. This was declared to be contributing to Japan's great task of bringing peace and happiness to the world. The book bore the calligraphy of such leaders in the Provisional Government as Wang Keh-min, Wang I-t'ang, and T'ang Erh-ho, together with that of the war-lord-scholar Wu P'ei-fu 吳佩孚 (1872-1939), the seventy-third lineal descendant of Mencius, Meng Ch'ing-t'ang 孟慶棠, and Japanese and Korean Confucianists.[170]

Such in general were the major aims and methods of the Japanese in their sponsorship of Confucianism in North China. As in the case of Manchuria, support for Confucianism abroad had a different significance when considered in the context of Japan proper. Conditions in 1937, however, had changed radically from those in 1931, for the militarists and ultra-nationalists had virtually taken over complete control of Japan, with the result that the country was no longer "spiritually unprepared" as had been the case earlier. This meant that Japan's war in China, along with the policies adopted by the Provisional Government of China and other Japanese activities on the Asiatic continent, would be made to play an integral part in arousing the loyalty and devotion of the people to the nationalist cause. It was particularly so in the case of Japanese expansion into China, since the conflict demanded increasingly greater sacrifices by the whole nation, while the anticipated quick victory and spoils did not materialize.

The struggle in China was pictured to the Japanese as a titanic conflict of cultures in which Japan was helping China rid herself of the cancers of Western penetration and Communism, and return to the traditional spiritual civilization of Asia. A spokesman for the National League of Japanese University Professors declared: "How could Japan remain patient? Chiang Kai-shek and his sympathizers are at variance with the 400 million Chinese. Let us state here again that the Chinese people

---

170. *K'ung Meng sheng-chi t'u-chien* 孔孟聖蹟圖鑑 (*Album of Plates of Sacred Remains of Confucius and Mencius*), (Tōkyō: Santō Bunka Kenkyūkai 山東文化研究會, 1940).

are not Japan's enemy, but the Kuomintang and the Communists are our deadly enemy."[171]

The Kuomintang was accused of attempting to destroy the cultural heritage of China by its selfish dealings with foreign powers and efforts to extend European culture to the exclusion of the teachings of Confucius and Mencius.[172] In contrast to this, the Japanese were showing great concern for the venerable civilization of China, even to having Japanese army personnel clean and sweep out Chinese cultural establishments.[173] A Chinese delegate of the Hsin-min-hui in North China was invited to Tōkyō where he spoke of the need for collective Japanese and Chinese action to bring about a cultural renaissance along traditional lines. "Japan and China together must cooperate and reconstruct Eastern culture.... From Han times Chinese and Japanese culture have been closely related; from T'ang and Sung times they have formed one harmonious body."[174] General Doihara Kenji, whose earlier association with the Manchurian incident was noted, described the China conflict in the strongest terms: "...this is a war for the renaissance of Oriental culture.... To lose this war will mean the eternal defeat and subjugation of the Orient to Western civilization."[175]

Confucianism in Japan, because of its background of consistent anti-Westernism and its importance in the traditional Asiatic cultural heritage, was naturally called on to help give an ethical justification for this "crusade" and in other ways attest to the high ideals of the Japanese sponsored Asiatic renaissance. Kawai Tatsuo 河相達夫 (b. 1889), director of the Information Bureau of the Foreign Office, constantly made use of Confucian

171. National League of Japanese University Professors, *The Japan China Conflict and the Attitude of Japan*, (Tōkyō: The Nippon Press, 1937), 52.

172. Fujisawa Chikao 藤澤親雄, "Shimmin shugi no tetsuriteki kiso" 新民主義の哲理的礎基 ("Philosophical Basis of the *Hsin-min-chu-i*"), *Gaikō jihō* 外交時報 (*Revue Diplomatique*), LXXXV, 796 (1938), 29-30.

173. Nakamura Yasaji 中村彌三次, "Tairiku bunka seisaku ni tsuite" 大陸文化政策に就て ("Concerning Cultural Policies on the Continent"), *Gaikō jihō*, LXXXV, 795 (1938), 41-42.

174. Fujisawa, *op. cit.*, 29-30.

175. Doihara Kenji 土肥原賢次, "Taishi kokumin kōryō no konkan" 對支國民綱領の根幹 ("Basis of the [Japanese] People's General Policy toward China"), *Chūō Kōronsha* 中央公論 LXIII, 11 (Nov., 1938), 116, 123.

concepts in his book *Hatten Nippon no mokuhyō* 發展日本の目標 (*The Goal of Japanese Expansion*) to explain the war in China.[176] In one passage concerning expansion for self-defense and culture, he spoke of how such expansion was not really war when based on Confucian moral precepts.

> The Oriental ideal of love, benevolence and mutual help condemns war for selfish ends. Japan's armament—always a "divine sword that slays not"—is dedicated to the peace of East Asia and to the welfare of the world; it is employed only against the forces inimical to international justice and to the common interests of East Asia. Japan's advance, inspired by humanity, should not be confused with aggression for gain at the expense of other nations.[177]

At the same time, however, Confucianism could justify war if the aims were good.

> The declaration of the Japanese Government of January 16 this year, which sets forth a determined stand against Chiang Kai-shek, heralds the birth of a new order in Asia. It is based on what is called *jen* in Confucianism, which means perfect virtue or humanity and requires one not only to love the good, but to hate the bad and to punish the wicked. It is this spirit of *jen* that compels Japan to reject and destroy the unethical Kuomintang regime.[178]

The final goals of Japanese expansion as envisaged by Kawai were likewise directly related to the plea of Confucianists in modern Japan to reject Western materialistic culture and return to Asiatic civilization.

> The Asiatic peoples should cast aside all the selfish individualism and materialism of Europe. They should embrace one common faith of Asia and live an Asiatic life. The Confucianism that originated in China and was perfected in Japan, as if anticipating the needs of

---

176. Kawai Tatsuo 河合達夫, *Hatten Nippon no Mokuhyō* 發展日本の目標 (*The Goal of Japanese Expasion*), (Tōkyō: Chūō Kōronsha, 1938): this book was translated in an abridged form under the title, *The Goal of Japanese Expansion*, (Tōkyō: Hokuseidō 北星堂, 1938), and it is from the latter that all quotations and references in this study are taken.

177. *Ibid.*, 63-64.

178. *Ibid.*, 95.

today, long ago laid down the stern and solemn code of "self-mastery and return to decorum." Herein lies the common ideal for Japan, Manchoukuo and China.[179]

Although Kawai Tatsuo was well acquainted with Confucian ideas, he was himself a career foreign service official and not a Confucianist. This adds weight to thesis that Confucianism in Japan after 1933 became a vehicle for nationalist propaganda, since in earlier periods, statements by responsible officials pitting Japan and Asiatic culture unconditionally against the West had been avoided. Once the extreme nationalists and radical army elements gained control in Japan, though, they found many of their criticisms of Japanese political and social conditions echoed by those of the Confucianists. In particular, their opinions were the same concerning the evils of Western materialism and the overadulation of Western culture and ideas. It is not surprising, then, to find that outstanding representative Confucianists were consulted and brought to the fore at this time, especially in matters dealing with a revival of Asiatic traditional culture and with the attempted establishment by Japan of a common anti-Western ideology with China.

For example, the scholar Hattori Unokichi 服部宇之吉 (1867-1939), who had a long association with Confucian organizations in Japan dating back to the Meiji period, made secret recommendations in 1938 to the Cultural Affairs Section of the Foreign Office concerning cultural policy toward China.[180] While admitting that a cultural program for China must allow for differences between China and Japan, he criticized the Western direction of scientific and industrial education in China and recommended that greater emphasis be put on Asiatic studies. A Wang-tao Research Institute, staffed by Chinese and Japanese, could carry on investigation into problems of politics, law, economics, morals, education, and history, and devise ways to encourage Confucian

---

179. Ibid., 113.
180. Gaimushō Bunka Jigyōbu 外務省文化事業部, Taishi bunka seisaku ni tsuite 對支文化政策に就いて (Regarding Cultural Policy Toward China), (Tōkyō: 1939), section by Hattori Unokichi; as referred to by Hilary Conroy, "Japan's War in China: An Ideological Somersault," The Pacific Historical Review, XXI, 4 (Nov., 1952), 371-372. The author is indebted to Conroy's article for a number of ideas and references in this section.

virtues associated with the *Wang-tao*, such as humaneness, filial piety, self-improvement, and respect for obligations and authority. The diffusion of these ethical precepts was to be the responsibility of local Chinese supervisory personnel. Cultural contact between Japan and China was to be maintained through exchange professorships, exhibits, and the interchange of library materials.[181]

Professor Inoue Tetsujirō 井上哲次郎 (1856-1944), another veteran Confucianist of distinction, in 1939 published a book of his essays concerning the China war and its related cultural problems entitled *Tōyō bunka to Shina no shōrai* 東洋文化と支那の將來 (*Asiatic Culture and the Future of China*). Because of the multitude of topics brought up in the book, it is difficult to summarize Inoue's views in detail. Nevertheless, among the recurrent themes are his apology for Japan's actions in China and his appeal for the rebirth of China through a renewed emphasis on the superior spiritual values of traditional Asiatic civilization, especially Confucianism. In justice to Professor Inoue, it must be pointed out that he did not simply advocate for China a blind return to Confucianism or other traditional modes of thought. He considered that certain characteristics of Confucianism, such as the overemphasis on filial piety, the degradation of women, or the tendency toward a narrow formalism, needed to be changed.[182] Despite such shortcomings, he declared Confucian ethics were the most suitable for China and praised the Provisional Government of North China for basing its ideology of *Hsin-min-chu-i* on forward-looking Confucian principles.[183] Without this foundation, Inoue claimed China could not exist as an independent nation. He adduced evidence for his point of view by showing how Chiang Kai-shek and the Nationalist government had alternately needed to depend on England, France, the United States, and Russia for its survival since the people no longer had any common ideals.[184]

Japan, however, was mindful of the debt she owed to China for her past cultural inheritance, and now that modern Japanese

181. Conroy, *op. cit.*, 371-372.
182. Inoue, *op. cit.*, 134-135.
183. *Ibid.*, 137.
184. *Ibid.*, 93-94.

civilization was much more advanced than the Chinese, Japan was seeking to repay China and help her attain real independence.[185] According to Inoue, Japanese civilization had reached such a superior level because Japan alone of all the nations in the Far East had been able to preserve and develop traditional Asiatic civilization while adopting the strong points of Western civilization. Specifically this meant that spiritual and ethical aspects of Indian Buddhism and Chinese Confucianism had been amalgamated through the genius of the Japanese spirit with the scientific and material advances of Western civilization. Inoue called the product of the fusion the Culture of New East Asia (*Shin Tōa no bunka* 新東亞の文化). He felt that it was Japan's destiny to propagate and spread this new unifying ideology to all Asia.[186] Professor Inoue's views concerning the dichotomy of Asiatic and Western civilizations and the need for the creation of a new culture by uniting their respective spiritual and material values were directly in the tradition of Confucianists in Japan, Korea, and China. It will be remembered that many of these men had been deeply disturbed by the breakdown of universal ethical, cultural, and spiritual values in Asia. Therefore one can see in the Japanese espousal of Confucianism in North China an effort to establish a type of cultural and spiritual unity between the two nations that would appeal to certain groups and lessen the attraction of Chinese nationalism. It was correctly reasoned that anti-Japanese feeling had been engendered by Chinese nationalist agitation, and consequently the replacement of this nationalist ideology by Confucianism was meant to make Sino-Japanese cooperation easier. This is evident in educational ordinances of the Provisional Government, ordering the teaching of the *Four Classics* to change the anti-Japanese ideas of the students, and directing the spread of China's traditional virtues in order to develop China's mission according to the spirit of unity among the nations of East Asia.[187]

---

185. *Ibid,*. 205.
186. *Ibid.*, 263-267. Inoue also quoted the opinions of various foreigners supporting his views concerning the destiny of Japan in synthesizing elements of Eastern and Western culture; 280-286.
187. Taylor, *op. cit.*, 222-223.

The ideal of an Asia led by Japan and unified on the basis of traditional Oriental culture does not appear to have had great success in the areas of central and southern China which the Japanese occupied in 1937 and 1938. Even in North China, the rise of Chinese resistance under the Border Government of Hopei, Shansi and Chahar 察哈爾 constantly threatened the Japanese forces and made tenuous the control by the Provisional Government of all but the major towns and cities on the rail lines and other arteries of communication.[188] The Japanese had expected the hinterland areas would naturally fall under their control once the main lines of communication were occupied. This is no doubt one of the reasons they directed their ideological program of reviving Confucianism to appeal to the landed gentry, since it was calculated that this group could best insure the stability and domination of the hinterland with its large peasant population.

The Border Government, however, sponsored a program of revolutionary economic and political reforms that successfully attracted the peasantry who otherwise might well have cooperated with the Japanese, had it been simply a matter of choosing between the old Kuomintang regime or the new order of the Japanese. This situation created a paradox, for it was in the vast hinterland of villages that the old traditional social and political forms were most alive. There the Japanese had anticipated obtaining passive if not active support for their revived Confucian ideology; and yet the hinterland became the center of anti-Japanese resistance, while the cities, organized along modern social and political lines least suited to the realization of Confucian ideals, were the basis of Japanese power.[189] The cities also became the refuge for the dispossessed gentry who were unable to carry out the role assigned to them in the hinterland by the Japanese. This group therefore became useless to the Japanese as a means of social and political control, and the positive value of Confucian-

---

188. *Ibid.*, 40. About half of Taylor's book deals with the development of Chinese resistance to the Japanese in North China, organized and known as the Border Government of Hopei, Shansi, and Chahar.

189. *Ibid.*, 198.

Wang Ching-wei (front right)

ism declined correspondingly because the group to which it had the most appeal was powerless.[190]

The comparative failure in achieving significant political and social aims through a revival of Confucian ideology in North China may have been one of the decisive factors mitigating against its use as the guiding political principle in other sections of China occupied by the Japanese. Additional factors, such as the rivalry of various Japanese armies over their respective spheres of influence in occupied China, and the possibility that some sort of *modus vivendi* might be arranged between Japan and China, also played a part in the relegation of Confucianism to a secondary role in Japan's attempts to dominate China.[191] Finally, Japanese negotiations with Wang Ching-wei, number-two man in the Kuomintang government at Chungking 重慶, succeeded in persuading him to break with Chiang Kai-shek on December 18, 1938. Wang fled to Hanoi 河內 and declared himself for peace with Japan, urging other Nationalist officials to follow his example. Japanese leaders realized, though sometimes reluctantly, that with this move they must acknowledge the paramount claims of nationalism in China over Confucianism and universal Asiatic ideologies.[192] In effect, the change in attitude meant that the Japanese had decided it would be easier to dominate and exploit China by giving lip-service to the forms of Chinese nationalism than by attempting the kind of experiments with reviving the past which were failing in North China. As Japanese armies became increasingly bogged down in China, the need to find a political alternative to military conquest became ever more pressing. The prospect of a rival nationalist government to Chungking, led by Wang Ching-wei, seemed to offer great hope. After prolonged discussions, the Central Government

---

190. *Ibid.*, 200-201. Graham Peck, *Two Kinds of Time*, (Boston: Houghton Mifflin Co., 1950), 577, indicates how in late 1944 the Japanese reversed their policy of supporting the gentry on a sector of the Hunan 湖南 front, and appealed to the peasantry with apparently devastating success.

191. Conroy, *op. cit.*, 367-379, gives a good picture of the competing Japanese groups in China. See also Taylor, *op. cit.*, 176-177.

192. The tortured process involved in this metamorphosis of attitudes is well described by Conroy, *op. cit.*, 367-379.

of China was inaugurated at Nanking on March 30, 1940, replacing the former Reformed Government of Nanking, the United Council of China, and the Provisional Government of China in the north.[193]

The Central Government of China was claimed to be no new government, but the old Kuomintang government returned from Chungking; Wang Ching-wei was acting president, pending the return of president Lin Sen 林森 (1862-1943), and the same fiction was maintained with other government offices whose heads were to be welcomed back from the wilderness in Chungking.[194] The important point to bear in mind is that the Central Government of China was meant to represent the true and orthodox line of Kuomintang succession under the leadership of the favorite disciple of Sun Yat-sen. There was never any question over the use of the *Hsin-min-chu-i* or other Confucian derived ideologies as the basic principles of the Central Government, for these were clearly unsuitable to the proposed nationalistic tenor of the new regime.[195] The Japanese themselves recognized this fact practically from the very day Wang made his break with Chungking, and in official statements openly supported such long-standing Chinese nationalist aims as the abolition of extraterritorial rights and the return to China of foreign concessions.[196] General Itagaki Seishirō 板垣征四郎 (1885-1948), Chief-of-Staff of the Japanese Expeditionary Forces in China in 1940, declared that

> The West wishes China to remain a colony of the Western powers, in order that it may continue its exploitation for its own selfish gains; it thus fears accomplishment of the Chinese emancipa-

---

193. Taylor, *op. cit.*, 177, 187. The Reformed Government of Nanking was established March 28, 1938, representing the Japanese occupied sections of central and south China. The United Council of China was created in September 22, 1938 as a means of effecting collaboration between the Provisional Government of China and the Reformed Government of Nanking. Its main function appears to have been to act in place of a united central government, especially in matters where it was necessary for the two Japanese-sponsored Chinese regimes to present a united front, such as foreign policy statements. Actually, however, it had no legal or constitutional basis; no governmental powers; nor was it even formally recognized by Japan.

194. *Ibid.*, 183.

195. *Ibid.*, 28, 183-184.

196. As stated in Prince Konoe's Declaration of December 22, 1938; quoted in the *Voice of New China*, VI, 4 (May, 1941), 106.

tion and independence through Japan's help....

When China becomes a united nationalistic country and determined to cooperate, Japan and China may become good friendly neighbors. If the Japanese deceive the Chinese, following Western example, by exploiting China as a colony, they are violating the Japanese character of reason and righteousness....[197]

Japan being ostensibly committed to Chinese nationalist aims,[198] one might wonder if Confucian ideas still had any value in promoting the rapprochement between the two nations or encouraging stability in Japanese occupied sections of China. The evidence seems to show that they did, although supporters of the Central Government described Confucianism more as a part of the Chinese nation's cultural heritage than as an all-embracing universal philosophy of life. In this sense, the difference between the attempted revival of Confucianism in North China is apparent, for the Provisional Government of China had sponsored the Confucian-based *Hsin-min-chu-i* as a way of life, in which Confucian ideals stood as the unifying bond cementing the nations of East Asia.

The make-up of the Central Government of China also clearly set it apart from that of the Provisional Government of China whose conservative character has already been pointed out. No attempt was made to dredge up Ch'ing dynasty relics, and on the contrary, the leaders of the Central Government had a background of long support for the nationalist revolution in China. Some, such as Chiang Kang-hu 江亢虎 (b. 1883),[199] Chen Kung-po 陳公博 (1890-1945),[200] and Wang Ching-wei[201] himself were known to have

---

197. From a pamphlet written by General Itagaki Seishirō, as quoted in the *Voice of New China*, VI, 4 (May, 1941), 106.

198. Shigemitsu Mamoru 重光葵, *Shōwa no dōran*, II, 160 ff. As one of the important framers of China policy, Shigemitsu says that he long felt the most effective means of improving Sino-Japanese relations was for Japan to become a champion of real Chinese independence. He claims to have attempted to implement this during the periods between 1941 and 1945 when he was minister of Foreign Affairs.

199. For brief biographical notes, see *Tōyō rekishi daijiten*, III, 54; also see Hashikawa Tokio 橋川時雄, *Chūgoku bunkakai jimbutsu sōkan* 中國文化界人物總鑑 (*General Mirror of Persons in the Chinese Cultural World*), (Peiking: Chunghua Fa-ling Pien-yin-kuan 中華法令編印館, 1940), 109.

200. For brief biographical notes, see *Tōyō rekishi daijiten*, VI, 222.

201. For brief biographical notes on Wang Ching-wei, see *Tōyō rekishi daijiten*, I, 358-359.

leftist tendencies.[202] Therefore an appeal to Confucian ideas by members of the Central Government could not be interpreted solely as an effort to gain the support of the old gentry class, as had been the case in North China.

Nevertheless, Confucianism as part of the national cultural heritage was useful for encouraging social stability. For example, Wen Tsung-yao 溫宗堯 (b. 1875), later President of the Judicial Yuan of the Central Government, wrote in December 1939 of how

> ...the ancient moral teachings of China are now vehemently discarded and then strongly recommended, so that China's cultural attainments dating back five thousand years are cast away or picked up at will and all at the whim and fancy of one or two individuals. Such is the chaotic state of China. If no attempt is made to start things anew, the world is going back to the dark ages and man [will] degenerate into lower animals.[203]

This was meant to be a criticism of conditions under the Chungking regime, in contrast to which Wen described the efforts of the Japanese to bring a "new order" to China. He also disparaged those who feared Japan, for he claimed the Japanese were anxious to see a strong, independent China, and had great respect for Chinese cultural attainments, particularly Confucianism.

> As to China's hereditary culture, not only is Confucius worshipped by Japan and China alike, but the Japanese show more respect for Confucius than the Chinese. Even the sage Wang Yang-ming, whose teachings are only respected by the Chinese on [the] lips, is followed in Japan by actual practice. Supposing Japan should be given the chance to handle the education of the Chinese, besides

---

202. Shigemitsu, op. cit., I, 201, mentions a number of other figures in the Central Government who had leftist leanings. In reference to these persons, the adjective leftist may have been used because most were once members of the Communist Party or sympathetic with it, and also because these individuals favored more radical land and industrial policies than those supported in ruling Kuomintang circles.

203. Wen Tsung-yao, "New Order Explained," Voice of New China, III, 7 (Dec., 1939), 7. At times, the English in this and other material quoted from the Voice of New China is awkward. Minor corrections in spelling and syntax have therefore been made and are indicated by words in brackets. For brief biographical notes on Wen Tsung-yao, see Tōyō rekishi daijiten, I, 397.

science and technical instructions, she will teach China spiritually after Confucius for ancient philosophy and after Wang Yang-ming for later ideals. Thus is it advantageous or destructive to China as far as Chinese ideals [are] concerned?[204]

After Wang Ching-wei left Chungking in December 1938, his party and his followers were recognized in the Japanese occupied sections of China as the orthodox Kuomintang, the dominant political party of China. The actual process, however, of forming a new unified Chinese government under Wang was a difficult matter because of the existence of earlier Japanese sponsored regimes, the Provisional Government of China in the north and the Reformed Government of Nanking in central and south China. Wang Keh-min and Liang Hung-chih 梁鴻志 (1882-1945),[205] the respective heads of these two puppet governments, were naturally apprehensive over their possible loss of power, and the situation was further complicated by rivalry among competing groups of the Japanese army in China.[206] Long negotiations ensued between Wang Ching-wei and the other parties in attempting to find a solution to the problem of unification. Finally, at a conference held at Tsingtao 青島 from January 24 to 26, 1940, a measure of accord seems to have been reached concerning the establishment of a unified central government.

In a significant statement at this conference, Wang Ching-wei elucidated the meaning of the *San-min-chu-i* so as to provide a basis for criticizing those who were opposed to his peace movement with Japan and for uniting divergent groups on the basis of national aims.

The *San-min-chu-i* are principles leading to the salvation of our nation. They aim at elevating China from a semi-colonial status to that of freedom and equality among the nations.... However, these principles do not contradict the ideal of East Asia or of Universalism. The fundamental spirit of these principles is based on Chinese ancient morals and its code is peace. It does not aim at aggression. Therefore, it is *Wang-tao*, the Way of Right, not the *Pa-tao*, the Way of

---

204. Wen, *op. cit.*, 7.
205. For brief biographical notes, see *Tōyō rekishi daijiten*, IX, 149.
206. Taylor, *op. cit.*, 179 ff.

Might. China must first have her freedom and equality before she can be a member in East Asia and a member among the [family] of nations. This is the same principle that world peace comes after the governing of a nation; the governing of a nation comes after the regulation of a family, and the regulation of a family comes after the cultivation of the individual.[207]

The curious combination in this statement of an appeal both to nationalism and to Asiatic universalism can best be understood by considering the position of Wang at this time. He had to rely on the Japanese for his military support, and yet his strength and popularity were dependent on those who believed in his sincere devotion to the welfare of the Chinese nation. Since the willingness of the Japanese to continue supporting Wang would depend on the effectiveness of his appeal to the national sentiments of the Chinese,[208] he had to prove that his policy of peace and cooperation with the Japanese was the most effective means for achieving national aims. In this light, the seemingly contradictory aspects of Wang's statements are resolved. The national aims represented by the *San-min-chu-i* are still foremost in the proposed program of the new government, but the welfare of the state is also declared to be in harmony with Confucian-based ideals of peace and universalism in East Asia.

The prominence given to the idea of universalism in East Asia is particularly important because this was one of the claims used by the Japanese in their efforts to promote a rapprochement with China. It had even been brought up as early as 1925 by Sun Yat-sen in a speech he had made at Kobe on Pan-Asianism. There he had said that the *Wang-tao* was the ethical and humane doctrine binding together the nations of Asia, especially Japan and China.[209] Wang Ching-wei echoed this idea in his Tsingtao

---

207. "The Tsingtao Conference," *Voice of New China*, III, 10 (Feb., 1940), 6. Note the paraphrase of the *Ta-hsüeh* 大學 (*Great Learning*), 6. as translated by Legge, *Chinese Classics*, I, 356-357, in the last part of Wang's statement that "world peace comes after the governing of a nation..."

208. Taylor, *op. cit.*, 183.

209. Léon Wieger, *Le Feu aux Poudres*, Chine Moderne series VI, (Sienhsien, Hopei province, China: Hienhien 獻縣 press, 1926), 125. Sun's complete speech at Kobe is recorded by Wieger in this book. For the latest and most thorough study of Sun Yat-sen's relations wit hthe Japanese an dits significance for Pan-Asianism, see: Marius

statement, and a little later, he made direct reference to Sun's Pan-Asiatic declaration in the epilogue to a book entitled *China and Japan: Natural Friends—Unnatural Enemies.*

> Now that [Japan and China] have come to realize their past mistakes, and are exerting their respective efforts for a common destiny, the Pan-Asiatic doctrine is, fifteen years after the death of Dr. Sun Yat-sen, revived with a bright future.
>
> The association of Japan with ourselves on a basis of equality is exactly the realization of the aim and hopes of Dr. Sun's Pan-Asiatic doctrine....[210]

Other cases of the encouragement of Confucianism under the Central Government of China indicate a similar trend to use its principles as the basis for increased Sino-Japanese cooperation and friendship or to justify the policies adopted by the Central Government. Wen Tsung-yao, for example, whose praise of Japanese respect for Chinese culture has been mentioned, also held up Japanese women as practicing those Confucian womanly virtues on which depended the strength or weakness of the family and the state. In an article written in 1941 calling for the improvement of feminine education in China, he delineated the proper duties and responsibilities of women by quoting statements from Confucius and Wen Wang 文王[211] and by taking illustrative cases from Chinese history. Docility, obedience, attention to housework, and proper care for the family were declared to be the highest ideals for women. Finally, Wen Tsung-yao recommended the women of Japan as models to the Chinese, saying:

B. Jansen, *The Japanese and Sun Yat-sen,* Harvard Historical Monographs XXVII (Cambridge: Harvard University Press, 1954), especially chapter 9.

210. Sun Yat-sen, *China and Japan: Natural Friends—Unnatural Enemies,* edited by T'ang Leang-Li (Shanghai: China United Press, 1940), as quoted by *Voice of New China,* VI, 4 (May, 1941), 108.

211. Wen Wang was the father of Wu Wang 武王, first king of the Chou 周 dynasty (1122-225 B.C.). He was held up by Confucianists as epitomizing the ideal ruler and man of virtue, for though he opposed the last infamous ruler of the Shang 商 dynasty (1766-1122 B.C.), Chou-hsin 紂辛, he did not take the throne from him. This action was considered to reflect the virtue of Wen Wang. See: *Mengtzu* 孟子 (*Mencius*), Liang Hui Wang 梁惠王, II, 5; 10; Kung-sun Ch'ou 公孫丑, I, 1; as translated by Legge, *Confucian Classics,* II, 161-162; 169: 182-183. Also see the reign of Wen Wang described in the *Shih-chi* 史記, Chou pen-chi 周本記, (Shanghai: Po-na-pen edition, 1930-37), IV chuan 卷, p. 4 b-7 b; as translated by Édouard Chavannes, *Les Memoires Historiques de Se-ma Ts'ien,* (Paris: Ernest Leroux, 1895), I, 217-227.

If anyone thinks that the sayings of Emperor Wen Wang and Confucius are out of date, then let him look at the women of Japan. Everything of Japan compares favorably with European and American standards. But the morality of the Japanese women is much superior to their European and American sisters. The Japanese woman has got the knowledge of an American or European woman. But the American or European women have not got the qualities of a good mother like those of a Japanese woman.... The Chinese women on the contrary learn the bad points of the Western women, but miss what is good in them. China and Japan both copied things from the West. But because of this difference, China has become weak and Japan strong. ...If China wants her people to be strong and intelligent, she must pay more attention to her feminine education. The best way to attain this is to look to Japan for an example.[212]

A case more directly related to the political problems facing the Central Government is found in the comments of the *Central China Daily News* on how to commemorate the birthday of Confucius in 1941. The newspaper first pointed out that Chinese resistance to the Japanese had been based on false premises. The Chinese had deceived themselves concerning the situation both in China and Japan; therefore to continue in this error would be to disregard the teachings of Confucius who had warned people against being too opinionated or too stubborn.[213] As a further reproof to those Chinese who desired to continue the war under the leadership of Chungking, the newspaper described the unjust and inequitable conditions in the interior, using a phrase from the Confucian *Analects* (*Lun-yü* 論語) to illustrate how such injustice inevitably brought instability to the state.

As the war of prolonged resistance is for [the] interest of a few individuals, it is only natural that only those few people will be benefitted; Confucius said: "In a country as in a family, what we are afraid of is not scarcity of goods, but unequal distribution of these goods; not poverty, but restlessness." In this time of war, a few people have billions of American dollars deposited in foreign

---

212. Wen Tsung-yao, "Improvement of Feminine Education China Advocated," *Voice of New China*, VII, 2 (Oct., 1941), 35-36.
213. *Central China Daily News*, (August 27, 1941), as quoted in the *Voice of New China*, VI, 12 (Sept., 1941), 359-360.

countries while the majority of the peeople do not have anything to eat and are fighting at the subsistence level. This situation of wealth will naturally create a general situation of restlessness.... Why is there such restlessness in the interior? The answer is that there is no equal distribution in the interior. In commemorating the birthday of Confucius, we regret to say that Confucius' teaching has not been faithfully carried out, and, as a result, this restless situation has cropped up.[214]

Meanwhile, on the actual day of the anniversary of Confucius' birthday, August 27, 1941, a national holiday was proclaimed at Nanking, the capital of the Central Government. High Chinese and Japanese officials were present at the ceremonies held in the Hall of Confucius,[215] and Wang Ching-wei delivered a speech on "The Change in Attitudes toward Confucius by People in the Last Hundred Years."[216] This event once again illustrates how Confucianism served a dual role in China under the Central Government, for while Confucius' birthday was celebrated as a national holiday, it was also an occasion at which Japanese and Chinese together showed their respect for the universal Asiatic sage.

It is worthwhile at this point to try and evaluate as a whole the character of Japanese sponsored Confucianism in Korea, Manchuria, and China. Each of these areas posed certain unique problems to the Japanese in terms of the most efficacious methods for maintaining and extending their domination. Confucianism was one of the means employed in attempts to bring social and political stability in the conquered territories. Two common denominators, however, may be singled out among the most important factors effecting Japan's use and encouragement of Confucianism in Korea, Manchuria, and China. They are the

---

214. *Ibid.*, 360. The quotation of Confucius is from the *Lun-yü* 論語 (*Analects*), Chi-shih 季氏, 10; the translation in the *Voice of New China* is quite different from that given by Legge for the same passage, but seems just as plausible. See Legge, *Confucian Classics*, I, 308.

215. *Voice of New China*, VI, 12 (Sept., 1941), 362.

216. *Ibid.*, (section in Chinese), "Wang chu-hsi yen-chiang chi-nien hsien-shih K'ung-tzu tan-ch'en ch'üan-wen" 主汪席演講紀念先師孔子誕辰全文 ("Complete Text of Speech of Chairman Wang Commemorating the Birthday of Our Ancient Teacher Confucius"), 189-192.

strength of the nationalist spirit, and the extent to which the advocates of a predominantly traditional type of agricultural economy were still dominant. Generally speaking, Confucianism was on the stoniest ground in those places where the flame of nationalism burned brightest; and likewise, Confucianism had the least appeal in places where the traditional pattern of agrarian economy had broken down. In one sense, it appears that the strength of nationalism and the strength of traditional agrarian society were simultaneously affected in inverse proportion by the progressive intrusion of Western political and economic systems. Nationalism increased as Western influences did, but these in turn challenged the static values and social organization forming the basis of traditional agrarian society.[217]

Korea offers a particularly clear example of the above situation because of its early annexation by Japan in 1910, before Western intrusions had made great inroads. Korea still represented *par excellence* a society in which the traditional agrarian economy was dominant. There was little real national feeling among the peasants, and the ruling gentry-bureaucratic classes were more united by their devotion to a Confucian ethic[218] than loyalty to the state. This fact is illustrated in the type of opposition to the Japanese in Korea,[219] especially in the period between 1905 and 1910, which witnessed the rise of the "Righteous Army" (*Ŭipyŏng* 義兵).[220] Although the "Righteous Army" actively

---

217. See Shikata Hiroshi 四方博, "Kyūrai no Chōsen shakai no rekishiteki seikaku" 舊來の朝鮮社會の歴史的性格 ("Historical Characteristics of Traditional Korean Society"), *Chōsen gakuhō* 朝鮮學報, 3 (May, 1952), 131-147, for an excellent analysis of the static quality of traditional Korean agrarian society and the role of Confucian concepts in impeding the growth of industry and commerce in Korea.

218. For a striking illustration of the persistence of Confucian ethical norms in Korea, even during a period of so-called administrative reforms around 1900, see Laurent Crémazy, *Le Code pénal de la Corée, Tai-Han Yyeng Pep* 大韓刑法, (Seoul: The Seoul Press, 1904), especially such sections as: "Blessures entre parents," 95-97; "Défaut d'observance des cérémonies rituelles du deuil," 76-77; "Exemption de peine en faveur du fils qui tue le meutrier de son père," 85.

219. *Chōsen minzoku kaihō tōsō-shi* 朝鮮民族解放鬪爭史 (*History of the Struggle for Liberation of the Korean People*), edited by the Chosŏn Yŏksa P'yŏnch'an Uiwŏnhoe 朝鮮歷史編纂委員會 and translated from the Korean by the Chōsen Rekishi Kenkyūkai 朝鮮歷史研究會 (Kyōto: San'ichi Shobō 三一書房, 1952), 156-157.

220. *Ibid.*, 162-168. Also see F. A. McKenzie, *The Tragedy of Korea*, (London: Hodder and Stoughton, 1908), 168-208, for a first-hand description of fighting between the Japanese and the "Righteous Army."

fought the Japanese in minor engagements all over Korea, it
represented primarily a movement of supporters of the Yi dynastic house and of the old bureaucracy, carried on by discharged
Korean soldiers, in which there was relatively little participation
by the mass of the peasantry.[221]

Under these circumstances, the encouragement of Confucianism by the Japanese may be considered to have naturally
suggested itself as a means of maintaining political stability and
establishing social control.[222] However, the conditions for the
optimum effectiveness of Confucianism in this role did not continue long, for with the very cruel and harsh administration
during the first few years of Japanese rule, Korean national
spirit was greatly stimulated. And together with this came the
increasing dissolution of the old pattern of agrarian economy
because the Japanese themselves, in order to develop and exploit
Korea efficiently, rapidly introduced modern commercial and
industrial techniques. This tended to make the appeal of Confucianism less influential after the first ten or fifteen years of the
annexation,[223] but by that time, Japanese domination and control
of Korea were complete. Therefore the continued espousal of
Confucianism in Korea by the Japanese became more for the
purpose of showing the unity of ideals between Japan and Korea

---

221. Hatada Takashi 旗田巍, *Chōsen-shi* 朝鮮史 (*History of Korea*), (Tōkyō:
Iwanami Shoten 岩波書店, 1951), 199-200. Even the Communist interpretations of recent
Korean history, which praise the "Righteous Army" movement as a precursor to a
"people's nationalist liberation movement," admit that it lacked popular support. See
Chōsen minzoku kaihō tōsō-shi, 168-169. Also *Chōsen shin minshu shugi kakumei-shi*
朝鮮新民主主義革命史 (*Revolutionary History of Korea's New Democracy*), edited by
Kim Chŏng-myŏng 金鐘鳴 (Tōkyō: Gogatsu Shobō 五月書房, 1953), 25-26. It is inter-
esting to note that the word for "Righteous Army," *Ŭipyŏng* 義兵 was used by the
North Koreans in reference to Communist guerrillas in South Korea after 1945.

222. It is significant that in the period immediately following the annexation, when
nearly all other Korean organizations were being dissolved, the Government General
of Korea sponsored the Keigakuin 經學院 to encourage Confucianism. See ch. IV, p.
166-167 of this study. Despite their avowed support for Confucianism, they Japanese
apparently did not trust strictly Korean Confucian associations, and many of the latter
seem to have suffered the same fate as other Korean organizations at this time. For
the suppression of organizations, see Takeuchi Tatsuji, *War and Diplomacy in the
Japanese Empire*, (Garden City: Doubleday, Doran and Co., 1935), 165; *Annual Report
on Reforms and Progress in Chosen (1910-11)*, (Seoul: Government General of Chosen,
1911), 85-86; *Annual Report on Reforms and Progress in Chosen (1911-12)*, 53-54.

223. Takahashi Tōru 高橋亨, "Chōsen ni okeru Jukyō" 朝鮮に於ける儒教 ("Confucianism in Korea"), *Shibun* 斯文, V, 1 (Jan., 1923), 88-89.

than to help preserve social order.

The same analysis used in the case of Korea may be applied to Manchuria and China, making allowances for the differences in the relative conditions of each area and the period of Japanese expansion. Manchuria in 1931 was predominantly agricultural,[224] and Chinese nationalism had not yet been able to make much headway because of the continuing dominance of warlords in the region since the revolution of 1911. Thus a favorable situation for the effective use of Confucianism in Manchuria was present, and in addition, following the return of the former Chinese Emperor to a position of nominal power, the symbolic head of the Confucian world, the *t'ien-hsia* 天下,[225] was restored. The conscious espousal of the *Wang-tao* 王道 and the use of *Ta-t'ung* 大同[226] as the "style" for the new era of government in Manchuria after 1932 show that the Japanese were very much aware of the appeal which Confucian concepts could have to the Chinese. In Manchuria, however, just as in Korea, the great gap between theory and practice seems to have belied the high ideals espoused by the Japanese,[227] and their development of commerse and industry in the area further created conditions which were not suited to the traditional Confucian social and economic pattern of life. Nevertheless, the Japanese continued assiduously to promote Confucianism in Manchuria, declaring its principles to be those guiding the nation.

It was important for the Japanese to do this in view of the assertions they increasingly made in the 1930's over their concern for the future of tradtional Oriental civilization. The climax to

---

224. Jerome B. Cohen, *Japan's Economy in War and Reconstruction*, (Minneapolis: University of Minnesota Press, 1949), 37.

225. See Joseph Levenson, "*T'ien-hsia* and *Kuo* and the 'Transvaluation of Values,'" *F.E.Q.*, XI, 4 (Aug., 1952), 447-451, for a discussion of the significance of *t'ien-hsia* and the Confucian values associated with it.

226. See ch. IV, footnote 121, of this study.

227. A granddaughter of Cheng Hsiao-hsu told the writer that by 1935, Cheng had become quite disillusioned with the state of affairs in Manchoukuo. Although he had tried to resign on various occasions before, he was not permitted to do so by the Japanese who no doubt wished to use his reputation as a scholar and Confucianist. Finally, in 1935, Cheng was allowed to resign after he made a speech indirectly ciriticizing the Japanese. He alluded to Manchoukuo as a child who must be allowed to walk alone and suggested that this time had arrived.

this policy came with the struggle for North China, after the Lukouchiao incident in 1937, when the Japanese attempted to make Confucian doctrines the basis of their ideological appeal to the Chinese. They realized that direct control over as populous and vast an area as North China would be very difficult, and hence were seeking some method of attracting an influential social group to the Japanese cause.

On the surface, conditions seemed propitious for the success of a political and social program based on Confucianism, for in all China, nationalism was weakest in the north, and the economy was characterized by the overwhelming predominance of the small, traditional agricultural village.[228] Once again, though, the excesses of the Japanese as well as the presence of many Japanese camp followers and carpetbaggers served to arouse Chinese nationalist sentiment,[229] imposing a serious obstacle to the effectiveness of Japanese-sponsored Confucian ideology. Perhaps equally important in causing the appeal of Confucianism to lag was the revolutionary program of social and economic reform sponsored by the Border Government of Hopei, Shansi, and Chahar. Apparently the mass of the peasantry were so drawn to this program that they gave up many of their old loyalties to actively participate in the struggle against the Japanese which had transcendent national objectives.[230] Since the Japanese could not directly contact the peasantry, they had hoped indirectly to do so through the gentry by promoting Confucianism which would strengthen the bonds of the traditional agricultural system.[231] A segment of the gentry seem to have been amenable to these aims, for it was to their benefit to maintain the *status quo;* but because of the rejection by the peasantry of the old ties, this gentry group became isolated and impotent as a social force.

The Japanese no doubt recognized the interaction of some of the factors described above. Such an assumption helps to explain

---

228. George Babcock Cressey, *China's Geographic Foundations,* first edition, fifth impression (New York and London: McGraw-Hill Book Co., 1934), 172.

229. Taylor, *op. cit.,* 26, 77, 115.

230. *Ibid.,* 109-110, 112-113, 116-117.

231. *Ibid.,* 76-77, 80-81.

why they did not try to push a political and social program based on Confucianism in Central and South China.[232] In particular, they appear to have become aware that the strength and parsistence of the Chinese nationalist movement ruled out the possibility of Confucianism being made the principal vehicle for uniting the aims of the two nations. It is here that one can grasp the significance of Japan's new role as the ostensible supporter of national liberation for China after 1940; for in this new situation, while Confucian ethical principles continued to be praised, Confucianism as an overall social philosophy was replaced by concepts with a more conscious national appeal.

---

232. It is also to the point to note the greater urbanization of Central and South China over North China, together with the deeper influence which Western industry and commerce had made on these areas. Cressey, *op. cit.*, 309, 367-368. Such developments often brought tension and dislocation to Chinese society on which nationalism tended to flourish.

The cultivatable land area per person was also much less in the south than in the north, which may have made the peasant in the south potentially more revolutionary and nationalistic than his brother in the north. Cressey, *op. cit.*, 297-298, 355.

CONCLUSIONS

In this study of Confucianism in modern Japan, an attempt has been made to trace in some detail the history of Japanese Confucian institutions and Confucian thought, particularly during the years from 1868 to 1945. Because the basis for the influence of Confucianism in modern Japan lay in the Tokugawa period, a brief outline of its developments at that time was also presented, but little attention was given to comparing this background to that of Confucianism in the corresponding period of Chinese history. Such a comparison, however, can reveal some of the fundamental underlying aspects of modern Japanese social and intellectual history, as well as help clarify certain factors which caused Japan's transition from a feudal agricultural society to a modern industrial state to be so different from China's.

The very fact that Tokugawa Japan was a feudal society should be mentioned first, for it set off Japan socially and intellectually from China. On the surface, Confucianism was the dominant intellectual creed in both countries, serving to rationalize and help perpetuate fixed social relationships, and providing the training for government administrators.

In Japan, however, status and position were determined by birth without reference to beliefs. Even in early attempts during the Nara period (710-782) to transfer the Chinese examination system to Japan, the equalitarian premises of the system were distorted to fit the hierarchical organization of Japanese society, and only nobles of the fifth rank and above were permitted to attend government schools and take the examinations for office.[1]

---

1. Kubomi Masayasu 窪美昌保, *Taihōryō shinkai* 大寶令新解 (*New Interpretation of the Taihōryō*), revised second edition (Tōkyō: Meguro Jinshichi 目黒甚七, 1916), II, 310, 318.

This emphasis on hereditary status was a characteristic of Japanese social order still persisting in the Tokugawa period, for even then, a man's position was not dependent on the possession of any particular corpus of learning, but primarily on birth. This is the antithesis of the situation in China where the qualification for office was not formally birth, but a knowledge of Confucianism. In the ordinary course of events, a man would have difficulty obtaining a position in the bureaucracy without it.

Nor was there present in Japan that type of basic combination between landholding and office which characterized Chinese traditional society, and to which Confucian social values fitted so well by their balancing of public and private interests. The sale or alienation of land was not permitted in Japan during the Tokugawa period,[2] and the ruling *daimyō* compensated their samurai by fixed rice incomes commensurate with their military and administrative duties. Landholding itself was not a characteristic of the ruling warrior class.

Furthermore, Tokugawa Japan, despite such institutions as the Seidō which trained officials in the Confucian canon,[3] was feudal in its basic organization and ideals, The significance of this can most easily be grasped by noting that the military class and not the scholar was at the apex of Japanese society. This meant that the martial virtues and military prowess would be valued above learning and academic pursuits, and is illustrated by the fact that most Japanese heroes were men of will rather than intellect, warriors rather than scholars. Under these circumstances, it is easy to understand why in Japan loyalty was considered higher in the scale of values than filial piety, a reversal of the pattern in China.

Although the Tokugawa Shōguns adopted Confucianism in order to inculcate ideas which would help stabilize the *status*

---

2. E. Herbert Norman, *Japan's Emergence as a Modern State*, I.P.R. Inquiry Series (New York: Institute of Pacific relations, 1940), 16, 20-21. Norman notes certain minor exceptions to this, but the prohibition against the sale or transfer of land was necessary for the maintenance of Tokugawa feudal hegemony.

3. See ch. I, footnote 38, of this study.

quo and maintain an effective administration, it was a conscious choice made because Confucian doctrines seemed the most useful and practical at the time. The spread of Confucianism in society might be expected to arouse greater interest in peaceful pursuits among the samurai, but the dominant position of the Tokugawa was still ultimately dependent on its military strength and that of its vassals and their samurai. Recognition of this may be found in the separation of the warrior from farming and other occupations in which he had often been engaged during peaceful periods before the Tokugawa.[4] The samurai's primary function was to fight loyally for his lord in return for a rice stipend. Confucianism could strengthen the bond of loyalty between the samurai and his lord, or provide him with a certain amount of learning through which he could better administer his lord's domain, but the samurai's commitment to Confucianism was fundamentally a secondary one, subordinate to the values and duties of a military code.

This situation is quite the opposite from that in China where a civilian bureaucracy constituted the fundamental ruling class, and where Confucianism rationalized the existence and permanence of Chinese gentry society through a universally accepted system of examinations expected to determine those best fitted to govern. Theoretically, at least, the examination system was open to all persons, selection being on the basis of ability, which gave Chinese society a measure of social mobility not present in Japan.

Although Japan had her die-hard Confucianists, many samurai leaders and the Tokugawa government itself realized that Confucianism alone was no longer adequate to deal with the problems facing the nation in the years immediately preceding the *Meiji Restoration*. Since Confucianism never was the essential concomitant of the political and social order of Tokugawa Japan, it is not surprising to find that once its practical value to that society declined, samurai and even some Confucianists became more interested in acquiring Western learning

---

4. Norman, *op. cit.,* 16-17.

than in studying the Confucian classics.[5] With the advent of the Meiji Restoration, there was relatively little difficulty in putting aside all vestiges of institutionalized Confucianism which the Tokugawa had maintained. Even more important was the fact that Confucianism as a system of thought fell into abeyance, and yet few people gave this more than passing notice.

In China, however, Confucianism was not simply a creed which had been selected from a number of competing philosophies to achieve particular objectives. It was a way of life encompassing the ultimate standards for Chinese social and political order, and possession of Confucian learning was universally recognized as a necessary prerequisite for holding office. Therefore Confucianism could hardly be cast aside in China as easily as it had in Japan, for it would mean a real alienation from values which had been accepted by the Chinese for nearly two thousand years. The reluctance of the Chinese to part with Confucian values for over seventy years after the Opium War is in strong contrast to the craze for Western learning which swept Japan immediately following the Meiji Restoration, only a little more than a decade after the opening of Japan by the West in 1854.

One further point needs to be elaborated in comparing the fortunes of Confucianism during the nineteenth century; namely, that Confucianism was Chinese in origin and background, and alien to Japan. Shintoism, as the native Japanese belief, never really competed with Confucianism in Japan until the rise of national consciousness in the latter part of the Tokugawa period. When Confucianism was proving itself increasingly inadequate to deal with the problems posed by the threat of the West to Japan, a revived Shintō tradition with the Emperor as the symbolic unifying head of the nation was ready at hand to replace

---

5. Honjō Eijirō 本庄榮治郎, *Economic Theory and History of Japan in the Tokugawa Period*, (Tōkyō: Maruzen 丸善, 1943), 19. Honjō makes a pointed statement of the fact that:

> ...It was under the stress of necessity that foreign ideas were imported. It was due to her desire to profit by the ideas of advanced countries that Japan adopted Confucianism in the Tokugawa period and imported Western economic thought after the Meiji Restoration. It was by no means out of curiosity or caprice that she did so.

the moribund foreign creed. It may be an exaggeration to say that Meiji leaders really were intellectually attracted to Shintō beliefs, but there can be no doubt that they found the prestige of the Emperor and appeal of Shintō mythology useful in unifying and strengthening the state.

On the other hand, Confucianism for China represented the most powerful and universally accepted indigenous tradition, one that Taoism and Buddhism, the latter of which had a foreign origin, were entirely incapable of replacing. This meant that there would be an intellectual vacuum in China if the Chinese ruling classes discarded Confucianism. Such a consideration helps explain their reluctance to do this and their efforts to "modernize" Confucianism, illustrated so well in Chang Chih-tung's 張之洞 (1837-1909) book *Ch'üan-hsüeh p'ien* 勸學篇 (*Exhortation to Study*).[6] Nevertheless, Confucianism had to be put aside as the basis for the Chinese way of life and as the ultimate source for the determination of knowledge and truth before China could make significant progress toward industrialization and modernization.[7] Yet exactly because Confucianism was so much more deeply rooted in China than Japan, such a change was correspondingly more difficult, and would imply a more fundamental renunciation of former values than the discarding of Confucianism had for Japan.

The truth of this assertion becomes evident in Japan by the middle of the Meiji period, after the first flush of Westernization and experimenting with various types of new educational, administrative, and social institutions had taken place. Following the adoption of modern industrial, financial, and commercial techniques essential to strengthening the state, Japanese leaders became aware of dislocation being caused by the process of modernization, particularly the lack of any fixed standard of ethical and

---

6. The *Ch'üan-hsüeh p'ien* 勸學篇 was published in 1898, shortly before the fateful "100 day reform." It was translated into English under various titles such as *Learn* and *China's Only Hope*. See Chang Chih-tung, *China's Only Hope*, translated by the Rev. Samuel I. Woodbridge (New York: Fleming H. Revel Co., 1900), 151.

7. Such a move on the part of the Chinese was only finally taken in 1904 when the traditional examination system, which principally tested a candidate's knowledge of the Confucian classics, was abolished.

social values. Despite the abolishment of clans and dissolution of
local ties which had divided the loyalties of the people during the
Tokugawa period, new cleavages among the agricultural population, urban workers, supporters of Christianity, advocates of
reforms along particular Western lines, and adherents of rising
political parties threatened the unity and social stability of the
state. It was at this point that men such as Motoda Eifu were
able effectively to reassert the need for Confucian ethical values
to bring back the acceptance of a universal moral standard among
the Japanese people. Confucian ideology, with its tradition for
upholding social harmony and exhorting individuals to carry out
their respective duties, naturally recommended itself to Japanese
leaders as a counterbalance against disruptive tendencies ap-
pearing in the second and third decade of the Meiji period.

But Confucian ethical principles had to be subordinated to
the claims of nationalism, for simply to bring Confucianism
back as another competing philosophy on the Japanese scene
would have been to further confuse and splinter men's loyalties.
By 1890, the material basis for a strong Japanese state along
modern lines had been established, and the pressing need, as
envisaged by the moulders of Japanese policy, was to find a
unifying force in the ideological realm such that people would
feel their primary loyalty was to the state. The Emperor, because
his position could be considered above criticism, was used as
the vehicle for accomplishing this end, and among the landmarks
pointing the way to the desired norms was the Imperial Rescript
on Education of the Emperor Meiji. In the Rescript, the five
Confucian virtues associated with the Confucian social relationships were declared to be a fundamental part of the Japanese
heritage, bequeathed to and implanted among the Japanese people
by the Imperial Ancestors. Confucian ethics were henceforth no
longer foreign, but a part of pristine Japanese traditions; and
while this did not automatically imply a revival of organized
Confucian institutions in Japan, it suggested that the most effective way for Confucianists to reestablish their prestige and influence was by having Confucianism serve the aims of the state.

This emphasis on the practical value of Confucianism in

modern Japan is crucial for understanding the development of Japanese intellectual history, for the situation in 1890 was basically a repetition of that in the Tokugawa period when Confucianism also had been adopted because it was deemed useful in achieving certain desired ends. Neither in Tokugawa Japan nor in Japan after 1868 did that particular type of social and political structure exist which was fundamental to the kind of all-embracing commitment to Confucian values characteristic of traditional China. Nevertheless, Confucian ethical principles were consciously chosen to be part of the Japanese moral code. To appreciate this process of borrowing, it may be useful to compare these circumstances with those involved in the use of Confucianism during the period of the Enlightenment in Europe by men such as Voltaire. Certainly the political and social structure of European nations at this time was most unlike that of China, but Confucianism was praised and declared worthy of emulation because it could serve to discredit the church and weaken the hold of superstitions associated with religion.[8] Such a use of Confucianism, however, did not indicate any real attachment to Confucian values, and once clericalism died out as a major issue in Europe, an active interest in Confucianism ceased.

Of course, Japanese social and political conditions, as well as the long Japanese tradition of Chinese studies, made Confucianism much less ephemeral in Japan than in Europe. Nevertheless, the essentially practical aspect of its appeal can clearly be seen in the history of Confucian organizations in modern Japan. Without exception, Confucian organizations gained in prestige and influence as they related their activities to current social and political problems. This did not mean that Confucianism became important in activating mass movements, for on the contrary, Confucianism was a philosophy which appealed to the ruling classes in their role as leaders and mentors of the state. For example, the Shibunkai, the most important Confucian organi-

---

8. See Adolf Reichwein, *China and Europe, Intellectual and Artistic Contacts in the Eighteenth Century*, The History of Civilization Series (New York: Alfred A. Knopf, 1925), 87 ff. Also see François Marie Arouet de Voltaire, *Dictionnaire Philosophe ou la Raison par Alphabet*, (Paris: Edition de Cluny, 1930), I, 196-201.

zation in modern Japan, never was large nor did it have many branches spread throughout Japan to help popularize its teachings. Its influence did not lie so much in numbers of members as in the type of men who supported it. Among its most ardent backers were important businessmen, influential political leaders, university professors, high-ranking military men, and noted scholars. In other words, the typical supporters of Confucianism in modern Japan represented a cross-section of the Japanese elite.

The attraction of the Shibunkai and similar Confucian organizations is difficult to understand unless one keeps in mind that Confucianism was essentially a call for an inner change of heart and purification of self. Confucianists in China as well as in Japan had always held that this was the really basic change necessary to attain an ideal society, and not simply a change of institutions or outward forms. In the *Analects* itself was the statement, "The Master said, 'A man can enlarge the principles which he follows; those principles do not enlarge the man'."[9] And this phrase was quoted by a Japanese writer in 1925 to corroborate his belief that the future of Confucianism in Japan was dependent on its role in fostering a spirit of conscious self-criticism.[10] The significance of this theory for Japan in the twentieth century was the use it could be put to in criticizing overly radical social, political, and economic change. In the hands of conservatives, as the great majority of the supporters of Confucianism were, it provided the basis for asserting that corruption, materialism, infatuation with individualism, Communism and other Western ideas were responsible for the nation's ills, which could be remedied only by a change in the hearts of men. Institutions of representative government, Western style houses, agencies for collective bargaining, and all similar types of outward forms were declared unimportant without a purification of self.

---

9. *Lun-yü* 論語 (*Analects*), Wei Ching Kung 衛靈公, 28; as translated by James Legge, *Confucian Classics*, second edition, revised (Oxford: Clarendon Press, 1893), I, 302.

10. Iwahashi Junsei 岩橋遵成 *Nihon Jukyō gaisetsu* 日本儒教概説 (*Outline of Japanese Confucianism*), (Tōkyō and Ōsaka: Hōbunkan 寶文館, 1925), 378.

Consequently these men tended to advocate traditional ways, for they considered the sloughing off of superficial modern habits as evidence that the proper emphasis was being put on inner spiritual transformation.

It was only a short step from the spiritual change deemed necessary by the supporters of Confucianism to the revival of the Japanese spirit demanded by the Japanese nationalists. Like the Confucianists, they claimed that an inner change was essential and that attention to outward material forms was superficial. This found an expression in the ideal of the soldier who was taught in the Imperial Rescript to Soldiers and Sailors that, "Duty is heavier than a mountain, but death is lighter than a feather."[11]

In line with the emphasis on spirit by Confucianists and nationalists, both also criticized Western civilization as being overly materialistic. The fact was that Japan by 1920 had come to suffer from many of the same internal economic and social problems as Western nations. Confucianists, however, blamed the difficulties arising from such problems as unemployment, corruption in government, agricultural dislocation, and labor unrest on the preeminence given to material considerations rather than to ethical and spiritual ones. This had been a standard Confucian explanation for many of the ills besetting Japan since Meiji times, but it became an increasingly popular and acceptable point of view after 1931 when Japanese nationalists found their forcible solutions to Japan's problems often blocked by Western powers.

The nationalists actively made use of many of the ethical values in Confucianism like loyalty, filial piety, sincerity, humaneness, and righteousness, associating them with duty towards the nation and devotion to the Emperor. They were thus able to

11. Teikoku Chihō Gyōsei Gakkai 帝國地方行政學會 Genkō hōren shūran 現行法令輯覽 (Compilation of Present-day Laws and Ordinances), Tōkyō: Naikaku Kampō Kiroku-ka 內閣官房記錄課, 1930), VI, Gunji 軍事 (Military Matters), 2. A reference to this ideal and the attitudes it engendered among Japanese soldiers fighting in China during the late 1930's may be found in Hanama Tasaki, Long the Imperial Way, (Boston: Houghton Mifflin Co., 1950), 13.

claim that the aims of the nation had a spiritual and ethical content which set them above the purely materialistic aims of most Western states. A definite overtone of this attitude may be found in a speech delivered by Prince Konoe Fumimaro 近衛 文麿, the Prime Minister, on September 11, 1937, at the opening of a National Spiritual Mobilization Drive in Tōkyō.

> A nation, in its essence, is a cooperative organism united by the common objective of achieving a cultural mission imposed on it. Every composing member of the nation, therefore, is not merely a material existence living in pursuit of personal gains alone, but a spiritual being willing to participate in the furtherance of humanity. This interpretation of the nation and its composing members has been gaining strength more and more of late after the peoples of the world have come to find something wanting in the material cul‑ ture of the Occident.[12]

This avowed concern for spiritual values not only charac- terized Japanese policy at home, but became a major tenet of the Japanese war aims in China, as described in the last chapter, and throughout the whole Far East after the outbreak of the Pacific War on December 7, 1941. Spiritual values were spoken of as the outstanding attribute of Oriental civilization which could unite all Asia.[13] One might question whether there was any significant connection between Confucian principles and Japanese wartime declarations concerning so-called spiritual values, were it not for the remarks made by Uzawa Sōmei 鵜澤総明 in the prelimnary statement of the Defense Summation at the Inter- national Military Tribunal for the Far East, held in Tōkyō from 1946 to 1948.

---

12. Kawamura Shōichi 川村彰一 (ed.), *The Truth Behind the Sino-Japanese Crisis*, (Tōkyō: The Japan Times and Mail, 1937), 3.

13. In the areas conquered by the Japanese, among the leaders who made state- ments concerning the need for stressing spiritual civilization as a means of unifying Asia against materialistic Western culture were: Jose P. Laurel, president of the Philip- pines; Wang Ching-wei 汪精衛, provisional president of the Central Government of China; his Royal Highness, Prince Wan Waithayakon of Thailand: and Subhas Chandras Bose, head of the Indian Provisional Government. *The Japan Year Book, 1943-44*, (Tōkyō: Foreign Affairs Association of Japan, 1943), 1029, 1057, 1060, 1075-76.

Uzawa Sōmei, it will be recalled,[14] was a lawyer who in the early 1920's had criticized Western civilization for its materialism and inability to resolve the conflict among radical Western philosophies. He had contrasted this situation in the West with conditions in Japan where the spirit of peace and harmony, known as *Wang-tao*, was dominant. Uzawa apparently maintained this conviction concerning conflict and impending chaos in the West, for in his preliminary statement at the International Military Tribunal for the Far East, he spoke of how circumstances in the world, beyond the control of individual men, had almost made inevitable the outbreak of the second World War and its extension to the Far East. Uzawa then pointed out the similarity between the tense situation existing in the world during the period from 1918 to 1939 and the general conditions described in the *I-ching* 易經 (*Book of Changes*), one of the Confucian classics, under certain of its hexagrams which warned of calamities.[15]

From here Uzawa continued his argument by claiming that the defendants were men whose thought was based on the spirit of peace found in antiquity when such books as the *I-ching* had been compiled.[16] They were men of Confucian culture[17] who used phrases such as *hakkō ichiu* 八紘一宇 (eight corners of the world under one roof), taken from the ancient classics of China and Japan, to indicate all-embracing peace, and not territorial aggrandizement as averred by the prosecution.[18] The Greater

---

14. See ch. III, 128-130, of this study. Uzawa who died only in 1957, was made Chairman of the University Councilors of the newly founded International Christian University in Tōkyō, founded in the early 1950's. This appointment seems rather inappropriate in view of Uzawa's earlier attitudes toward Western philosophy and thought.

15. *IMTFE*, Defense Summation, Introductory Statement, Defense Document, # 3054, 10-15. Uzawa referred to the *pi* 否 hexagram as one example. For a description of conditions under *pi*, see Z. D. Sung (trans.), *The Text of the Yi King, Chinese Original with English Translation*, (Shanghai: The China Modern Education Co., 1935), 59-62.

16. *IMTFE*, Defense Summation, Introductory Statement, Defense Document, # 3054, 10, 23-29.

17. *Ibid.*, 31-36.

18. *Ibid.*, 24-29. Uzawa went through a long and complex phonetic-semantic analysis to prove this point, quoting from many Chinese and Japanese sources. The phrase *hakkō* 八紘 first occurred in a Han dynasty work, the *Huai-nan tzu* 淮南子. See *Huai-nan tzu* 淮南子, tsu-bu-tsung 四部叢 edition (Shanghai: Commercial Press, 1922), chuan I, 5 a; chuan IV, 3 b, 4 a; The *Nihon shoki* 日本書紀 (*Chronicle of Japan*) is the first Japanese work in which *hakkō* appears, although the characters are read *ame no*

East Asia Coprosperity Sphere was nothing more than an attempt
to establish the independent existence of Asia, based on the
Wang-tao ideal of peace which had originated in Asia and "flowed
into Japan for consummation."[19]

Uzawa's assertions that it was impossible to accuse the
defendants of criminal responsibility and plotting of aggression
because of their sincere devotion to Confucian ideals[20] went
almost unnoticed by the prosecution. It is doubtful if more than
a few members of the prosecution even were aware of the impli-
cations in Uzawa's appeal. In any case, the defendants were
being tried for specific actions they had committed or were
responsible for, and not for their ethical beliefs or cultural
heritage. Perhaps Uzawa was more concerned in justifying the
defendants in the eyes of the Japanese, under which circumstances his appeal to Confucian principles may well have struck
a responsive cord. This, however, brings up the question of
whether the avowed suporters of Confucian ideals in modern
Japan were sincere and actually trying to put theory into practice.

It would be difficult to question the beliefs of old-line Confucian scholars and educators such as Hattori Unokichi or Inoue
Tetsujirō, although their Confucian tradition gave them an anti-
Western bias which was susceptible to use by nationalists and
militarists. In contrast to these men of intellect, there were men
of action like General Araki Sadao 荒木貞夫 or Ōkawa Shūmei
大川周明 who spoke in terms of Confucian ethical priciples, but
whose deeds were so far removed from Confucian ideals as to
make their sincerity seem superficial. An extreme example of
the gulf separating Confucian theory from practice was General
Matsui Iwane's 松井石根 (1878-1948) description of Japanese military action in China in the 1930's as the punishment by an elder
brother meted out to an obstreperous younger brother, motivated

---

shita according to Iida Takesato 飯田武郷, *Nihon shoki tsūshaku* 日本書紀通釋 *(Explanation of the Chronicle of Japan)*, fifth printing (Tōkyō: Daitōkaku 大鐙閣, 1927),
II, 1208.

19. *IMTFE*, Defense Summation, Introductory Statement, Defense Document, #
3054, 29.

20. *Ibid.*, 34-35.

by love.[21] Matsui was in charge of the Japanese forces in the Nanking area during the grisly so-called "rape of Nanking" in December, 1937,[22] but could nevertheless characterize such brutality against the Chinese using Confucian terminology.[23]

A commentary on this type of shallow devotion to Confucian principles is found in a statement of Shigemitsu Mamoru 重光葵 wartime Foreign Minister of Japan who himself was in prison two and a half years as a convicted war criminal. He said, remarking on the Japanese defeat, that Japan had rejected the *Wang-tao* or way of leadership through the example of virtue, and chosen instead the *Pa-tao* or way of leadership through force.[24] With statement, Confucianism had completed a cycle of adaptation in Japan, for from a source to justify Japanese expansion, it had become a basis for criticism of that expansion.

21. *IMTFE*, Exhibits, Defense Document 2738, exhibit # 3498, 3-4.

22. *IMTFE*, Proceedings, 3894-3944, give a number of first-hand accounts of Japanese atrocities in Nanking after its fall on December 13, 1937.

23. For references in the Confucian classics to the proper relations between elder and younger brothers see *Lun-yü* 論語 (*Analects*), II, 8; as translated by Legge, *op. cit.*, I, 148. *Lun-yu*, IX, 15; as translated by Legge, *op. cit.*, I, 222; *Ta-hsüeh* 大學 (*Great Learning*), IX; as translated by Legge, *op. cit.*, I, 370-372.

24. Shigemitsu Mamoru 重光葵, *Shōwa no dōran* 昭和の動亂 (*The Upheavals of the Showa Period*), (Tōkyō: Chūō Kōronsha 中央公論社, 1952), I, 257.

BIBLIOGRAPHY

The following bibliography is simply a list of the books and articles used in the preparation of this study, and no attempt has been made to cover comprehensively all materials pertaining to Japanese Confucianism. Also, since many of the books and articles referred to have only a passing connection with Japanese Confucianism, annotations have been limited to those dealing directly with Confucianism in modern Japan. In the case of articles taken from the magazine *Shibun* 斯文, however, few annotations are given because the magazine itself was the major organ of Japanese Confucianism from 1919 to 1945, and as such it deserves to be considered as a whole. Many of these articles, though, are discussed in the text and footnotes of the study, together with other books and articles on which no comments are made in the bibliography below. The abbreviations mentioned in the preface have also been used in the bibliography.

ORIENTAL LANGUAGE — BOOKS

Arai, Tsuneyasu, 新井恒易. *Nippon chihō bunka dantai sōran* 日本地方文化團體綜覽 (*General View of Japanese Local Cultural Organizations*). Tōkyō: Nippon Bunka Chūō Remmei 日本文化中央聯盟, 1942.

Ashikaga, Enjutsu 足利衍述. *Kamakura Muromachi jidai no Jukyō* 鎌倉室町時代之儒教 (*Confucianism of the Kamakura and Muromachi Periods*). Tōkyō: Nihon Kotenzenshū Kankōkai. 日本古典全集刊行會. 1932.

A Brief Survey of Recent Sinological Study in Japan. Compiled and edited by Ku-lu Wang. Shanghai: Life Publishing Co., 1935.
   Despite the English title, this book is written entirely in Chinese.

It includes in its survey of Sinological studies in Japan useful sections describing the Shibun Gakkai, the Shibunkai, and similar important Confucian organizations in Japan since the Meiji period.

Bamba, Masatomo 萬羽正朋. *Nippon Jukyōron* 日本儒教論 (*Theory of Japanese Confucianism*). Tōkyō: Mikasa Shobō 三笠書房, 1939.

A short but good interpretive history of Japanese Confucianism, with emphasis on the Tokugawa period. The author seems to have been influenced by Marxist thought in the manner in which he relates ideology to particular social and economic groups, but this treatment of the subject is stimulating and a change from the usually dry, unanalyzed mass of details found in many histories of Japanese Confucianism.

Buya shokudan 武野燭談 (*Candlelight Talk from Musashi*). Kokushi sōsho 國史叢書 series. Tōkyō: Kokushi Kenkyūkai, 國史研究會, 1917.

Chōsen jimmei jisho 朝鮮人名辞書 (*Korean Biographical Dictionary*), 2nd edition. Keijō: Chōsen Sōtokufu Chūsūin 朝鮮總督府中樞院, 1938.

Chōsen minzoku kaihō tōsō-shi 朝鮮民族解放闘爭史 (*History of the Struggle for Liberation of the Korean People*). Edited by the Chosŏn Yŏksa P'ŏnch'an Uiwŏnhoe 朝鮮歷史編纂委員會, and translated from the Korean by the Chōsen Rekishi Kenkyūkai 朝鮮歷史研究會. Kyōto: San'ichi Shobō 三一書房, 1952.

Chōsen no kyōdo jinshi, dai nibu: sekiten, kiu, antaku; fu, kyōdo jinshi bunken 朝鮮の郷土神祀第二部；釋奠，祈雨，安宅；附郷土神祀文獻 (*Local Korean Temples, part two: Confucian Ceremonies, Prayers for Rain and Safeguarding the Home; supplement, Records on Local Temples*), Chōsa shiryō 調査資料 no. 45, Keijō: Chōsen Sōtokufu, 1938.

This book contains detailed statistical information and historical data on Confucian temples throughout Korea. The Confucian ceremonies carried out in these temples during the period of Japanese control of Korea are also described, as well as other non-Confucian ritual practices common among the people.

Chōsen no ruiji shūkyō 朝鮮の類似宗敎 (*Korean Quasi-religions*). Chōsa shiryō 調査資料 no. 34, Keijō: Chōsen Sōtokufu, 1935.

This book is based on comprehensive research carried out by the Korean Government-General concerning the "quasi-religions" existing in Korea in the early 1930's. There is a special section on Confucian inspired "quasi-religions," but Confucian influences will be found to permeate many of the other types discussed. An excellent work useful for both historical and sociological study.

Chōsen no shūraku 朝鮮の聚落 (*Korean Villages*). Research series no. 38, Keijō: Chōsen Sōtokufu 朝鮮總督府, 1933.

Chōsen Shi Henshūkai 朝鮮史編修會. *Kindai Chōsen shi kenkyū* 近代朝鮮史研究 (*Study of Recent Korean History*). Keijō: Chōsen Sōtokufu, 1944.

Chōsen shi taikei 朝鮮史大系 (*Outline of Korean History*). Keijō: Chōsen shi Gakkai 朝鮮史學會, 1927. 5 vols.

Chōsen shin minshu shugi kakumei-shi 朝鮮新民主主義革命史 (*Revolutionary History of Korea's New Democracy*). Edited by Kim Chong-myŏng 金鐘銘. Tōkyō: Gogatsu Shobō 五月書店, 1953.

Chōsen Shina bunka no kenkyū 朝鮮支那文化の研究 (*Studies of Korean and Chinese Culture*). Edited by the Keijō Teikoku Daigaku Hōbun Gakkai 京城帝國大學法文學會. Tōkyō: Tōkō Shoin 刀江書院, 1929.

This book consists of a series of essays, including Takahashi Tōru's 高橋亨, "Richō Jugakushi ni okeru shuriha shugiha no hattatsu" 李朝儒學史に於ける主理派主氣派の發達, dealing with the development of the Schools of form and matter in the history of Korean Confucianism. This cleavage was of great importance in the history of Korean thought, influencing political factions up to the present day. Takahashi's article is considered one of the best studies of the subject.

Chosŏn sŭngmu Yuhyŏn nyŏnp'yo, pu shipp'al sŏnsaeng nyŏnpo 朝鮮陞廡儒賢年表, 附十八先生年譜 (*Chronological Table of Canonized Korean Confucian Sages, supplement*: *Chronological Biographies of the Eighteen Masters*. Keijō: Taedong Samunhoe 大東斯文會, 1928.

This book was published to commemorate the Emperor Shōwa's ascending the throne, and it was hoped that by making known the details of the lives of Korea's canonized Confucian Sages, public morality would be improved. The chronological tables in the book are very useful for research, and the book itself is a good example of Japanese attempts to support traditional values in Korea.

Chosŏn sŭngmu Yuhyŏn nyŏnp'yo 朝鮮陞廡儒賢年表 (*Chronological Table of the Canonized Korean Confucian Sages*). Keijō: Taedong Samunhoe 大東斯文會, 1928.

See *Chosŏn sŭngmu Yuhyŏn nyŏnp'yo, pu shipp'al sŏnsaeng nyŏnpo*. In addition, this volume contains an appendix with speeches, lists of members, and other useful information concerning the Korean Confucian organization Taedong Samunhoe.

Dai hyakka jiten 大百科辞典 (*Great Encyclopedia*). Tōkyō: Heibonsha 平凡社, 1931-35. 28 vols.

Hashikawa, Tokio 橋川時雄. *Chūgoku bunkakai jimbutsu sōkan* 中國文化界人物總鑑 (*General Mirror of Persons in the Chinese Cultural World*). Peking: Chung-hua Faling Pien-yin-kuan 中華法令編印館, 1940.

Hatada, Takashi 旗田巍. *Chōsen-shi* 朝鮮史 (*History of Korea*). Tōkyō: Iwanami Shoten 岩波書店, 1951.

Hattori sensei koki shukuga kinen rombunshū 服部先生古稀祝賀記念論文集 (*Collection of Commemorative Essays Congratulating Professor Hattori on his Seventieth Year*). Tōkyō: Fusambō 富山房, 1936.

Hioki, Shōichi 日置昌一. *Kokushi dainempyō* 國史大年表 (*Great Chronology of National History*). Tōkyō: Heibonsha 平凡社, 1935-36. 7 vols.

Horiuchi, Tateki 堀内干城 *Chūgoku no arashi no naka de* 中國の嵐の中で (*In the Midst of the Maelstrom of China*). Tōkyō: Kangensha, 乾元社 1950.

Huai-nan tzu 淮南子. Tsu-bu-t'ung 四部叢 edition. Shanghai: Commercial Press, 1922.

Iida, Takesato 飯田武郷. *Nihonshoki tsūshaku* 日本書紀通釋 (*Explanation of the Chronicle of Japan*). Fifth printing. Tōkyō: Daitōkaku 大鐙閣, 1927.

Iijima, Tadao 飯島忠夫. *Nippon no Jukyō, Kokutai no hongi kaisetsu sōsho* 日本の儒教, 國體の本義解說叢書 (*Japanese Confucianism, Explanatory Series on the Meaning of National Polity*). 5th edition. Tōkyō: Mombushō Kyōgakukyoku 文部省教學局, 1941.

A short survey of the history of Japanese Confucianism by a scholar who was associated with the writing of *Kokutai no hongi*. The book has a nationalist interpretation, but is useful because of the clarity with which the author expresses himself and his good choice of illustrative material.

Inoue, Tetsujirō 井上哲次郎. *Nippon Yōmei gakuha no tetsugaku* 日本陽明學派の哲學 (*The Philosophy of the Japanese Yōmei School*). 3rd edition. Tōkyō: Fusambō 富山房, 1901.

————. *Tōyō bunka to Shina no shōrai* 東洋文化と支那の將來 (*Asiatic Culture and the Future of China*). Tōkyō: Risōsha 理想社, 1939.

Inoue Tetsujirō was a well-known professor of philosophy and veteran supporter of Confucianism in Japan. This book is a collection of his essays written for the most part after the outbreak of Sino-Japanese hostilities in July, 1937. In general, he is critical of Chinese iconoclasm and advocates Sino-Japanese rapprochment on the basis of a revival of Confucianism and Asiatic spiritual civilization. A valuable book for gaining an insight into the Japanese attempts to create a universal Asiatic ideal.

Iwahashi, Junsei 岩橋遵成. *Nihon Jukyō gaisetsu* 日本儒教概説 (*Outline of Japanese Confucianism*). Tōkyō and Ōsaka: Hōbunkan 寶文館, 1926.

A historical survey of Confucianism in Japan from the time of its introduction into the country down to about 1920. This book includes many details concerning Japanese Confucianism, but it is weak on interpretation and is often confused. It also tends to consider events from a nationalist point of view. There is a useful chapter, however, on Confucian developments in Japan since the Meiji period.

Katō, Seiichi 加藤盛一 and Takahashi, Shunjō 高橋俊乘. *Yontei Dainihon rekishi teiyō* 四訂大日本歷史提要 (*Summary of the History of Great Japan, Fourth Revision*). Approved by the Korean Government-General; fifth printing. Tōkyō: Fuzambō 富山房, 1936.

Kim, Kyŏng-t'ak 金敬琢. *Yugyo chŏlhak sasang kaeyo* 儒教哲學思想概要 (*Outline of Confucian Philosophical Ideas*). Seoul: Sŏnggyun'gwan 成均館, 1950.

From this work, written by a contemporary Korean Confucianist, one can gain an idea of how Confucianism is being adjusted to and changed by Western philosophical beliefs in Korea.

Kiyowara, Sadao 清原貞雄. *Kaishū Nippon dōtoku shi* 修改日本道德史 (*History of Japanese Morality, Revised edition*). Tōkyō: Chūbunkan Shoten 中文館書店, 1937.

This is a long book covering the major changes which have occurred in the formulation of morality throughout Japanese history. Its particular value for this study lies in its description of the reaction by traditionalists and Confucianists to developments in the Meiji and Taishō periods.

Kokushi Jiten 國史辭典 (*Dictionary of National History*). Tōkyō: Fuzambō 富山房, 1940-43. 4 vols.

Ku, Chieh-kang 顧頡剛. *Ku-shih-pien* 古史辨 (*Symposium on Ancient Chinese Culture*). Peiping: P'u-she 樸社, 1926. 7 vols. in 9.

Kubomi, Masayasu 窪美昌保. *Taihōryō shinkai* 大寶令新解 (*New Explanation of the Taihōryō*). Tōkyō: Meguro Jinshichi 目黒甚七, 1916. 4 vols.

Kung Meng sheng-chi t'u-chien 孔孟聖蹟圖鑑 (*Album of Plates of Sacred Remains of Confucius and Mencius*). Tōkyō: Santō Bunka Kenkyū-kai 山東文化研究會, 1940.

A handsome book of pictures, rubbings, and reproductions from Confucian temples in North China, accompanied with explanatory comments. The Japanese devoted considerable sums to restoring and preserving historical remains in China such as appear here, often with political considerations in mind. This album is a good example of such a work.

Kuzū, Yoshihisa 葛生能久. *Tōa sengaku shishi kiden* 東亞先覺志士記傳 (*Biography of Pioneer-patriots in East Asia*). Tōkyō: Kokuryūkai 黒龍會, 1933-36. 3vols.

Motoda, Eifu and Sugi, Magoshichirō 元田永孚, 杉孫七郎. *Yōgaku kōyō* [and] *Fujokan* 幼學綱要, 婦女鑑 (*Essentials of Learning for the Young, Mirror of Womanhood*). 5th edition. Tōkyō: Kunaishō 宮内省, 1915.

These two books were written by two of the most important Japanese Confucianists during the Meiji period in an effort to provide basic books on ethics and morality for the rising generation. They are examples of the type of code of conduct considered desirable by Confucianists in an era when many of the old values were being threatened or swept away.

Nakamura, Kyūshirō 中村久四郎. *Nippon bunka to Jukyō* 日本文化と儒教 (*Japanese Culture and Confucianism*). Tōkyō: Tōkō Shoin 刀江書院, 1935.

A short book attempting to assess the influence of Confucianism on Japanese culture. The author takes the view that the Japanese have chosen those elements of Confucianism which were compatible with the Japanese national polity, and rejected the rest. This process, he claims, has been going on for centuries, until the basis of Confucianism has been fully assimilated in Japan.

Nakayama, Yasumasa 中山泰昌. *Shimbun shūsei Meiji hennen shi* 新聞集成明治編年史 (*Meiji Chronological Collection of Newspapers*). Tōkyō: Zaisei Keizai Gakkai 財政經濟學會, 1935-36. 15 vols.

Nihonbunka Kenkyūkai 日本文化研究會. *Nihon Jukyō* 日本儒教 (*Japanese Confucianism*). Tōkyō: Tōyō Shoin 東洋書院, 1936.

Nihon Jugaku nempyō 日本儒教年表 (*Chronological Table of Japanese Confucianism*). Tōkyō: Shibunkai 斯文會, 1923.

This book is useful primarily as a reference work. It lists important events related to the history and development of Confucianism in Japan from 200 A.D. through 1922, arranged in chronological order. References are concise, and the sources of information are usually listed under each item. Thirty pages are devoted to the period after 1868, but many important events are left out which are significant for Japanese Confucianism during these years, such as the promulgation of the Imperial Rescript on Education of the Emperor Meiji and the landmarks leading to it.

Nihon kyōiku bunko 日本教育文庫 (*Library of Japanese Education*). Tō-kyō: Dōbunkan 同文館, 1913. 12 vols.

Nihon no Jukyō 日本の儒教 (*Japanese Confucianism*). Tōkyō: Nippon Jukyō Sen'yōkai 日本儒教宣揚會, 1934.

The Nippon Jukyō Sen'yōkai was an important Japanese Confucian organization founded in 1934. This volume includes an assorted collection of speeches, essays, and other materials related to the founding of the organization and its activities.

Oda, Shōgo 小田省吾 and Ǒ Yun-jǒk 魚允迪. *Chōsen bunbyō oyobi shōbu Juken* 朝鮮文廟及陞儒廡賢 (*Korean Confucian Temples and Canonized Confucian Sages*). Keijō: Chōsen Shi Gakkai 朝鮮史學會, 1924.

This is a valuable book for doing research on Korean Confucianism, for it contains a brief history of the Sǒnggyun'gwan, the center of Confucianism in Korea; a list of canonized Korean Confucianists with brief biographies; a chronology listing events of major importance in the history of Confucianism in Korea; the regulations established by the Japanese for the Keigakuin which replaced the Sǒnggyun'gwan; and collections of some of the writings of outstanding Korean Confucianists.

Ōkawa, Shūmei 大川周明. *Shintei Nippon nisen roppyakunen shi* 新訂日本二千六百年史 (*The Two Thousand Six Hundred Year History of Japan, Newly Revised*). 21st edition. Tōkyō: Daiichi Shobō 第一書房, 1940.

Otsuka, Tatsuo 大塚龍夫 and Uematsu, Yasushi 植松安. *Kojiki zenshaku*

古事記全釋 (*Complete Explanation of the Kojiki*). 5th edition. Tō-kyō: Fukyūsha 不朽社, 1935.

Shinsen dai jimmei jiten 新撰大人名辞典 (*Newly Edited Great Biographical Dictionary*). Tōkyō: Heibonsha, 平凡社, 1937-41. 9 vols.

Shibunkai 斯文會. *Kinsei Nihon no Jugaku* 近世日本之儒學 (*Recent Japanese Confucianism*). Tōkyō: Iwanami Shoten 岩波書店, 1939.

A valuable collection of essays on Confucianism during the Tokugawa period. The contents are divided into essays dealing with official Tokugawa Confucianism; aspects of Confucianism among the clans; and problems of Confucianism in Edo.

Shibunkai 斯文會. *Shibun rokujūnen shi* 斯文六十年史 (*A History of Sixty Years of Confucian Studies*). Tōkyō: Shibunkai 斯文會, 1929.

This book is a history of Confucian studies and events related to its encouragement from 1868 through 1928. There is, however, little attempt at interpretive analysis in the work, and it might be more appropriately characterized as a collection of important primary sources and documents than as a history. The arrangement of materials in the book is topical, and special attention is given to the development of Chinese studies in various universities and institutes throughout Japan.

Shigemitsu, Mamoru 重光葵. *Shōwa no dōran* 昭和の動亂 (*The Upheavals of the Shōwa Period*). Seventh printing. Tōkyō: Chūō Kōronsha 中央公論社, 1952. 2 vols.

Shotō kokushi 初等國史 (*Elementary National History*). 2nd edition; revised. Keijō: Chōsen Sōtokufu 朝鮮總督府, 1937.

Shotō kokushi 初等國史 (*Elementary National History*). Fifth grade; fourth printing. Keijō: Chōsen Sōtokufu 朝鮮總督府, 1942.

Shōwa jūkyū-nijū nendo Toyōshi kenkyū bunken ruimoku 昭和十九・二十年度東洋史研究文獻類目 (*Bibliography of Oriental Historical Studies for 1944 and 1945*). Kyōto: Kyōto Daigaku Jimbun Kagaku Kenkyū-jo 京都大學人文科學研究所, 1951.

Takada, Shinji 高田眞治. *Nippon Jugaku shi* 日本儒學史 (*History of Japanese Confucianism*). Tōkyō: Chijin Shokan 地人書館, 1941.

A short history of Japanese Confucianism written by a member of the Shibunkai. Under these circumstances, it is not strange to find that the author describes the development of Confucianism in modern

Japan in terms of the overadulation for Western materialism which was only overcome when spiritual culture began to be revived in Japan. Despite this point of view, the book is clear and presents a useful over-all survey of Japanese Confucianism.

Takahashi, Shunjō　高橋俊乘.　*Nihon kyōikushi*　日本教育史　(*History of Japanese Education*).　Revised, 2nd edition.　Tōkyō: Kyōiku Kenkyūkai 教育研究會, 1934.

Takahashi, Tōru　高橋亨.　*Richō Bukkyō* 李朝佛教 (*Buddhism of the Yi Dynasty*).　Chōsen shisōshi taikei series no. 1 朝鮮思想史大系第一.　Tōkyō and Ōsaka: Hōbunkan 寳文館, 1929.

This is the most authoritative study of Yi dynasty Buddhism available. It deals historically and topically with the subject, but much information on Confucianism in Korea is included because the decline of Buddhism during the Yi dynasty was largely due to the opposition of Confucianists. There is a section on developments in the modern period of Japanese control of Korea.

Teikoku Chihō Gyōsei Gakkai 帝國地方行政學會.　*Genkō hōrei shūran* 現行法令輯覽 (*Compilation of Present-day Laws and Ordinances*).　Tōkyō: Naikaku Kambō Kirokuka 內閣官房記錄課, 1930. 12 vols.

Tokutomi, Iichirō　德富猪一郎.　*Motoda sensei shinkōroku* 元田先生進講錄 (*Record of Lectures before the Emperor of Mr. Motoda*). 2nd popular edition, with supplement. Tōkyō: Min'yūsha 民友社, 1934.

Motoda Eifu was one of the most important Confucianists in Japan in the first half of the Meiji period because of the favored position he held with the Imperial house. His lectures provide one of the best sources from which to gain an insight into how Japanese Confucianists of this period viewed the rapid changes taking place in their country. Included in the book are a sketch of Motoda's life and comments on the part he played in drawing up the Imperial Rescript on Education of the Emperor Meiji.

Toriyama, Kiichi 鳥山喜一.　*Joshi shingaikoku rekishi, Tōyō no bu* 女子新外國歷史東洋の部 (*New History of Foreign Nations for Women, Section on Asia*).　Third revised edition.　Tōkyō: Teikoku Shoin 帝國書院, 1939.

Toyoda, Takeshi 豊田武.　*Nippon Shūkyō seido shi no kenkyū* 日本宗敎制度史の研究 (*A Study of the History of Japanese Religious Systems*).　Tōkyō: Meguro Shoten 目黒書店, 1935.

Tōyō rekishi daijiten 東洋歷史大辭典 (*Historical Dictionary of East Asia*).

2nd printing. Tōkyō: Heibonsha 平凡社, 1938-39. 9 vols.

Uda, Hisashi 宇田尚. *Nihon bunka ni oyoboseru Jukyō no eikyō* 日本文化に
及ぼせる儒教の影響 (*The Influence of Confucianism on Japanese Culture*). Tōkyō: Tōyōshisō Kenkyūkai 東洋思想研究會, 1935.

Yamada, Yoshio 山田孝雄. *Jinnōshōtōki jutsugi* 神皇正統記述義 (*Explanation of the Jinnōshōtōki*). Tōkyō: Min'yūsha 民友社, 1932.

Yun Munbaksa yuko 尹文學士遺稿 (*Posthumous Works of Mr. Yun, M.A.*).
Keijō: Chōsen Insatsu Kabushiki Kaisha 朝鮮印刷株式會社, 1933.

Mr. Yun was a promising young Korean scholar who unfortunately
died before he was thirty, and this volume was published to commemorate him. It includes his M.A. thesis which deals brilliantly with
the rise and influence of Neo-Confucianism in Korea. There is also
a study of a nineteenth century Korean Confucianist, Kim Yak-yong
金若鏞, and his proposals for land reform.

Watanabe, Ikujirō 渡邊幾次郎. *Nippon kempō seitei shikō* 日本憲法制定史講
(*Lectures on the History of the Formulation of the Japanese Constitution*). Tōkyō: Chigura Shobō 千倉書房, 1937.

This book deals primarily with the problems and personalities involved in the formulation of the Japanese constitution, but since
the Imperial Rescript on Education of the Emperor Meiji was closely
related to this attempt to stabilize the philosophy and institutions
of government, much material on the formulation of the Rescript is
included. In particular, the conflict between the ideas of Motoda Eifu
and Itō Hirobumi are discussed, showing the divergence between
the ethical interpretation of events characteristic of Confucianists
and the interpretations of more practical men of that day.

Zenkoku kyōka dantai meikan 全國教化團體名鑑 (*Register of Cultural
Organizations throughout the Country*). Tōkyō: Chūō Kyōka Dantai
Rengōkai 中央教化團體聯合會, 1929.

Zokkokushi taikei 續國史大系 (*Continuation of the Outline of National
History*). Tōkyō: Keizai Zasshisha 經濟雜誌社, 1902. 15 vols.

ARTICLES

"Abbreviated Regulations of the Shibunkai," *Shibun*. I, 1 (Feb., 1919), 1-2.

Abe, Munetaka 阿部宗孝. "Koten no sonchō," 古典の尊重 ("Reverence for the Classics"), *Shibun*. XV, 12 (Dec., 1933).

"Chūgakkōrei shikō kisoku kaisei ni kan shi Mombudaijin e no gushin" 中學校令施行規則改正に關し文部大臣への具申 ("Representation to the Minister of Education Concerning a Reform of the Regulations for Carrying Out the Middle School Law"), *Shibun*. XIII, 7 (July, 1931), 539-594.

Department of Research of the Shibunkai. "Concerning the *kambun* course in Middle Schools," *Shibun*. I, 2 (April, 1919), supplement.

Doihara, Kenji 土肥原賢次. "Taishi kokumin kōryō no konkan" 對支國民綱領の根幹 ("Basis of the Japanese People's Policy toward China"), *Chūō Kōron* 中央公論. LXIII, 11 (Nov., 1938), 116-124.

Egi, Kazuyuki 江木千之. "Kokka toshite no sekiten" 國家としての釋典 ("The Confucian Ceremony as a National [Ceremony]"), *Shibun*. XII, 10 (Oct., 1930), 3-5.

Fujisawa, Chikao 藤澤親雄. "Shimmin shugi no tetsuriteki kiso" 新民主義の哲理的基礎 ("Philosophic Basis of the *Hsin-min-chu-i*"), Gaikō *jihō* 外交時報 (*Revue Diplomatique*). LXXV, 796 (Feb., 1938), 1-32.

Hagura, Shin'ichirō 羽倉信一郎. "Yoshida Shōin no Jukyō shichō to sono kokkakan" 吉田松陰の儒教思潮と其國家觀 ("The Confucian Intellectual Trend of Yoshida Shōin and his National Views"), *Shibun*. XV, 1 (Jan., 1932).

Hattori, Unokichi 服部宇之吉. "Democracy and Confucianism," *Shibun*. I, 4 (Aug., 1919), 327-334.

———. "Meaning of Confucianism for the Present," *Shibun*. I, 1 (Feb., 1919), 19-36.

———. "Radical Thoughts as Seen from the Point of View of Confucianism," *Shibun*. II, 6 (Dec., 1920), 375-386.

Hayashi, Yasakichi 林彌三吉, "Seiken no gaku wo shinki seyo" 聖賢の學を 振起せよ ("Let Us Encourage the Learning of the Sages"), *Shibun.* XV, 11 (Nov., 1933), 7-8.

Hongō, Fusatarō 本郷房太郎. "Seishinteki ni fukkō seyo" 精神的に復興せよ ("Let Us Have a Spiritual Renaissance"), *Shibun.* XII, 10 (Oct., 1930).

Ichimura, Sanjirō 市村瓚次郎. "Confucianism and General Elections," *Shibun.* II, 3 (June, 1920); II, 4 (Aug., 1920).

————. "The System of Confucianism as seen from a Cultural Standpoint," *Shibun.* VIII, 2 (April, 1925).

————. "Kokutai to chūkō" 國體と忠孝 ("The National Polity and Loyalty and Filial Piety"), *Kokugakuin zasshi* 國學院雜誌. XXXIII, 1 (Jan., 1917), 17-29.

Ichinoe, Hyōe 一戸兵衛. "Arasowazu Seidō wo funde susume" 爭はず正道を 踏んで進め ("Step Forward on the True Way without Quarreling"), *Shibun.* XII, 10 (Oct., 1930).

Ienaga, Saburō 家永三郎. "Kyōiku chokugo seiritsu no shisōshiteki kō-satsu" 教育勅語成立の思想史的考察 ("Historical Examination of the Ideological Formation of the Imperial Rescript on Education"), *Shigaku zasshi* 史學雜誌. LVI, 12 (Dec., 1946).

An excellent interpretive study of the ideology on which the Imperial Rescript on Education is based. It is doubtful if such a lucid analysis could have been safely made by a Japanese before 1945. The article supplements and enlarges many ideas which appeared in Watanabe Ikujirō's *Nippon kempō seitei shikō,* and should be read in conjunction with it.

Iijima, Tadao 飯島忠夫. "Kōshi no michi" 孔子の道 ("The Way of Confucius"), *Shibun.* XII, 9 (Sept., 1930), 631-642.

Inoue, Tetsujirō 井上哲次郎. "Ōdō shugi ni tsuite" 王道主義に就いて ("Concerning the Doctrine of the Kingly Way"), *Shibun.* XIV, 4 (April, 1932), 1-10.

Kaneko, Kentarō 金子堅太郎. "The Development of Japan and the Power of Chinese Studies," *Shibun.* I, 1 (Feb., 1919), 5-18.

Komatsubara, Eitarō 小松原英太郎. "Purpose of this Organization," *Shibun.* I. 1 (Feb., 1919), 1-4.

"Kōshi no taigi meibun setsu ni tsuite" 孔子の大義名分説に就いて ("Concerning Confucius' Theory of the Relations between Sovereign and Subjects"), *Shibun.* XI, 6 (June, 1929).

Koyanagi, Shigeta 小柳司氣太. "Characteristics of Confucianism," *Shibun.* IX, 3 (Mar., 1927), 1-23.

————. "Japanese *Kangaku* and the World Situation," *Shibun.* II, 2 (April, 1920), 89-94.

————. "Jukyō no seiji shisō" 儒教の政治思想 ("The Political Thought of Confucianism"), *Tōhō gakuhō* 東方學報. VI, (Feb., 1936), 830-831.

Meng, Ch'i 孟祁. "Chi Ku Hung-ming wen" 記辜鴻銘翁 ("Recollections of the Venerable Ku Hung-ming"), *Jen-chien-shih* 人間世. I, 12 (June, 1934), 44-45.

Mizuno, Rentarō 水野錬太郎. "The Way of Confucius," *Shibun.* IX, 12 (Dec., 1927), 721-727.

Nakamura, Kyūshirō 中村久四郎. "Manshūkoku to Kōshikyō no shinshimei" 滿洲國と孔子敎の新使命 ("Manchoukuo and the New Mission of Confucianism"), *Shibun.* XV, 8 (Aug., 1933), 1-12.

Nakamura, Yasaji 中村彌三次. "Tairiku bunka seisaku ni tsuite" 大陸文化政策に就いて ("Concernig Cultural Policies on the Continent"), *Gaikō jihō* 外交時報 (Revue Diplomatique). LXXXV, 795 (Jan., 1938), 41-81.

Ōki, Tōkichi 大木遠吉. "*Kangaku* and Ideological Problems," *Shibun.* II, (1920).

The exact reference to this article in the *Shibun* was lost by the writer, but as each volume of *Shibun* includes a table of contents for the numbers of the whole year, this article, as well as any others from *Shibun* without exact pagination in the bibliography, may be easily pin-pointed.

Sakatani, Yoshio 阪谷芳郎. "Discussion of the Need for Chinese Studies from the Standpoint of the Ideas of the People of the Empire," *Shibun.* I, (May, 1919), 213-227.

Sekiya, Ryūkichi 關谷龍吉. "Shakai kyōka no kihon toshite no Jukyō" 社會敎化の基本としての儒敎 ("Confucianism as the Basis of Social Cultivation"), *Shibun,* XIII, 5 (May, 1931).

Sera, Ryōichi 世良亮一. "Concerning the *Kambun* Textbooks of Middle School," *Shibun.* XXI, 5 (May, 1930), 36-40.

Shibunkai 斯文會. "History of the Shibun Gakkai," *Shibun*. I, 1 (Jan., 1919), 105-108.

Shibusawa, Eiichi 澁澤榮一. "Morality and Economics," *Shibun*. I, 1 (Feb., 1919).

Shikata, Hiroshi 四方博. "Kyūrai no Chōsen shakai no rekishiteki sei-kaku" 舊來の朝鮮社會の歷史的性格 ("Historical Characteristics of Tradi-tional Korean Society"), *Chōsen Gakuhō* 朝鮮學報. 3 (May, 1952), 131-147.

Shionoya, On 鹽谷溫. "Kamakura tsūshin" 鎌倉通信 ("News of Kama-kura"), *Shibun*. XIII, 9 (Sept., 1933), 1-9.

———. "Hijōji to Kangaku" 非常時と漢學 ("Critical Times and Chinese Studies"), *Shibun*. XV, 9 (Sept., 1933), 1-10.

———. "Kōfushi to waga kokutai" 孔夫子と我が國體 ("Confucius and our National Polity"), *Shibun*. XI, 9 (Sept., 1929), 687-704.

———. "Confucius and the Japanese National Polity," *Shibun*. VIII, 5 (Aug., 1926), 305-308.

———. "Nankō to San'yō Sensei" 楠公と山陽先生 ("Kusunoki Masashige and Rai San'yō"), *Shibun*. XIII, 7 (July, 1931).

Shiratori, Kurakichi 白鳥庫吉. "Kokutai to Jukyō" 國體と儒教 ("The National Polity and Confucianism"), *Kokugakuin zasshi* 國學院雜誌. XXIII, 1 (Jan., 1917), 1-16.

Since Shiratori was a scholar, ethnologist, and linguist of standing, it is surprising to find him writing here what seems like a nationalist tract. In this period, nationalism was not the intimidating force it was to become twenty years later in Japan; yet Shiratori associates Japan's national polity with a superior spiritual force which he claims gives Confucianism greater strength and permanence in Japan than China.

Takahashi, Tōru 高橋亨. "Chōsen ni okeru Jukyō" 朝鮮に於ける儒教 ("Con-fucianism in Korea"), *Shibun*. V, 1 (Jan., 1923).

Takahashi, who had been a teacher in Korea for nearly twenty years at this time, wrote that there was little interest in Confucianism among the young people of Korea. He felt that only with Japanese support could Confucianism continue to exert an influence. The article also includes a brief resume of the history of Confucianism in Korea.

Uda, Hisashi 宇田尚. "Kōkoku no shimei to shin Jukyō seishin no sai-teishō" 皇國の使命と新儒教精神の再提唱 ("The Readvocacy of a New Confucian Spirit and the Mission of the Imperial Nation"), *Shibun*. XV, 11 (Nov., 1933).

Uno, Tetsuto 宇野哲人. "Freedom and Equality," *Shibun*. II, 5 (Oct., 1920).

Uzawa, Sōmei 鵜澤總明. "On the *Wang-tao*," *Shibun*. I, 4 (Aug., 1919), 313-336; I, 5 (Oct., 1919), 393-402.

Wang, Ching-wei 汪精衞. "Wang chu-hsi yen-chiang chi-nien hsien-shih Kung-tzu tan-ch'en ch'üan-wen" 汪主席演講紀念先師孔子誕辰全文 ("Complete Text of Speech of Chairman Wang Commemorating the Birthday of Our Ancient Teacher Confucius"), *Voice of New China*. VI, 12 (Sept., 1941), 189-192.

Yamada, Chisaburō 山田智三郎. "Japanese Modern Art," *Monumenta Nipponica*. V, 2 (Dec., 1942), 114-125.

Yamamoto, Kunihiko 山本邦彦. "Shibun Gakkai jidai no kaiko" 斯文學會時代の回顧 ("Recollections of the Period of the Shibun Gakkai"), *Shibun*. IIX, 4-9 (1926); IX, 1-12 (1927); X, 1-12 (1928); XI, 1 (1929).

Much of the literature and many of the records dealing with the Shibun Gakkai, one of the leading Confucian organizations in Japan from 1880 to 1918, were destroyed in the great Tōkyō earthquake and fire of 1923. Yamamoto Kunihiko, however, had been associated with this organization in its early years, and in this series of articles he wrote the most detailed history of the Shibun Gakkai and description of its members that is available, drawing on his memory to fill in gaps where written materials no longer existed.

"Zenkoku chūtō gakkō kambunka kyōin kyōgikai" 全國中等學校漢文科教員協議會 ("Nation-wide Conference of Middle-School *Kambun* Teachers"), *Shibun*. XV, 12 (Dec., 1933).

WESTERN LANGUAGE — BOOKS

Allen, G. C. *A Short Economic History of Modern Japan.* London: George Allen and Unwin Ltd., 1946.

Anesaki, Masaharu. *History of Japanese Religion.* London: Kegan Paul, Trench, Trübner and Co., 1930.

Armstrong, Robert C. *Light from the East.* University of Toronto Studies; University of Toronto, 1914.

Aston, W. G. "Nihongi," *Translation and Proceedings of the Japan Society.* London: Kegan Paul, Trench, Trübner and Co., 1896. 2 vols.

Bernard, Henri. *Sagesse Chinoise et Philosophie Chrétienne (Chinese Wisdom and Christian philosophy).* Série Culturelle des Hautee Etudes de Tientsin. Paris: Cathasia, 1935.

Bisson, T. A. *Japan in China.* New York: The Macmillan Co., 1938.

Brinkley, F. *History of the Japanese People.* New York, London: Encyclopedia Britannica Co., 1915.

Bruce, J. Percy. *Chu Hsi and His Masters.* Probsthain Oriental Series. London: Probsthain and Co., 1923.

Bureau of Education. *Manual of Education in Chosen.* Keijō, Korea: The Government-General of Chosen, 1920.

Chamberlain, Basil H. *Translation of Kojiki.* Annotated by W. G. Aston, 2nd edition. Kōbe: J. L. Thomson and Co., 1932.

Chang, Chih-tung. *China's only Hope.* Translated by Samuel I. Woodbridge. New York: Flemming H. Revel Co., 1900.

Chavannes, Edouard. *Les Memoires de Se-ma Ts'ien.* Paris: Ernest Leroux, 1895. 5 vols.

Cohen, Jerome B. *Japan's Economy in War and Reconstruction.* Minneapolis: University of Minnesota Press, 1949.

The Comintern's Activity in Manchuria. Hsinking: Manchuria Daily News, 1940.

Crémazy, Laurent. *Le Code Pénal de la Corée, Tai-Han Hyeng Pep*

大韓刑法. Seoul: The Seoul Press, 1904.

Cressey, George Babcock. *China's Geographic Foundations*. 1st edition, fifth impression. New York and London: McGraw-Hill Book Co., 1934.

Dickins, V. *Chiushingura* 忠臣藏: *The Loyal League*. London: Allen and Co., 1880.

Eberhard, Wolfram. *A History of China*. Berkeley and Los Angeles: University of California Press, 1950.

Fung Yu-lan. *A Short History of Chinese Philosophy*. Edited by Derke Bodde. New York: Macmillan Co., 1948.

Gardner, Charles S. *Chinese Traditional Historiography*. Cambridge: Harvard University Press, 1937.

Grajdanzev, Andrew J. *Modern Korea*. New York: Institute of Pacific Relations, 1944.

Hall, Robert King. *Shūshin: the Ethics of a Defeated Nation*. New York: Columbia University, 1949.

In 1941, the teaching of ethics consumed approximately 6.7 per cent of the actual teaching time devoted to classroom subjects in elementary schools in Japan. Some idea of the importance of Confucian ethical norms in these ethics courses can be gained by reading the sections of the pre-war Japanese ethics textbooks translated in this work. It also includes a valuable interpretive chapter on "Kōdō: The Imperial Way" in which Hall discusses the use of ethical indoctrination in Japanese education. A review of this book by Edwin O. Reischauer may be found in *H.J.A.S.*, XIII (June, 1950), 249-253.

Holton, D. C. *Modern Japan and Shinto Nationalism*. Revised edition. Chicago: The University of Chicago Press, 1947.

Honjō, Eijirō 本庄榮治郎. *Economic Theory and History of Japan in the Tokugawa Period*. Tōkyō: Maruzen 丸善, 1943.

Hu, Shih. *The Chinese Renaissance*. Chicago: University of Chicago Press, 1933.

Hummel, Arthur W. *Eminent Chinese of the Ch'ing Period*. Washington: United States Government Printing Office, 1943-44. 2 vols.

Ike, Nobutaka. *The Beginning of Political Democracy in Japan*. Baltimore: The John Hopkins Press, 1950.

I.M.T.F.E. Defense Summation, Introductory Statement, Defense Document no. 3054.

This introductory statement by the defense at the International Military Tribunal for the Far East is permeated with Confucian ideas which were claimed to be the basic beliefs of the defendants. The defense claimed this commitment to Confucian values made it impossible for the defendants to have planned aggression or committed crimes against humanity.

I.M.T.F.E. Exhibits, Defense Document 2738. Exhibit number 3498.
————. Proceedings. 3894-3944.

The Japan Year Book, 1943-44. Tōkyō: Foreign Affairs Association of Japan, 1943.

Jansen, Marius B. *The Japanese and Sun Yat-sen.* Harvard Historical Monographs XXVII. Cambridge: Harvard University Press, 1954.

Johnston, Reginald F. *Confucianism and Modern China.* London: Victor Gollanez, 1934.

Johnston was a long-time resident of China who felt that traditional Confucian values still had importance for China. This attitude is clearly expressed in this book which briefly traces the fortunes of Confucianism in modern China. The footnotes to the book are a useful source of information difficult to obtain elsewhere.

————. *Twilight in the Forbidden City.* London: Victor Gollanez, 1934.

Jones, F. C. *Manchuria since 1931.* London: Royal Institute of International Affairs, 1949.

Kawai, Tatsuo 河相達夫. *The Goal of Japanese Expansion.* Tōkyō: Chūō Kōronsha, 1938.

Kawai Tatsuo was a Japanese foreign service officer and therefore his views may be considered as unofficially representing the Japanese government. In this book, he sought to justify Japanese expansion, particularly in China, and liberally used Confucian principles to show how Japan was motivated only by the highest ideals.

Kawakami, K. K. *Manchoukuo, Child of Conflict.* New York: Macmillan Co., 1933.

Kazin, Alfred. *On Native Grounds.* New York: Reynal and Hitchcock, 1942.

Keenleyside, Hugh and Thomas, A. F. *History of Japanese Education and Present Educational System.* Tōkyō: Hokuseidō Press, 1937.

Keith, Elizabeth and Scott, E. K. Robertson. *Old Korea, the Land of Morning Calm.* London and New York: Hutchinson and Co., 1946.

Kiang, Wen-han. *The Chinese Student Movement.* New York: King's Crown Press, 1948.

Kikuchi, Dairoku. *Japanese Education.* London: John Murray, 1909.

Kokutai no Hongi: Cardinal Principles of the National Entity of Japan. Translated by John Owen Gauntlett and edited with an introduction by Robert King Hall. Cambridge: Harvard University Press, 1949.

Korea: Bureau of Education. *Manual of Education in Chosen.* Seoul: Government-General of Chosen, 1920.

Korea: Government-General of Chosen. *Annual Report on Reforms and Progress in Chosen (1910-11).* Seoul: 1911.

————. *Annual Report on Reforms and Progress in Chosen (1911-12).* Seoul: 1912.

————. *Annual Report on Administration of Chosen, 1930.* Keijō: 1931.

Korea: Government-General of Tyosen. *Annual Report on Administration of Tyosen, 1936-37.* Keijō: 1937.

Ku, Chieh-kang. *The Autobiography of a Chinese Historian.* Translated and annotated by Arthur W. Hummel. Leyden: E. J. Brill, 1931.

Ku, Hung-ming. *Papers from a Viceroy's Yamen.* Shanghai: Shanghai Mercury, 1901.

————. *The Spirit of the Chinese People.* Peking: The Peking Daily News, 1915.

Kuno, Yoshi S. *Japanese Expansion on the Asiatic Continent, A Study in the History of Japan with Special Reference to Her International Relation with China, Korea, and Russia.* Berkeley and Los Angeles: University of California Press, 1937-40. 2 vols.

League of Nations. *Manchuria. Report of the Commission of Enquiry Appointed by the League of Nations.* Washington: 1932.

Legge, James. *The Confucian Classics.* 2nd edition; revised. Oxford:

Clarendon Press, 1893-95; and H. Frowde. 5 vols. in 8.

Longford, Joseph H. *Japan.* The Nations of Today Series. Boston and New York: Houghton Mifflin, 1923.

Manchoukuo. *Manchoukuo, Handbook of Information.* Hsinking: Manchoukuo Government, 1933.

Manchoukuo: Department of Foreign Affairs. *The Chief Executive's Proclamation; the Organic Law of Manchoukuo and other Laws Governing Various Government Offices.* Series 2. Hsinking: Manchoukuo Government, 1932.

Manchoukuo. *Manchoukuo, Handbook of Information.* Hsinking: Manchoukuo Government, 1932.

————. *Proclamations, Statements and Communications of the Manchoukuo Government.* Series 1. Hsinking: Manchoukuo Government, 1932.

Manchoukuo State Council. Bureau of Information. *An Outline of the Manchoukuo Empire.* Dairen: Manchuria Daily News, 1939.

McCune, George M., with the collaboration of Arthur L. Grey, Jr. *Korea Today,* Cambridge: Harvard University Press, 1950.

McKenzie, F. A. *The Tragedy of Korea.* London: Hodder and Stoughton, 1908.

Mitford, A. B. *Tales of Old Japan.* London: Macmillan and Co., 1876.

Murdock, Joseph. *A History of Japan.* Revised and edited by Joseph Longford. London: Kegan Paul, Trench, Trübner and Co., 1926. 3 vols.

Murray, Emmett L. *Early Russian Contacts with the Japanese to 1855.* Unpublished M. A. Thesis. University of California in Berkeley, 1950.

National League of Japanese University Professors. *The Japan China Conflict and the Attitude of Japan.* Tōkyō: The Nippon Press, 1937.

Norman, E. Herbert. *Japan's Emergence as a Modern State.* I.P.R. Inquiry Series. New York: Institute of Pacific Relations, 1940.

Obata, Kyūgorō. *An Interpretation of the Life of Viscount Shibusawa.* Tōkyō: Tōkyō Printing Co., 1939.

Osuga, William M. *The Establishment of State Shinto and the Buddhist Opposition in the Early Meiji Period.* Unpublished M. A. Thesis. University of California in Berkeley, 1949.

Pan Ku. *The History of the Former Han Dynasty.* Translated by Homer Dubs. Baltimore: Waverly Press, 1938-44. 2 vols.

Peck, Graham. *Two Kinds of Time.* Boston: Houghton Mifflin Co., 1950.

Reichwein, Adolf. *China and Europe, Intellectual and Artistic Contacts in the Eighteenth Century.* The History of Civilization Series. New York: Alfred A. Knopf, 1925.

Sansom, G. B. *The Western World and Japan.* New York: Alfred A. Knopf, 1950.

Seventh Biennial Conference of the World Federation of Education Association. *Education in Japan.* Tōkyō: The World Conference Committee of the Japanese Education Association, 1938, 2 vols.

Sharman, Lyon. *Sun Yat-sen, his Life and its Meaning.* New York: The John Day Co., 1934.

Sheen, Fulton J. *Communism and the Conscience of the West.* New York: The Bobbs Merrill Co., 1948.

Shryock, John. *The Origin and Development of the State Cult of Confucius.* New York: The Century Company, 1932.

Spae, Joseph John. *Itō Jinsai.* Monumenta Serica Monograph Series, XII. Peiping: The Catholic University of Peking, 1948.

While this monograph deals primarily with the Tokugawa Confucian philosopher Itō Jinsai and his doctrines, the first chapter presents a valuable historical survey of Confucianism in Japan through the end of the Tokugawa period. A knowledge of this Confucian background is very helpful in studying modern Confucian developments. A review of this book by Donald H. Shively may be found in *H.J.A.S.*, XI (Dec., 1948), 456-464.

Stephenson, E. S. and Asano, W. *Famous People of Japan.* Yokohama: Kelly and Walsh Ltd., 1911.

Sun, Yat-sen. *Memoirs of a Chinese Revolutionary.* London: Hutchinson and Co., 1919.

Suzuki, Daisetz. *Zen Buddhism and its Influence on Japanese Culture.* Kyōto: The Eastern Buddhist Society, Otani Buddhist College, 1938.

Takeuchi, Tatsuji. *War and Diplomacy in the Japanese Empire.* Garden City: Doubleday, Doran and Co., 1935.

T'ang, Leang-li. *China in Revolt.* London: Noel Douglas, 1927.

————. *The Foundations of Modern China.* London: Noel Douglas, 1928.

Tanin, O. and Yohan, E. *Militarism and Fascism in Japan.* New York: International Publishers, 1934.

Tasaki, Hanama. *Long the Imperial Way.* Boston: Houghton Mifflin Co., 1950.

Taylor, George E. *The Struggle for North China.* Institute of Pacific Relations Enquiry Series. New York: Institute of Pacific Relations, 1940.

A brilliant analytical first-hand study by Taylor of conditions in North China between 1937 and 1940. Taylor had the opportunity to travel throughout the Japanese occupied and free areas of North China, and his book contains an enormous amount of information on the Japanese attempts to revive Confucianism as the basis for their puppet regime.

The Text of the Yi King, Chinese Original with English Translation. Translated by Z. D. Sung. Shanghai: The Chinese Modern Education Co., 1935.

Third Report on Progress in Manchuria to 1932. Dairen: South Manchuria Railway, 1932.

Tōa Keizai Chōsakyoku 東亞經濟調查局. *Manchoukuo Yearbook.* Tōkyō, 1934.

Tolischus, Otto D. *Tokyo Record.* New York: Reynal and Hitchcock, 1943.

The Truth behind the Sino-Japanese Crisis. Edited by Kawamura Shōichi 川村彰一. Tōkyō: The Japan Times and Mail, 1937.

Voltaire, François Marie Arouet de. *Dictionnaire Philosophe ou la Raison par Alphabet.* Paris: Editions de Cluny, 1930.

Wang, Siu-chi. *Lu Hsiang-shan, a Twelfth Century Chinese Idealistic Philosopher.* New Haven: American Oriental Society, 1944.

Wieger, Léon. *Chaos.* Chine Moderne series, VIII. Sienhsien, Hopei province, China: Hienhien Press, 1931.

————. *Le Feu aux Poudres*. Chine Moderne Series, V. Seinhsien, Hopei province, China: Hienhien Press, 1926.

Wilhelm, Richard. *The Soul of China*. Translated by John H. Reece and Arthur Waley. New York: Harcourt Brace and Co., 1928.

Wong, William. *Henry Pu Yi, and the Japanese 1924-45: a Study in Puppetry*. Unpublished M. A. Thesis. University of California in Berkeley, 1951.

Yamada, K. *Two Lectures*. Translated by K. Matsuda. Shanghai: Tung Wen College, 1926.

These two lectures provide an example of how die-hard Confucianists attacked Western civilization after the first World War as being overly materialistic and inferior to the traditional spiritual culture of the Orient, represented by Confucianism. Yamada also felt that China's problems had arisen because she was trying to imitate the West, and he urged a return to traditional Confucian values in order to ameliorate the situation. This appeal is reminiscent of the line taken up by the Japanese in Manchuria and China in the 1930's.

Yanaga, Chitoshi. *Japan since Perry*. New York: McGraw Hill Co., 1949.

Young A. Morgan. *Imperial Japan, 1926-38*. London: George Allen and Unwin Ltd., 1938.

ARTICLES

Asaji, N. and Pringle, J. C. "Lectures Delivered in the Presence of His Imperial Majesty the Emperor of Japan," *T.A.S.J.*, series 1, XL, (1912), 44-113.

A partial translation of some of Motoda Eifu's lectures before the Emperor Meiji. See Tokutomi Iichirō's book, *Motoda sensei shinkō-roku*.

Ballard, S. "A Sketch of the Life of Noboru Watanabe," *T.A.S.J.* 1st series, XXXII, (1905), 1-23.

Cheng, Hsiao-hsu. "Wang-tao or the Kingly Way," *Manchuria*. II, 24 (Dec., 1937), 843.

Ch'i, Ssu-ho. "Professor Hung on the Ch'un Ch'iu," *The Yen ching Journal of Social Studies*. I, 1 (June, 1938), 49-71.

Clement, Ernest. "Chinese Refugees of the Seventeenth Century in Mito," *T.A.S.J.*, 1st series, XXIV, (1896), 12-20.

Conroy, Hilary. "Japan's War in China: an Ideological Somersault," *The Pacific Historical Review.* XXI, 4 (Nov., 1952), 367-379.

This article ably analyzes the attempts of the Japanese to use traditional Confucian ideology and similar ideas in order to obtain support from the Chinese between 1937 and 1940. The study is made from the standpoint of the conflicting Japanese attitudes concerning the best solution to the "China problem."

Dore, R. P. "The Ethics of the New Japan," *Pacific Affairs.* XXV, 2 (June, 1952), 147-159.

In 1951, the Japanese Minister of Education proposed that the old Imperial Rescript on Education of the Emperor Meiji be replaced by an "Outline of Ethical Practice for the Japanese People," since it was felt that some code of ethical behavior was needed and the old Rescript was no longer suitable to the times. The great debt which the new "Outline" owed to Confucianism is analyzed in this article, which includes a translation of the "Outline" and a consideration of its general philosophical premises.

Dull, Paul S. "The Assassination of Chang Tso-lin," *F.E.Q.* XI, 4 (Aug., 1952), 453-463.

Feldman, Horace Z. "The Meiji Political Novel," *Far Eastern Quarterly.* IX, 3 (Many, 1950), 245-255.

Fung, Yu-lan. "The Philosophy of Chu Hsi," translated from Chinese by Derke Bodde, *H.J.A.S.* VII (April, 1942), 1-51.

————. "The Rise of Neo-Confucianism and its Borrowings from Buddhism and Taoism," translated from Chinese by Derke Bodde, *H.J.A.S.* VII (July, 1942), 89-125.

Gale, James S. "Selection and Divorce," *T.A.K.B.R.A.S.* IV, pt. 3 (1913), 17-22.

Gaspardone, Émile. "La Chronologie Ancienne du Japon," *Journal Asiatique.* CCXXX, (April-June, 1938), 235-277.

Haga, T. "Notes on Japanese Schools of Philosophy," *T.A.S.J.* 1st series, XX, pt. I, (1893), 134-147.

Hu, Shih. "The Establishment of Confucianism as a State Religion during the Han Dynasty," *J.N.C.B.R.A.S.* XL, (1929), 20-41.

Hulbert, Homer. "National Examination in Korea," *T.A.K.B.R.A.S.* XIV, (1923), 9-23.

A historical study of the national examination system in Korea, which like its Chinese model, primarily tested a man's knowledge of the Confucian classics. This system was abandoned after 1894 as a method for choosing candidates for government office.

Levenson, Joseph. *"T'ien-hsia* and *Kuo* and the Transvaluation of Values," *F.E.Q.* XI, 4 (Aug., 1952), 447-451.

The Japan Weekly Mail. (Yokohama), July 29, 1899.

————. (Yokohama), Oct. 17, 1908.

Kiyowara, Sadao. "Japanization of Oriental Thoughts," *Contemporary Japan.* XIII, 7-9 (July-Sept., 1944), 725-736.

Kiyowara, a well-known scholar, outlines in this article how religions and philosophical thought, brought to Japan from abroad, has been modified to fit the Japanese *kokutai.* Confucianism is discussed in some detail, but the interpretation is slanted to support Japanese nationalist views. It is a good example, however, of this type of polemical writing.

Knox, George A. "Autobiography of Arai Hakuseki, Hyōchū oritaku Shiba no ki," *T.A.S.J.* 1st series, XXX, pt. II, (1902), 89-211.

————. "Ki, ri, and ten," *T.A.S.J.* 1st series, XX, pt. I, (1892), 157-177.

Kumagai, Kōjirō 熊谷幸次郎. "Ōcho jidai no Daigaku to shigaku" 王朝時代の大學と私學 ("The University and Private Schools in the Nara and Heian Periods"), *Rekishi chiri* 歴史地理 (*History and Geography*), translated and summarized in the *H.J.A.S.* II, (March, 1937), 68-73.

McLaren, W. W. "Japanese Government Documents, 1868-89," *T.A.S.J.* 1st series, XLII, pt. 1, (1914), 1-681.

Sargent, Clyde B. "Subsidized History," *F.E.Q.* III, (Feb., 1944), 119-143.

Simmons and Wigmore. "Land Tenure and Local Institutions," *T.A.S.J.* 1st series, XIX, pt. 1, (1891), 37-246.

"The Tsingtao Conference," *Voice of New China.* III, 10 (Feb., 1940), 6-7.

Van Gulik, R. H. "Kakkaron, a Japanese Echo of the Opium War,"

Monumenta Serica. IV, (1939-1940), 478-545.

Wen, Tsung-yao. "Improvement of Feminine Education in China Advocated," *Voice of New China.* VII, 2 (Oct., 1941), 35-37.

———. "New Order Explained," *Voice of New China.* III, 7 (Dec., (Dec., 1939), 6-8.

Wright, W. B. "The Capture and Captivity of Pere Giovanni Batista Sidotti in Japan from 1700 to 1715," *T.A.S.J.* 1st series, IX, (1881), 156-172.

APPENDIX

A. Imperial Rescript on Education of the Emperor Meiji.

Know ye, Our Subjects:

Our Imperial Ancestors have founded our Empire on a basis broad and everlasting, and have deeply and firmly implanted virtue; Our subjects ever united in loyalty and filial piety have from generation to generation illustrated the beauty thereof. This is the glory of the fundamental character of Our Empire, and herein also lies the source of Our Education. Ye, Our Subjects, be filial to your parents, affectionate to your brothers and sisters; as husbands and wives be harmonious, as friends true; bear yourselves in modesty and moderation; extend your benevolence to all; pursue learning and cultivate arts, and thereby develop intellectual faculties and perfect moral powers; furthermore advance public good and promote common interests; always respect the Constitution and observe the laws; should emergency arise, offer yourselves courageously to the State; and thus guard and maintain the prosperity of Our Imperial Throne coeval with heaven and earth. So shall ye not only be Our good and faithful subjects, but render illustrious the best traditions of your forefathers.

The Way here set forth is indeed the teaching bequeathed by Our Imperial Ancestors, to be observed alike by Their Descendants and the subjects, infallible for all ages and true in all places. It is Our wish to lay it to heart in all reverence, in common with you, Our subjects, that we may all attain to the same virtue.

The 30th day of the 10th month of the 23rd year of Meiji.

[G. B. Sansom, *The Western World and Japan,* (New York: Alfred A. Knopf, 1950), 464.]

B. Aims of the Shibunkai.

As transportation between the East and the West has fully opened up and European power has proceeded eastward, of the various Asiatic nations, there is only one which has avoided either having its independence threatened or having its territory seized. This lone one, Japan, has excelled majestically among these nations, being headed by its eternally changeless Imperial family.

And the fact of its not only having preserved the flawless golden vessel of its national polity, but also developing and expanding its power, to what has it been due? In the final analysis, it has been because after the [Meiji] Restoration, high and low were united in making the essence of the national polity its foundation, in widely seeking knowledge all over the world, and in reforming evil ways from the past, therewith splendidly carrying our statesmanship.

In the overzealousness, however, of borrowing strong points and supplementing weak ones, the "mean" was destroyed, and the correction of distortions immediately was overdone. There was a disposition towards uselessly putting values in materialistic culture. With this, although the knowledge and skills of the people advanced by tremendous strides, and projects useful for them and for their well being arose greatly, their faith in time-honored morality gradually declined and often the signs of the shock could be perceived. In addition, there were those who, taking advantage of the common feelings of dislike for the old and exaltation for the new, preached vitriolic opinions and tried to disturb our intellectual world. This was indeed an autumn period deserving of the anxiety and warnings of our men of intelligence.

The reflux of raging waves after they have broken is never an easy thing, but the removal of a vine before it has become long is certainly not difficult. Fortunately, the good ways and beautiful customs of our nation since its founding still exist in our villages, and with public-spirited, patriotic men as the immovable rock in midstream, those who took responsibility on themselves also were numerous. Today, men with the same feelings have united their hearts and pooled their strength, and so have formed a great organization here. With this they will clarify the morality peculiar to us, and in planning its propagation and diffusion, it is not difficult to expect their achieving the prevention of the deterioration of public morals.

Respectfully considering the promulgation of the Rescript on Education of the Emperor Meiji, although being the morality peculiar to our nation originating in the instructions of Imperial ancestors, yet it also nearly entirely agrees with the spirit of the Confucian way. In the final analysis, since our exemplary sages have already taken the Confucian way as both a means for self-discipline and a rule for governing peacefully, it has been from the beginning fused and blended with our morality. Therefore the Imperial instructions of the Rescript on Education, under the cloak of the Confucian way, should become more and more clear, and through the Rescript on Education the fundamental meaning of the Confucian way should gain strength. This is the reason why we are expecting that the Imperial instructions of the Rescript on Education will be enhanced through this mutual planning of those of the same mind and the mutual organization of those who with similar anxieties are greatly promoting the Confucian way.

When, forty years ago, various outstanding men in the government and among the people organized the Shibun Gakkai for the purpose of stressing the Confucian way and preserving public morals, the late Emperor especially donated money from the Imperial Privy Purse and bestowed the Imperial favor of praise and encouragement [on it]. As time passed, however, the old scholars gradually faded away and the work [of the society] declined so that looking at matters today, its scope was narrow, and it could not fulfill the needs of the day. Men of intelligence, finding this deplorable, hereupon changed the organization of the society [Shibun Gakkai] and newly set up this association which by continuing its tasks and planning again a renovation and expansion, above, was able to return the Imperial favor of the late Emperor, and below, was able to hand on the cherished objects of its predecessors.

Considering matters, the great war of the world today is without parallel in history, and it goes without saying that it will bring great changes in every sphere. And especially in its influence on the intellectual world, it will demand deep consideration anew from men of intelligence. At this juncture, this association, with the approval and help of many talented men in the government and among the people, has taken the Confucian way for spreading our nation's characteristic morality and for endeavouring to arouse spiritual culture in order to attain [in this area] progress corresponding to that of the utility and well being of the people connected with materialistic culture. And by carrying this out and achieving these [ends], for ages it will further the flourishing of the destiny of the nation and not fail to elevate the brilliancy of our national polity that excells among the ten thousand nations of the post-war world.

[Shibunkai 斯文會, *Shibun rokujūnen shi* 斯文六十年史 (*A History of Sixty Years of Confucian Studies*), (Tōkyō: Shibunkai 斯文會, 1929), 317-318.]

C. Opening address by Katō Masanosuke outlining the aims of the Nippon Jukyō Sen'yōkai, given January 27, 1934, at the founding ceremonies of the society.

As for spiritual and material culture, they are to the nation like the two wings of a bird or the two wheels of a cart which cannot do without one of its [members] for even an instant. However, at the time of the Meiji Restoration, promoted by the urgency for introducing material culture, we neglected attention towards our spiritual culture which has been traditionally handed down from the time of the establishment of the nation. In the fields of education, industry, and politics, due to introducing exclusively European material culture for the last fifty or more years, material culture made rapid strides. Our country changed its appearance in communications, transportation, architecture, construction, industry, and all fields, so that in comparison to Europe and America, we were in no way inferior. And rather than not being inferior, in some types of industrial production, their quality and value reached the point of being superior to that of Europe and America. The result was that in fear of not being able to endure the competition, some countries cried out about the Yellow peril and went as far as planning the exclusion of Japanese commodities.

In this short space of forty or fifty years, threatened by the people of Europe and America, we realized rapid progress which, needless to say, was felicitous for the nation. But what I feel is most deplorable is that together with the advance of material culture, every type of evil that should have been avoided was introduced. This was so-called individualism and utilitarianism. The result of revering individualism was that our traditional national principles were relegated to a secondary place; and the result of being infatuated with utilitarianism was that fame and profit occupied the foremost position, while justice and humanity were discarded. Without reflection, we have amplified the mad condition in which we have nothing but fame and profit in mind. And capitalists exploiting the flesh and blood of laborers, while laborers unite and strike in opposition; landlords and tenants each wishing their own havest to be large, with tenant disputes arising constantly; politicians taking advantage of their positions and yearning for unfair profits; the problem of the sale of doctor's degrees at the Nagasaki Medical College; the problem of the buying and selling of Tōkyō school principalships; and the problem of Communist influence at Kyōto University and Nagano elementary school; all these are the poisons of following material culture.

Amongst the European nations, these various evils have grown, until today, many are in extreme circumstances. And this, in the final analysis is due to their thirsting eagerly for material culture and lacking spiritual culture which is [like] one of the wings of a bird or wheels of a cart.

In our country, however, there is an Imperial way and a *kokutai* which have not changed since the founding of the nation; and also there is Confucianism that has been amalgamated into the Imperial way and *kokutai;* and a spiritual culture that traditionally has had no equal in all the countries of the world. Only due to the urgency of importing material culture, for a while dissension arose concerning instruction in traditional spiritual culture, and unfortunately, the evils of material culture spread throughout the country.

Therefore, as a way of purifying the land of Japan and cleaning out these poisons, the arousing of traditional feelings of humaneness, righteousness, loyalty, and filial piety, and the promotion of Confucianism is the first [essential].

In order to revere the Imperial way and the *kokutai*, there is no better way than offering worship to Imperial ancestors and arousing a spirit of veneration; in order to perpetuate family rules and laws, there is no better way than offering worship to ancestors and stimulating a spirit of reverence. And also, in order to spread Confucianism which has become amalgamated into the Imperial way and the *kokutai*, there is no better method than sacrificing to past sages and developing a spirit of respect. For this, we members of the Daitō Bunka Gakuin have gathered together a teaching staff, and organized a Confucian promotion society, and beginning in Tōkyō, we will open up Confucian promotion lecture societies all over the country, spread our characteristic spiritual culture, and expect to sweep clean the poisons that have followed material culture. Today we are carrying out here a ceremony to Confucianism and past sages.

Today I presented to each one of you gentlemen a pamphlet entitled the *Seiyūki*. In this pamphlet there are the questions asked by the Emperor Meiji on November 5, 1886, when he called his brilliant scholar of Chinese studies, Motoda Eifu, into conference and [expressed] his uneasiness over there being no actual Japanese or Chinese course at the University on his visit to the Imperial University. "The University is a Japanese institution of higher learning for developing superior men of talent. However, through the present curriculum, if one wished to obtain talented men who could teach the basis of the way of governing, it would be impossible. Even if one were to graduate from the physics, chemistry, or medical course, and were a man of character, one would not be able to become a [government] minister. At the present time, meritorious ministers of the Restoration [period] are in the cabinet, and although they are handling governmental matters, they cannot go on forever.... Therefore I believe there is a need to set up a course for Japanese and Chinese studies. What do you think of this?"

According to Motoda's answer, the Emperor dispatched the chief chamberlain, Tokudaiji, to transmit his views to the head of the University, Watanabe, and [this pamphlet] is a record of the course of these events.

I again today, with the memory of the Emperor Meiji who forty years ago was inspired concerning the need for Confucianism to help in preserving the Imperial way and the *kokutai*, deeply feel that the Emperor was an enlightened ruler without peer in the world for sagaciousness and wisdom. If the Emperor were alive now, I believe that he would have taken preventive measures against the radical thoughts and scandals of today. When I reminisce on this, feelings of pain at the Emperor's death fill my breast, and I have thoughts of endless tears.

We scholars, when we read this *Seiyūki* and think of the present-day conditions of our nation, cannot help but feel the increasing burden of responsibility for spreading Confucianism. We have organized a society for the promotion of Confucianism with this in mind, and carried out ceremonies today for past sages. Despite everyone being very busy, and in spite of the intense cold, the fact that so many of you have attended gives us [of this society] great satisfaction.

I, as a representative of the whole group, deeply and warmly express my thanks here. If all of you are in agreement with the aims that have been outlined and will assist directly and indirectly in this work, it will be felicitous for the nation.

[*Nihon no Jukyō* 日本之儒教 (*Japanese Confucianism*), (Tōkyō: Nippon Jukyō Sen'yōkai 日本儒教宣揚會, 1934), 6-11.]

INDEX

Confucianism, as a special topic, has not been included in the index because it is the subject of the book and is referred to on nearly every page. There are, however, such general topics as capitalism, nationalism, etc. included in the index, and these are discussed in relation to Confucianism on the pages noted.

278 INDEX

著者の書翰

　拝　啓　四月二十日カラカスで進藤様と面会して貴方と原島教授が私の論文の印刷に
どれ程尽力をなされたか初めて分りました。誠に有り難う御座居ます。進藤様と色々話
して彼が私の論文を出版する主なる理由は次の様に言はれました。その国の歴史を理解
するには外国人は時として本国の史家より洞察力が有ります，それは外国の学者がもつ
と客観的に国史の大勢を観察出来るからです，私の論文には最近日本史に対する外国学
界の客観的思想と分析があるとの意見は本当に思ひ掛けないことで感謝する次第で御座
居ます。

　御存じの通り私は此の論文を一九五四年正月頃書き上げました。主に加州大学に有る
史料を使ったので未熟な点が多いと思ひます。例へば論文の第四章には日本軍に占領さ
れた支那地域の政府に就いての史料が少い事はよく分りました。丁度論文が出来上ると
Frederick W. Mote, *Japanese Sponsored Governments in China 1937—1945*,
Hoover Institute and Library bibliographical series III (Stanford: Stanford
University Press, 1954) と言う書籍目録が出ました。その副題は An Annotated
Bibliography Compiled from Materials in the Chinese Collection of the Hoover
Library ですから必ず論文の第四章の欠点を補ふ資料を示すと思ひましたけれども書き
直す機会がありませんでした。勿論それ許りで無く又論文に短所が多いと思ひますが進
藤様はその儘論文を印刷したら良いと主張されましたから簡単な書き改めの部分だけで
彼にお渡ししました。史料をもう少し捜し当てゝも自分の解釈は変りませんと思ひまし
たからです。

　此の論文は或る程度迄に American historian の精進の結晶として認められたら良
いと思います。又その結果で日本と米国には歪曲されていない儒教の理想をお互いにも
つと理解すれば私の希望以上と存じます。　敬　具

於カラカス市　一九五八年四月二十四日

Warren　W.　Smith　Jr.

末　松　保　和　学兄